Understanding and Healing Emotional Trauma

Understanding and Healing Emotional Trauma is an interdisciplinary book that explores our current understanding of the forces involved in both the creation and healing of emotional trauma. Through engaging conversations with pioneering clinicians and researchers, Daniela F. Sieff offers accessible yet substantial answers to questions such as: What is emotional trauma? What are the causes? What are its consequences? What does it mean to heal emotional trauma? How can healing be achieved?

These questions are addressed through three interrelated perspectives: psychotherapy, neurobiology and evolution. *Psychotherapeutic perspectives* take us inside the world of the unconscious mind and body to illuminate how emotional trauma distorts our relationships with ourselves and with other people (Donald Kalsched, Bruce Lloyd, Tina Stromsted, Marion Woodman). *Neurobiological perspectives* explore how trauma impacts the systems that mediate our emotional lives and well-being (Ellert Nijenhuis, Allan Schore, Daniel Siegel). And *evolutionary perspectives* contextualise emotional trauma in terms of the legacy we have inherited from our distant ancestors (James Chisholm, Sarah Blaffer Hrdy, Randolph Nesse).

Transforming lives affected by emotional trauma is possible, but it can be a difficult process. The insights shared in these lively and informative conversations can support and facilitate that process. This book will therefore be a valuable resource for psychotherapists, psychologists, counsellors and other mental health professionals in practice and training, and also for members of the general public who are endeavouring to find ways through their own emotional trauma. In addition, because emotional trauma often has its roots in childhood, this book will also be of interest and value to parents, teachers and anyone concerned with the care of children.

Daniela F. Sieff is an independent writer and scholar, with a PhD in biological anthropology, and an active interest in the dynamics of the psyche.

Understanding and Healing Emotional Trauma

Conversations with pioneering clinicians and researchers

Daniela F. Sieff

LONDON AND NEW YORK

First published 2015
by Routledge
27 Church Road, Hove, East Sussex, BN3 2FA

And by Routledge
711 Third Avenue, New York, NY 10017

Routledge is an imprint of the Taylor & Francis Group, an informa business

British Library Cataloguing in Publication Data
A catalogue record for this book is available from the British Library

Library of Congress Cataloging in Publication Data
Understanding and healing emotional trauma : conversations with pioneering clinicians and researchers / edited by Daniela F. Sieff.
p. ; cm.
ISBN 978-0-415-72081-6 (hbk) -- ISBN 978-0-415-72084-7 (pbk) --
ISBN 978-1-315-74723-1 (ebk)
I. Sieff, Daniela F., editor
[DNLM: 1. Stress, Psychological--physiopathology. 2. Stress, Psychological--psychology. 3. Biological Evolution. 4. Stress Disorders, Traumatic--physiopathology. 5. Stress Disorders, Traumatic--psychology. WM 172.4]
RC552.T7
616.85'21--dc23
2014021390

ISBN: 978-0-415-72081-6 (hbk)
ISBN: 978-0-415-72084-7 (pbk)
ISBN: 978-1-315-74723-1 (ebk)

Typeset in Times
by Saxon Graphics Ltd, Derby

For the contributors,
with deep gratitude for their work

Contents

Acknowledgements

First and foremost, I want to thank the contributors to this book. Irrespective of whether they first met me as a graduate student 25 years ago, or when I turned up with a list of questions and a digital voice recorder, they were generous and gracious in their support of this project.

The beginnings of this book were serendipitous. Sarida Brown inadvertently planted the seeds when she invited me to interview Donald Kalsched for *Caduceus*, the magazine she had founded. I circulated that article to women who have completed the leadership training programme with the Marion Woodman Foundation. Their enthusiastic response inspired this book. I am grateful to Sarida for her initial invitation and to the women of the Marion Woodman Foundation for their encouragement.

During the eight years it has taken me to put together this book, I have been accompanied, supported and encouraged by many different people in many different ways. They include, Laura Bear, Angela Bernstein, Evelyn Brown, Ray Bunce, Barbara Chapman, Marco Compagnoni, Marian Dunlea, Judith Harris, Dave Henry, Louise Holland, Graham Hull, Bobbie Lloyd, Paula Mahoney, Tania Matos, Punita Miranda, Madeleine O'Callaghan, Maja Reinau, Bruce Sansom, Amanda Sieff, Christina Shewell, Tina Stromsted, Jane Warren, Margaret Wilkinson, Tony Woolfson and the late Ross Woodman. Each of them has made a unique and vital contribution.

Phil Chalmers and Nicki Lee have helped me to remain embodied while working on this book, and their contribution has been equally important.

In recent years my thinking has been enriched by stimulating discussions with the members of my evolutionary psychotherapy group: Jim Hopkins, John Launer, Graham Music, Michael Reiss, Annie Swanepoel and Bernadette Wren. They have also offered me much appreciated support and encouragement.

As each chapter moved towards being finalised, I asked friends and colleagues for feedback. They were extraordinarily generous with their time and care, and this book is better for their suggestions. They include: Kent Anderson, Barbara Chapman, Louise Holland, Isabelle Laurent, Annie Swanepoel, Bruce Sansom and Maja Reinau. In this context, I especially want to thank my half-sister, Amanda Sieff, who read nearly every chapter – I am touched and indebted to her for all that she has contributed.

Antony Gormley was incredibly generous in allowing his work to be used on the front cover. I am thrilled that people will have their first encounter with this book through an image that speaks so powerfully to both mind and body. I also want to thank Meirian Jump at Antony Gormley's studio for her assistance regarding the cover, and Marco Compagnoni who helped to make this possible.

Joanne Forshaw and Kirsten Buchanan, at Routledge, guided this book's journey into the world.

I want to thank the leaders of the various different BodySoul Rhythms® workshops that I have attended over the years: Marian Dunlea, Mary Hamilton, Judith Harris, Ann Skinner, Paula Reeves, Meg Wilber and Marion Woodman. The container which they created offered me a safe, healing and vibrant environment in which to explore how the dynamics elucidated in these conversations are embodied in my own internal world. There is another who played an equally vital role in my inner journey which underpins these conversations; without his wisdom and fierce compassion the me who created this book would never have come into being.

Other individuals who enabled the me who created this book to exist include DD, Julian Hosking, Michael and Betty Hounsell, Bridie Russell and Tasbec. Three of them passed away long before this book was conceived, but that does not make their contribution to it any less important.

My parents, Marcus and Lily Sieff, also passed away before I began this book; nevertheless their support, values and love are present in every page.

Contributors

Sarah Blaffer Hrdy, PhD, anthropologist and primatologist, is Emeritus Professor of Anthropology at the University of California Davis, Associate in the Peabody Museum at Harvard, Professor-at-Large at Cornell University and a fellow of the US National Academy of Sciences. She has written several books including, *Mother Nature: A History of Mothers, Infants and Natural Selection* (1999, Chatto and Windus) and *Mothers and Others: The Evolutionary Origins of Mutual Understanding* (2011, Harvard University Press). Both books have been awarded multiple prizes. Hrdy's work integrates modern evolutionary theory with empirical research in primatology, animal behaviour, anthropology, attachment theory, developmental psychology, demography, palaeontology, archaeology and history to offer a new understanding of the nature of mothers and infants.

James S. Chisholm, PhD, is a developmental psychologist, an evolutionary anthropologist and a humanist. He is Professor Emeritus in the Department of Anatomy, Physiology, and Human Biology at the University of Western Australia. He has written numerous scholarly articles and two books: *Navajo Infancy: An Ethological Study of Child Development* (1983, Aldine Transaction) and *Death, Hope and Sex: Steps to an Evolutionary Ecology of Mind and Morality* (1999, Cambridge University Press). He was one of the first researchers to bring a modern evolutionary perspective to the study of human development.

Donald E. Kalsched, PhD, is a clinical psychologist and Jungian analyst in private practice in Albuquerque, New Mexico. He is the author of several articles and two books: *The Inner World of Trauma* (1996, Routledge) and *Trauma and the Soul* (2013, Routledge). He is a senior training analyst with the Inter-Regional Society of Jungian Analysts, where he teaches and supervises. He teaches, lectures and runs workshops internationally, pursuing his interdisciplinary interest in early trauma and dissociation theory, and its archetypal manifestations.

J. Bruce Lloyd, PhD, a biologist by origin, is a psychotherapist who is influenced by interpersonal, psychodynamic, existential and humanistic perspectives. He has taught on both diploma and postgraduate psychodynamic courses in the UK, lectured publicly and was the founding chairman of the British arm of the

National Association of Alcohol and Drug Abuse Counsellors. Most importantly, he has voyaged, and continues to voyage, through the territory explored in his conversation.

Randolph M. Nesse, MD, is Professor of Life Sciences, Arizona Foundation Professor, and Founding Director of the Center for Evolution, Medicine, & Public Health at Arizona State University. He was previously Professor of Psychiatry, Professor of Psychology and Research Professor at the University of Michigan. He is a founder of the field of evolutionary medicine, editor of *The Evolution & Medicine Review*, and president of the Foundation for Evolution, Medicine, & Public Health. His research has ranged from studies of neuroendocrine responses to anxiety, to the evolutionary origins of capacities for altruism and the origins and functions of emotions, especially anxiety and depression. He has written and edited several books including *Evolution and the Capacity for Commitment* (2001, Russell Sage Foundation) and *Understanding Depression* (2009, Oxford University Press).

Ellert R.S. Nijenhuis, PhD, is a psychologist and psychotherapist who has spent more than 30 years working with profoundly dissociated patients. He is also an award-winning clinician and researcher in the field of dissociation. He has written many professional articles and book chapters. He is author of *Somatoform Dissociation: Phenomena, Measurement, and Theoretical Issues* (2004, Norton) and a co-author of *The Haunted Self: Structural Dissociation and the Treatment of Chronic Traumatisation* (2006, Norton). He is a former Director of the Executive Council of the International Society of the Study of Trauma and Dissociation.

Allan N. Schore, PhD, is a practising psychotherapist and an interdisciplinary theoretician. He is on the clinical faculty of the University of California at Los Angeles David Geffen School of Medicine. He is author of numerous scholarly articles and his books are *Affect Regulation and the Origin of the Self* (1999, Psychology Press), *Affect Regulation and the Repair of the Self* (2003, Norton), *Affect Dysregulation and Disorders of the Self* (2003, Norton) and *The Science of the Art of Psychotherapy* (2012, Norton). He is editor of the Norton Series on Interpersonal Neurobiology, and lectures and teaches internationally.

Daniela F. Sieff, PhD, is an independent writer and scholar, with a doctorate in biological anthropology from Oxford University, and an active interest in the dynamics of the psyche. She has always sought to understand what it is that makes us who we are, and from early in her career has been drawn to thinking about this from an interdisciplinary perspective. Her doctoral research explored how evolutionary processes contribute to shaping human behaviour. Her research took her to a wilderness region of Tanzania to live with a traditional cattle-herding people. In recent years she has focused on what it means to be emotionally traumatised, and how we can change, heal and grow. This book has emerged from that work.

Daniel J. Siegel, MD, is a child psychiatrist, a researcher in the field of attachment and a proponent of the role of mindfulness in healing early trauma. He is clinical professor of psychiatry at the UCLA School of Medicine, where he is on the faculty of the Center for Culture, Brain, and Development and the Co-Director of the Mindful Awareness Research Center. He lectures internationally and has published extensively; his many books include: *Parenting from the Inside Out* (2004, Jeremy P. Tarcher), *The Mindful Brain* (2007, Norton), *The Mindful Therapist* (2010, Norton), *Mindsight: The New Science of Personal Transformation* (2010, Oneworld Publications), *The Whole-Brain Child* (2011, Robinson), *The Developing Mind* (2012, 2nd edition, Guilford Press) and *Pocket Guide to Interpersonal Neurobiology* (2012, Norton).

Tina Stromsted, PhD, MFT, BC-DMT, is a somatic psychotherapist, a board-certified dance/movement therapist and a Jungian psychoanalyst with a private practice in San Francisco. With roots in theatre and dance and nearly 40 years of clinical practice, she has a deep interest in the creative process, neuroscience and attachment theory, and in the integration of these and other realms in healing and development. She was co-founder of the Authentic Movement Institute in Berkeley, California, senior faculty in the Marion Woodman Foundation, and teaches at the C.G. Jung Institute of San Francisco, Pacifica Graduate Institute, and at universities and healing centres internationally. Her articles and book chapters explore the integration of body, psyche and soul in clinical work.

Marion Woodman, LLD, DHL, PhD, is a Jungian analyst, inspirational teacher and founding chairman of the Marion Woodman Foundation. She is author of several books including: *The Owl was a Baker's Daughter* (1982, Inner City Books), *Addiction to Perfection* (1983, Inner City Books), *The Pregnant Virgin* (1985, Inner City Books), *The Ravished Bridegroom* (1990, Inner City Books), *Leaving my Father's House* (1993, Shambhala Publications) and *Bone* (2000, Arkana). Woodman has walked – and continues to walk – through the territory she explores in her chapter. Now in her eighties, she shares some of the experiences and wisdom that she has accumulated as a result.

Introduction

Daniela F. Sieff

This interdisciplinary book explores our current understanding of emotional trauma through conversations with pioneering clinicians and academics. It brings together leading figures from psychotherapy, neurobiology and evolution to offer answers to questions such as: What is emotional trauma? What causes it? What are its consequences? What does it mean to recover from the impact of emotional trauma? How can that recovery be achieved?

Facing emotional trauma, both personally and professionally, is extremely challenging. However, due, in large part, to the innovative work of the contributors, we now have a better understanding of the forces involved in both the creation and healing of emotional trauma. This book invites a broad readership into that understanding. It is written for all those who are struggling with their own emotional trauma, as well as for the therapists, counsellors, social workers and others who accompany people through the process of healing. Because so much emotional trauma has its roots in childhood, this book is also written for parents, teachers and anyone engaged in the care of children.

Emotional trauma

Emotional trauma is defined not only by painful and frightening experiences, but also by the *impact* these experiences have on us and by their long-term *effects* on our lives. When our experiences are unbearably painful or frightening, particularly if there is nobody to whom we can turn for emotional support, a damaging imprint is left on our mind, brain and body, sending our lives onto a different path. Just how different our life-path turns out to be depends on the extent of the damage. However, instead of developing in a way that would allow us to become emotionally secure, and to fulfil our potential, crucial aspects of our lives become organised around the traumatising experiences. We are driven by a hidden fear of retraumatisation which is burnt deeply into our brains and bodies. We dissociate from our emotions, as well as from any parts of our personality which have attracted disapproval. We come to experience ourselves within the distorting framework of shame, believing that we are fundamentally defective and inadequate. As a result, the way that we relate to ourselves, to other people and to the world around us is compromised and distorted.

These responses are primarily unconscious. They are expressed through the neural networks and hormonal systems that are invisible to everyday awareness. All that we know is that life is a struggle. We feel empty and unable to engage with the world. We sense that our lives are somewhat false – that we are not being quite true to ourselves. We exist within an omnipresent haze of anxiety. We feel a gnawing sense of inadequacy. We harbour a fear of being uncovered as a fraud. We hate what we have become. We loathe our bodies. We see ourselves and others through a lens of blame and fault. We develop a victim mentality. We become addicts. We disappear into a world of fantasy. We descend into depression and hopelessness. We develop painful and unexplained physical symptoms. We behave self-destructively. We are drawn to damaging relationships. We are paralysed when we need to speak out. We explode with rage when we need to reflect. Our personality fragments and dissociates and we find ourselves absent while some apparent invader directs our actions. Living in any of these states can leave us wishing that we were dead, and that wish may beckon us towards suicide.

The overwhelming pain and fear at the root of trauma can have many different origins. Sometimes it is the result of a single dramatic event; other times it is a response to the underlying and ongoing attitudes and ways of relating which are implicit in our family, school, religion or culture. Sometimes our pain and fear results from overt physical or sexual violence; other times it is a response to being an unwanted or orphaned child, or to being repeatedly undermined, invalidated and shamed.

In some instances the original painful experiences happened to previous generations rather than directly to us. In these cases it is the hidden fears and distorted ways of relating that our recent ancestors developed which are surreptitiously and unconsciously passed on to us, and which lie at the root of our trauma.

Our evolutionary heritage, spanning millions of years, also influences the dynamics of emotional trauma, leaving us predisposed to find certain experiences particularly painful and frightening, as well as to respond to such experiences in the ways that enabled our distant ancestors to survive and parent children. Typically, these ancient responses create additional layers of suffering. Sometimes they are inappropriate in today's environment.

Although emotional trauma can occur at any point during our lives, the consequences of suffering trauma during infancy and childhood are particularly significant and long-lasting. That is because early relationships with parents and other caregivers (known as 'attachment relationships') influence the development of our emotional brains, fear response and reproductive physiology. Thus, young children who are abused, neglected or who simply have parents who are unable to attune to them – perhaps because they themselves are depressed, stressed or traumatised – will develop along different biological pathways to children whose parents are sensitive and responsive to their needs.

Our early attachment relationships are also important because they are the basis upon which we build unconscious mental models regarding the world and our place in it. If our caregivers are responsive to us we come to experience ourselves as lovable, relationships as trustworthy and the world as safe, but if our caregivers are not attentive then we come to experience ourselves as inherently unlovable, relationships as untrustworthy and the world as hostile. Unless these mental models are explicitly brought into consciousness and challenged, they may last a life-time. And because they determine how we behave, they create painful, repetitive and self-fulfilling cycles.

Unconscious mental models are not only formed in the context of our early attachment relationships, they are also formed in response to other environments, including that of our school, religion and culture. In addition, experiences that we have as older children, teenagers and adults can create powerful mental models about the world and our place in it. Mental models formed later can be just as limiting as those formed earlier in our lives.

One of the most damaging aspects of emotional trauma is that its consequences become so deeply ingrained within our minds, brains and bodies that we are unable to step aside from the trauma and see its impact on us, let alone change it. Instead we mistakenly believe that our suffering is the result of 'who we are' at some innate and immutable level.

Equally problematic is that being unaware of the trauma buried in our unconscious, we have little choice but to focus our energy on trying to alleviate the visible surface symptoms, perhaps through short-term therapy or psychotherapeutic drugs, or by pinning our hopes to something like a new romantic relationship or cosmetic surgery. These kinds of surface measures can give us temporary respite, but they do not touch the trauma which lies at the root of our distress, so in time we will fall back into our suffering.

Ultimately, the only way to recover from emotional trauma is to go beneath the surface, enter the world of the unconscious, and explore our wounds from inside our emotional self. We need to slowly make our way to the heart of our wounds, develop an embodied and experiential consciousness of how they play out in our lives, and find new and healthier ways to relate to them. We cannot do this work alone. To safely enter the world of the unconscious, and to build the new neural networks which will allow us to move beyond our trauma, we need to be working with somebody who can offer us an attuned, mindful, compassionate and therapeutic relationship.

Even then, healing does not necessarily mean that we will reach a place where trauma no longer has any effect on our lives. We cannot change the past. We cannot un-experience what we have already experienced. We are not machines and we cannot replace old, broken parts with new, shiny ones. What is more, we have evolved to remember, often at an unconscious and embodied level, anything that caused us unbearable pain and fear. We have also evolved to react automatically to anything that resembles our traumatising experiences. These reactions can be seen as the enduring legacy of our wounds, and render us particularly vulnerable under certain situations. However, if we do the inner work required to travel to the heart of our wounds, then we can reduce the impact of earlier trauma to create more fulfilling, authentic and meaningful lives.

There are many ways in which the wisdom embodied in the conversations that constitute this book can help us to do that inner work. First, by describing the systems constellated by trauma in terms of their psychology, neurobiology and evolution, these conversations enable us to step outside our trauma-derived existence and recognise what we are living. Second, the truths presented in these conversations act as magnets which reach deep below the surface of consciousness and pull our hidden traumatic reality into our awareness. Third, these conversations help us to change how we experience ourselves by explaining that we behave as we do not because there is something intrinsically wrong with us, but because this is how human beings respond to trauma. Fourth, these conversations allow us to know that we are not alone with our suffering, and that there are people who do understand. And fifth, these conversations show us that there is a way beyond our trauma and they offer us maps of the territory that we need to traverse.

We can recover from the impact of emotional trauma, but recovery is neither a quick nor an easy process. There is light to be found at the end of the tunnel, but the tunnel is often long, dark and frightening, both for those making their way through the tunnel and for those who accompany them. The aim of this book is to provide points of illumination in that darkness.

The perspectives

The contributors to this book have their roots in what can loosely be described as three different perspectives: psychodynamic psychotherapy, neurobiology and evolution. The book is structured accordingly. At the beginning of each chapter there is a summary which I will not repeat here. Instead, I will highlight some of the questions addressed by each perspective.

Part I: psychodynamic perspectives

These four chapters explore the psychological dynamics that emerge in response to emotional trauma, and show us how these dynamics influence the way we relate both to ourselves and to others. The psychotherapists contributing to this part of the book are Donald Kalsched, Bruce Lloyd, Tina Stromsted and Marion Woodman. Drawing on professional and personal experience, case studies, myths, poetry and fairy tales, their chapters take us into the inner world of the unconscious mind and body to illuminate what happens following emotional wounding, and how that affects our lived experience. As importantly, they bring to life the work we need to do if we are to heal. Collectively, these chapters invite us to look deeply within ourselves, and they show us how we might go about that. Some of the questions they address include:

- What are the unconscious systems that emerge as a result of emotional trauma? What does it feel like to live a life built around these systems?
- Why does the traumatised psyche become self-traumatising? How do the systems created to defend our psyche create new layers of suffering?
- Why is shame – a feeling of being fundamentally defective and inadequate – an inevitable consequence of emotional trauma? How are our lives affected when we experience ourselves through shame?

- What is the difference between blame and responsibility? Why is this distinction important for healing trauma?
- What is the link between emotional trauma and addiction?
- How does emotional trauma affect our physical bodies, as well as our relationship with our bodies?
- How does the trauma of our parents and grandparents affect us?
- How do we get to know the unconscious mind–body systems that we created in the wake of our traumatic experiences?
- How do we create real, lasting and meaningful change? What does it feel like to go through a process of change? What is required of us? What is required of those who accompany us?
- If we have suffered emotional trauma, then what does it mean to be well?

Part II: neurobiological perspectives

These three chapters explore the biological systems that come into play with emotional trauma, and they describe how these systems are expressed in our lives. The therapist-academics contributing to this section are Ellert Nijenhuis, Allan Schore and Daniel Siegel. Drawing on professional experience, case studies and literature, attachment theory, developmental psychology, interpersonal neurobiology and endocrinology, these contributors take us into the physical substrate of brain and body. This helps us to understand the neurobiological underpinnings of what happens to us both in the aftermath of unbearable pain and fear, and during healing. Collectively, these chapters enable us to understand our subjective experiences within the current scientific framework. Some of the questions addressed in these chapters include:

- How do our brains and bodies mediate emotions? What does it take to feel emotionally secure? What causes emotional insecurity?
- Why is dissociation intrinsic to trauma? What neurobiological processes underlie dissociation?
- How do the right and the left hemispheres of the brain differ? Why are these differences important in understanding emotional trauma?
- What is the 'attachment system'? How do early attachment relationships shape our developing brains, nervous and hormonal systems? How does this affect our lives?
- How do our brains and bodies store the unconscious mental models formed during infancy, childhood and beyond? When models are formed during trauma, what does that mean for us?
- What are the biological mechanisms by which traumas suffered by previous generations are passed on?
- With severe emotional trauma an entire personality may fragment and become divided and dissociated in extreme ways – what biological processes underpin this?

- How can we restructure a brain and nervous system that has been shaped by trauma? What role do therapeutic relationships play? How can mindfulness practices contribute?
- Why is it impossible to heal trauma if we simply talk about our past experiences? Why must we enter into our unconsciously embodied experience to repair the damage?

Part III: evolutionary perspectives

These three chapters explore the ways in which our species' evolutionary past has shaped the dynamics of emotional trauma, and show us how that past is visible in our lives today. The academics contributing to this part of the book are James Chisholm, Sarah Blaffer Hrdy and Randolph Nesse. Drawing on studies of hunter-gatherers, Western societies, non-human primates and other mammals, as well as on modern evolutionary theory, attachment theory and developmental psychology, these chapters take us into the world of our distant ancestors to show us how the challenges they faced have left imprints on our minds and bodies. Collectively, these chapters enable us to understand our trauma in the wider context of our evolved humanity. Some of the questions addressed in these chapters include:

- Why do we have emotions? For what purpose did they evolve?
- Are happiness and emotional well-being goals of evolution?
- How can we ascertain whether an emotional state is pathological or normal?
- How has the deep history of our species shaped the relationship between human mothers and their children? Do mothers instinctively love all their children?
- Why are human infants so sensitive to the way their parents and other caregivers relate to them?
- Children follow different developmental trajectories depending on the quality of their early attachment relationships; can evolution help us to understand why these different pathways exist?
- Could the developmental trajectories that result from childhood emotional trauma be evolutionarily adaptive?
- Are there evolutionary reasons why we care so much about what others think of us, as well as about the quality of our social relationships?
- Why are we prone to becoming trapped in cycles of self-blame and shame?
- How can an evolutionary perspective on development, attachment and emotions contribute to the alleviation of suffering?

Part IV: concluding perspective

When we are emotionally traumatised, we live in an inner world built around the implicit conviction that some aspect of our survival is at risk. As a result, we have no choice but to experience ourselves, others and the world around us through the distorting dynamics of fear, dissociation and shame. This final chapter explores how a broad and integrated understanding of trauma can help us to dismantle these dynamics, transform our 'trauma-worlds' and build a more enriched life.

By way of illustration, this chapter addresses three questions by linking together the insights gleaned from the contributors:

- Why are particular types of childhood experiences likely to leave us traumatised?
- Why does emotional trauma leave us prone to reacting in ways that create new suffering?
- Why is it so hard to make the changes that take us out of our trauma-worlds?

These questions were chosen because they represent different stages in the process of trauma and healing, and because they create an opportunity to discuss important principles that are relevant to working with emotional trauma more generally.

Constructing the conversations

I invited these contributors to participate in this book because their work has made a profound and innovative contribution to our current understanding of emotional trauma and its healing. The chapters emerged from ongoing dialogues that drew on a variety of sources: personal conversations during our meetings; notes I made during seminars and workshops; and passages taken from existing writings. I constructed each chapter by interweaving material from these different sources in order to introduce the contributors' ideas in a manner that is both accessible and has substance. Once each chapter draft had been completed, it was passed back and forth between me and the contributor until the two of us were happy that it expressed both the essence and the depth of their work.

This is essentially a personal book which has been eight years in the making. The deep understanding of the contributors has had a powerful impact on me as I worked through my own experience of trauma. As I engaged with my healing journey, their insights provided me with a feeling of being seen and accompanied, enabled me to shed some of my shame, encouraged me connect to what I carried in both my mind and body, and freed me to experience myself differently. Their understanding also gave me hope that real change was possible and showed me what I needed to do to make that change happen. I sincerely hope that these conversations will be equally inspiring to others who are on a healing journey.

Part I
Psychodynamic perspectives

1 Uncovering the secrets of the traumatised psyche

The life-saving inner protector who is also a persecutor[1]

Donald E. Kalsched and Daniela F. Sieff

Summary

The psychological system created when a child is traumatised is life-saving, but has a terrible down-side. The normal reaction to unbearable pain is to withdraw from the cause of that pain; however, when we are children, and it is our caregivers who are causing pain, we cannot physically withdraw, so withdrawal happens at a psychological level instead. We dissociate. Our relational and creative potential, which in happier circumstances would animate and vitalise our life, goes into hiding in the unconscious. At the same time, another part of the psyche moves to the forefront to become its protector.

This protective system vehemently avoids anything that appears to carry a risk of retraumatisation, but tragically it sees danger in the very opportunities that would bring us healing, fulfilment and meaning. Thus it sabotages these opportunities, perhaps by creating an insidious belief in the hopelessness of our life, or by fostering a vicious, scare-mongering inner critic. It may also sabotage these opportunities by spiriting us into a world of fantasy or addiction.

Rather than providing genuine protection, this psychological system is ultimately life-denying and self-traumatising. The inner protector becomes an unwitting inner persecutor. Healing requires that we move beyond the protector/persecutor, enter into our brokenness and reconnect to our buried potential, as well as to the original pain. It is a difficult and challenging process. The fairy story of 'The Handless Maiden' brings the archetypal dimensions of this system to life, and describes how we can move beyond it.

---

1 Earlier versions of this chapter, entitled 'Unlocking the Secrets of the Wounded Psyche,' appeared in *Caduceus* (2006) 69:10–14 and 70:16–20, and in *Psychological Perspectives* (2008) 51 (2): 190–199. We are grateful to both publishers for their permission to use some of that material in this book.

Daniela Sieff: Your work focuses on the psychological defence system that is created when we undergo some kind of childhood trauma. What is the essence of the system?

Don Kalsched: If, as children, our social and emotional environment is good enough, we will develop as an integrated whole. Our creativity, confidence and sense of self will unfold organically, and as we grow we will learn how to protect our emotional self in a healthy way. However, healthy development is compromised when our sense of self is repeatedly threatened. That can happen if we are abused or neglected, if our needs are invalidated or if we are made to feel inadequate and missing in some essential value. In particular, if our sense of self is threatened and there is nobody who can help us to metabolise our pain, we will enter the realm of psychological trauma.

At this point a psychological survival system kicks in – I call it the archetypal 'self-care system'. The problem is that when we are children this survival system has only a very limited number of options available to it. After all, a normal reaction to unbearable pain is to withdraw from the scene of injury, but because we depend on our caregivers we cannot leave, and so a part of the self withdraws instead. Our essence – the creative, relational, authentic spark of life which lies at our very core – goes into hiding deep in the unconscious. At the same time, another part of our psyche grows up prematurely. It becomes the inner caretaker and protector of our hidden essence, while complying with outer requirements as best it can.

The initial split in our psyche is miraculous because it averts psychological annihilation and saves our psychological essence in a protected and encapsulated state. However, it is also tragic in that it leaves us dissociated from what is most vital and creative in us, as well as from the experiences that make up our daily lives. The emotionally painful experiences continue, but they are not happening to 'me', because the essential 'me' is hidden away.

Dissociation is an unconscious process that goes on outside awareness. It seems to be a hard-wired capacity in the human psyche, like the circuit breaker installed in the electrical panel of a house. If too much current comes in (trauma), then the circuit-breaker trips. That said, we now know that the painful experiences do not disappear but are encoded in the body and unconscious brain.

Daniela: Can you talk about the belief system that children constellate around psychological trauma?

Don: If, as children, our life is sufficiently painful to require a lot of dissociation, and if our painful experiences are not made understandable by our parents, or other caregivers, then we develop a distorted interpretation of our experiences. Striving to understand why we are being neglected or abused, we are likely to believe there is something faulty with who we are: *'I would not be suffering this if I was an adequate person.... There must be something wrong with me.... Mummy and Daddy are right, I am not loveable....'* These beliefs constitute shame – a core conviction of our own defectiveness. As children, we come to these distorted beliefs for several reasons. First, this is typically the explanation given to us by parents – either explicitly or implicitly – and we do not have the knowledge which could help us refute it. Second, our psyche's self-care system can wrestle an (illusionary) feeling of control out of this belief, and create a hope that something can be done to change the situation: *'If only I can become "good enough" then maybe my pain will stop.'* Third, self-blaming beliefs are protective in that they prevent us from becoming angry with our parents and blaming them, and because we depend on our parents for survival we cannot afford to do that. In short, this self-blaming, shameful belief system is the best that our psychological self-care system can do.

However, when we turn our childhood anger away from our abusers, we have little choice but to turn it inwards onto ourselves, whereupon the psyche is split yet again, this time between a critical inner protector and a supposedly inadequate inner child. This splitting of the psyche is a violent process, just like the splitting of the atom, and the fallout is equally destructive and toxic. The split is cemented into the fabric of our being and a (false) shame-based identity becomes the filter through which we see our life. Simone Weil wrote that 'the false god turns suffering into violence; the true god turns violence into suffering'.[2] The self-care system of the traumatised child becomes the 'false god' that turns suffering into violence.

A client that I worked with remembered that when she was four years old her family moved to its first real home. She had been promised a room of her own and a backyard in which to play. On arriving at the new home, she spontaneously picked a bunch of flowers to give to her mother to show her excitement and joy. However, when her mother realised that these flowers had come from the neighbour's yard she went mad. She asked her bewildered daughter: *'What is the matter with you? How could you do that? You must go and apologise to the neighbour now!'* The love, excitement and spontaneous joy that the young girl was trying to express got cruelly quashed. Episodes like this, which happen in every child's life, do not matter too much if they are occasional occurrences or if the mother's empathy intervenes, but this client was frequently shamed when expressing her emotions, and in time she learnt to dissociate them. To achieve that, she buried the vibrant, spontaneous and feeling child, while at the same time another part of her grew up prematurely, developing a self-sufficient armour and becoming identified with her very good mind. However, at the hands of her inner protector, my client began to hate both her body with its emotional feelings, and the expressive, vibrant little girl who lived in that body and seemed to cause all her trouble. By the time she was in her thirties she was a very successful journalist; however, her hatred of her body was expressed through a secret eating disorder. By this point she was living in a world that was severely compromised by her psychological self-care system, even though that system had been created to help her survive her childhood.

---

2 Simone Weil, *Gravity and Grace*, translated by Friedhelm Kemp, Munich 1952, p. 104.

Daniela: You talk about the traumatised psyche becoming self-traumatising – can you elaborate on this?

Don: Once the inner protector has been constellated by the self-care system, it will do all it can to prevent any possible retraumatisation. In doing so, it becomes an unwitting, tyrannical and violent inner persecutor, inflicting more pain, trauma and abuse upon us than the original trauma, and external world, ever did. I like to use the analogy of auto-immune disease. In such disease – AIDS, for example – the killer T-cells 'think' they are attacking destructive intruders but they have been tricked and are really attacking healthy tissue. In the same way, the inner protector thinks the excitement or hope presented by a new life opportunity is dangerous, so does all that it can to sabotage such opportunities. Thus it becomes a pathological anti-life force within the psyche.

In short, the inner protector turns against the very person it is supposed to be protecting to become an inner persecutor. This makes the pain carried by the trauma survivor much worse.

Daniela: How does the inner protector sabotage new opportunities, and keep our essence locked away from the supposed dangers of life?

Don: The primary method used by the inner protector is a self-persecutory inner voice. This voice will say whatever is needed to prevent our essential self from leaving its hiding place in the unconscious and venturing out into a world where it could be retraumatised. For example, if we were abandoned as a child, it might say something like *'You are not lovable, and never will be'* in its determination to prevent our adult self from opening to love, and thus risk being abandoned once again. Or, if during our childhood we were repeatedly told we were stupid, it might convince us that we have nothing interesting or original to say so that we turn down an invitation to lecture, and thus avoid the risk of exposing our supposed stupidity. However, rather than providing us with protection, these negative, demoralising inner attacks often result in deep and overwhelming feelings of hopelessness and despair – a sense that life is for others and not for us.

This negative inner voice is not the only method of 'self-defence' used by the inner self-care system, and although other strategies are less immediately obvious, they are equally powerful, life-denying, self-destructive and self-traumatising.

One key strategy is to create additional layers of psychological splitting and dissociation. Not only do we split into a hidden inner child and a protector/persecutor, but our actual traumatic experiences are dismembered so that our experience is not felt. When a jigsaw puzzle is lying in 500 pieces we cannot see the big picture. In addition, we learn how to move out of our bodies so that we do not feel the full emotional and physical impact of what is happening to us. Once we are able to do that, we feel as though we are not actually there during our ordeals. Rather, we have become a disembodied observer – one step removed from what is happening to us. However, there are costs: dissociated from our experiences, our bodies, our feelings and our lives, we become like zombies – numbed and entranced. In one of her poems, Emily Dickinson described this powerfully:[3]

> There is a pain – so utter –
> It swallows substance up –
> Then covers the Abyss with Trance –
> So Memory can step
> Around – across – upon it –
> As one within a Swoon –
> Goes safely – where an open eye –
> Would drop Him – Bone by Bone.

The inner self-care system is the 'trance' covering the unbearable abyss of unmediated traumatic experiences. It descends whenever earlier trauma is retriggered.

Another method commonly used by the protector/persecutor is to encapsulate us in fantasy. Living a real life leaves us at risk of being retraumatised, so the psychological self-care system recruits the inner imaginal world which can provide a vibrant private space, where the sprit can live safe from the onslaughts of reality. In the fairy story of Rapunzel, the tower in which Rapunzel is imprisoned represents the fantasy world, and the witch personifies the archetypal protector/persecutor who is determined to keep Rapunzel (safely) out of real life. She is known as a sorceress, that is, a spell-caster – an expert in trance states. Peter Pan's Neverland may have been created to serve a similar purpose by author James Barrie. When Barrie was seven years old, his older brother, who was his mother's favourite child, died. Barrie's mother became depressed. In the fictionalised version of Barrie's life, portrayed in the film *Finding Neverland*, Barrie is describing this episode when he poignantly says: *'... that was the end of the boy James. I used to say to myself that he had gone to Neverland.'* In other words, the film portrays Neverland and Peter Pan as the fantastical creation of the young James Barrie, who needed a safe, magical world into which he could retreat, following overwhelming trauma. Stories about fairies stealing children are another way that this archetypal dynamic has come to light, and *'away with the fairies'* means literally that for a traumatised child! The child has taken refuge in the world of fantasy, imagination and dreams. The refrain of Yeats' poem, tellingly entitled 'The Stolen Child', beautifully expresses this:

> For he comes, the human child,
> To the waters and the wild
> With a faery, hand in hand,
> From a world's more full of weeping than he can understand.

3 Reprinted by permission of the publishers and the Trustees of Amherst College from *The Poems of Emily Dickinson: Variorum edition*, edited by Ralph W. Franklin, Cambridge, MA: The Belknap Press of Harvard University Press, Copyright © 1998 by the President and Fellows of Harvard College. Copyright © 1951, 1955, 1979, 1983 by the President and Fellows of Harvard College.

There is something wonderful in our psyche's capacity to invent fantastical worlds which give our threatened spirit a meaningful place in life and therefore some hope – but a high price has to be paid in terms of our adaptation to reality. When a temporary world of fantasy becomes a permanent inner state of being, it takes over. At this point fantasy has become a hypnotic spell that creates a 'comfortable' prison. We are encapsulates in limbo-land; neither dead, nor alive.

Finally, the self-care system may take us into the substitute world of addiction. Instead of real-life nourishment, the system says *'Have another drink'* or *'One more chocolate brownie.'* I often use the image of a hydroponic garden I once saw that was growing the most incredible strawberries. Those plants had their roots in circulating water that was highly mineralised – it was like the ambrosia of the gods – analogous to the mythic world of pure fantasy. The only problem was that these plants were slowly losing their capacity to root in real soil … in real life. Addiction is similar: we are fed on the mind-altering substitutes of pure 'spirit' and so we have the most magnificent experiences, or so we think. But meanwhile we become weaker and weaker. And the more we are fed by our addiction, the less able we become to take root in the world.

Daniela: For me, a verse of 'The Rose'[4] encapsulates the self-care system in a very poignant way:

> It's the heart, afraid of breaking
> That never learns to dance
> It's the dream, afraid of waking
> That never takes a chance
> It's the one who won't be taken
> Who cannot seem to give
> And the soul, afraid of dying
> That never learns to live

Don: Yes, indeed. And those last lines are especially relevant because 'dying' means surrender to the body – to our emotional feelings, but when we are traumatised that means opening to our suffering, which is exactly what the protector/persecutor system is designed to prevent.

Daniela: Is this defence system limited to those who suffered trauma? Have you met anybody who does not have this system?

Don: No – myself included! I lay awake the night before my last lecture listening to a bedtime story from the inner protector/persecutor about how I did not have anything new to say and how my talk was so disorganised that nobody would be

---

4 'The Rose' words and music by Amanda McBroom © 1977 Warner-Tamerlane Publishing Corp. (BMI) and Third Story Music, Inc. (ASCAP). All rights administered by Warner-Tamerlane Publishing Corp. Reprinted with permission.

able to follow it. That is a minor form of this system and I think that it is universal. Not all of us have unbearable trauma, but we are all injured to some degree. We all grow up in a home, or society, where only parts of ourselves are allowed to blossom, while other unacceptable parts are locked away in a hidden recess of our being. Few of us move into the second half of life having lived the first half in an environment where we were fully seen, mirrored, validated and allowed to live. So we all have some kind of protector/persecutor system – what psychoanalysts call a 'sadistic superego'. If we have not suffered trauma as a child the system will not be so extreme, primitive or rigid, but it will still limit our potential and prevent us from being fully alive.

Daniela: You describe the self-care system as archetypal; what do you mean by 'archetypal'?

Don: I use the word 'archetypal' in a Jungian context, by which I mean that the energy that animates the system lays deep in the unconscious, that it is 'archaic', 'primitive', and also 'typical' of humans. Archetypal energies tends to operate on the basis of polar opposites or extremes; good or bad, strong or weak, victim or perpetrator – 'fundamentalist categories' we might say. Moreover, archetypal energies exist in a raw, unconscious, unmediated form, so they are not easily assimilated by the conscious mind and tend to be overpowering. Volcanic rage is an example; when it pours through, we are possessed. Archetypal energy is high-voltage stuff – let us say 440 volts – and in order to be integrated into a conscious human ego it needs to be transformed into a more manageable 220 volts. That transformation occurs through bringing the energy to consciousness, and through human relationships. Without that transformation, archetypal energy cannot be integrated into our normal identity and then, when it is triggered, it can knock out the ego, so we effectively become possessed by it.

Because archetypal energy is located deep in our unconscious, the psyche's way of making it visible is to personify the energy and project it onto either imaginal or real people. Characters in myths, fairy tales, theatre and film portray archetypes. Our unconscious imagination also projects an archetypal veneer onto real human beings such as celebrities or politicians whom we either idealise or diabolise. Turning to the inner world, archetypal figures populate our dreams and fantasies, and are heard through some of our subtle, or not-so-subtle, inner voices.

The archetypal energy behind the psychological self-care system is typically personified by an inner figure that swings between being protective and being persecutory. At times it may take the form of a benevolent angel, a wise old man, a befriending fairy or a great good mother; but at other times it will take a form that is characterised by hostility, violence and malevolence. *The Phantom of the Opera* vividly portrays both sides of this archetype in relationship to an orphaned girl. In the film *I, Robot* the protector/persecutor is personified as the central computer.

Being a raw, unmediated, unintegrated, unconscious system, once the archetypal self-defences have been mobilised the system ossifies into a closed, rigid paradigm which is shut off from human influence. The system resists being educated. This leads to tragedy: because the system is stuck at the original trauma it does not take account of the fact that as we grow, other defences become available, and so our innocent, creative, relational, essence remains forever locked away for safe-keeping. The energy that should be propelling us to grow into who we really are – a process that Jungians call 'individuation' – is diverted into the process of survival, and into maintaining the protector/persecutor.

Daniela: How important is it to you to put this psychological system into a spiritual framework?

Don: The spiritual dimension of the archetypal self-care system has become increasingly important to me because I have become very interested in the process of what we might call 'ensoulment', meaning the way that our essence takes up residence. The psychoanalyst Donald Winnicott called it 'indwelling', by which he meant a gradual inhabiting of the infant's body by the spirit. In theological language we speak of the 'incarnation'. The way I now see the process is best told through a Gnostic myth: at birth, a spark of the divine comes into each of us. If our childhood was well enough mediated, the divinity incarnates and animates our life, guiding us towards individuation. But if the pain we suffered when we were children was too great, and if we developed a powerful self-care system, then that spark of divinity never makes the journey to ensoulment. Instead, it becomes cloistered in an autistic enclave: it is split off into the psyche's deepest recesses. It is kept safe until such time as we can find mediation for the pain that could not be suffered at the time that it was experienced.

This way of seeing has become important to me because I have been impressed that people who have been driven into an inner world through trauma often have mystical and life-saving experiences of the numinous – typically through the flowering of a rich inner life. For example, one client, in a moment of life-threatening childhood illness, had a vision of an angel who said: '*You can leave (i.e. die) or you can stay in life. If you stay it will be hard and painful.*' She chose to live, and her life has been hard, but since that experience she has had a powerful sense that she is companioned, knowing that there is something numinous and sacred in her psyche that holds a larger picture of her whole self. That is very reassuring to her.

It is my experience that the divine often comes to us through the broken places, through those split off and shameful places which are almost always traumatic. When the exiled parts of us are re-membered, and re-collected, and we can welcome them into our lives, there is profound healing. When the banished parts of us return and we can hold them with compassion, a sense of the divine often enters our lives as a sense of wholeness.

Daniela: How do we move beyond the prison of the psychological caretaking system?

Don: It takes great patience, great perseverance and a willingness to suffer the unknown in ourselves and in the world. In short it takes great tolerance for feelings but that is challenging because feelings are what the self-care system is least tolerant of. For the trauma survivor connecting to feelings is a very frightening process, so we need compassionate 'containers' to do this work – by that I mean therapists, friends and sometimes spiritual systems that can help to support us.

It also requires that we travel beyond the familiar story of our own suffering. We live in a very therapeutic culture and almost everyone has a story about having been victimised. We are a survivor of incest, or the child of an alcoholic, or a victim of physical abuse. At the same time, the distorted shame-based belief that we formed as children searching to understand our pain – that we are inadequate and that it is our fault – remains in the background of our psyche. However, the conviction of being a victim, both to our own inadequacy and to the external world, is a story created by the self-care system to give meaning to our pain and to prevent the deeper, original pain from surfacing. In the words of Emily Dickinson, the victim story 'covers the abyss (of the original splits) with trance'. In fact, although thinking of our self as a victim creates a dull, chronic misery, in time this misery becomes comfortable and familiar and it is all too easy to become trapped in it. Therapy, too, can get bogged down in this misery, but ultimately this is 'false grief' because it is the result of the self-care system.

Thus, to leave the prison of the self-care system, we have to awaken from the trance, go beneath our false grief, and connect to the more profound original pain; the pain of the threatened part of our childhood psyche that was banished to the unconscious for fear of annihilation. This is the pain of the 'lost heart of the self' that was innocent and yet suffered terribly. When the innocent parts of us are able to emerge from hiding and enter into consciousness we start to suffer 'true grief'. True grief is feeling the pain held in the innocent parts themselves. When we open to this deeper pain with self-compassion, we begin to cry the tears that reconnect us to our essence. In time we discover a new sense of aliveness and healing.

Daniela: The trance created by seeing ourselves as a victim to either our own innate badness or to an external source also prevents healing because it shields our inner protector/persecutor from our awareness. Any kind of victim or blame story enables us to avoid the disturbing fact that it is our own traumatised psyche which has become self-traumatising. However, until we see our own inner protector/persecutor for what it is, there can be no healing. To find healing we must know our protector/persecutor from the inside, accept that it is our own creation and appreciate its survival value. At the same time we must realise that it is outdated and let it go. In my experience, change only becomes possible once we are able to take responsibility and grieve for the life-denying and self-traumatising system that we ourselves have constructed.

Don: That is very well expressed and original. It is hard to move away from blaming either others, or our supposed badness, and to find the courage to take responsibility for the pain that we have caused ourselves by participating in the cover-up of the original pain (colluding with the self-care system, as it were). But unless we make this difficult shift, we remain stuck in a false grief and are unable to reach our more profound wounds: both the wounds that were unbearable to us because we were so little, and the wounds that our own self-care system inflicted upon us. And unless we reach these wounds, we remain in the prison erected by the self-care system. That said, we can only make this vital shift once we have become able to look at ourselves with deep compassion and forgiveness, realising that our collusion with the self-traumatising system was the only way that we could ensure our psychological survival and protect the animating spark of life at our core.

Once we have recognised our collusion with the self-care system, and once we are strong enough to feel the original pain of our young self, then we can open the doors to the lost spark of life that is imprisoned within us. In so doing, we begin to connect to an authentic experience of our own innocence. As a trauma-survivor who is stuck in false grief, we may tell a story about our suffering that includes 'innocence', but it is a kind of righteous or malignant innocence and often we do not really believe it. Underneath, we still feel convinced of our own innate badness, and although we can see the goodness and innocent suffering in others, we cannot see it in ourselves. However, if we can suffer the deeper pain of true grief, and by suffer I mean really allow it in and share it with another, then we can reconnect to our genuine innocence whereupon an unexpected dimension of the psyche opens to us. A powerful healing presence makes itself felt deep inside of us; a sense of real love and gratitude. Almost all mythology shows that embracing true suffering brings a revelation of the divine. This is why (mythologically) the Christ child, the child of light, is always born at the darkest time of the year in the least likely place, a stable. And why this same Christ figure finds a resurrected life in the Spirit after volunteering to suffer real pain – even death – in the service of truth.

Daniela: In order to reach that place of healing, the whole story on which we have built our life, and the system that enabled us to survive our childhood, has to be dismantled. That is terrifying. It does not change without enormous resistance, pain, fear and a huge fight.

Don: Yes, and it happens one step at a time; there is no quick way through. Most of us come into therapy because something has happened that makes us realise that we cannot continue as we are – something needs to change. But understandably, we are very ambivalent about giving up the defensive system that has ensured survival. In fact, every time the protector/persecutor is challenged, it goes into overdrive. And the protector/persecutor is most often challenged when we start to care about the therapist, or rather, when the wounded little child hidden inside of us starts to make a new attachment to a real person. When this happens, the protector/persecutor will try to sabotage the therapy and the relationship with the therapist in a determined effort both to prevent that part of us from risking possible retraumatisation, and to regain control of our inner world.

I was about to go on holiday and a client, who I had worked with for a year, finally let down her self-sufficient, fortress-like defences. With tears in her eyes she said that she would miss me, and her therapy, while I was away. In voicing this, she moved beyond the clutches of her self-sufficient but isolating protector/persecutor. She took the risk of allowing her wounded, vulnerable and previously hidden child to come to the surface and to express its feelings for another person.

We then discussed ways that she could keep connected to me during my holiday, but that night her protector/persecutor returned with a vengeance: she wrote me a long letter explaining that she could not continue therapy because she had become 'too dependent' on me. Through that letter a panicking protector/persecutor tried to backtrack by slamming the door shut on our relationship. The self-care system went all-out to prevent this woman from living her need to engage in meaningful relationships, because as a child the only way that she could survive was to bury that need.

In this case we were able to work through the attempted sabotage, but this kind of dynamic runs though the lives of almost everybody who has suffered trauma, and in some cases the protector/persecutor system does manage to sabotage the healing journey. Then the person is caught in a tragic and repetitive self-traumatising cycle. Even with those who do successfully challenge the system, every step of the journey involves a huge inner struggle, and enormous fear, requiring tremendous courage

Daniela: You describe the process of healing as one that happens in stages. Can you describe these stages?

Don: Let me try to portray the broad outline of these stages through the Grimm fairy tale *The Woman Without Hands*. This story is an archetypal illustration of how suffering is turned into violence, and how that violence is then redeemed. The central image is a young woman whose father chops off her hands in order to escape possession by the devil. The young woman is thus traumatically dismembered, cut off from her wholeness, her creativity, her agency – dissociated we might say.

In the fairy story, the father offers to keep his mutilated daughter handsomely for as long as she lives, but the dismembered young woman chooses to leave her father's house, and sets off with her stumps exposed. Thus her healing journey begins. Instead of masochistically and passively accepting the protection of the father who has maimed her, she takes the first steps towards finding her own unique life. In terms of healing trauma, this early part of the story symbolises the need to leave the dubious, life-denying safety offered by our inner protector/persecutor. What is more, in setting off with her stumps exposed, the story tells us that it is important to accept our own shamed, 'crippled' condition, with its attendant sense of being unworthy and unlovable. We have to be willing to walk forward into our life despite our wounds, rather than hide from them.

Starving, the Handless Maiden comes to a garden belonging to a king. It is full of fruit trees, but she is blocked from entering it. She falls on her knees and prays for help, whereupon an angel appears and helps her to enter the garden and take a piece of fruit. True to mythology the world over, and true to the human psyche, acknowledging our own brokenness and our need for help opens up deeper resources in our own inner psyche, and often in the external world as well.

When the Handless Maiden returns to the garden the following night, the king witnesses this, and despite her disfigurement he sees her as 'whole', and falls in love with her. Healing begins in earnest. She also, of course, falls in love with him. He holds an image that no-one else has ever held of her beauty and wholeness. In the analogous situation of psychotherapy, the therapist sees our wholeness, despite our dismembered and dissociated state. This can have a profound effect on the healing process.

In the fairy tale, the king then makes the Handless Maiden a pair of silver hands – substitutes for what she has lost. Thus, she is half-way healed. She and the king live together and a child, symbolising the true potential in this situation, is born. Similarly, when as a client we risk letting down our defensive guard and begin to work with our therapist, we are accepting the equivalent of silver hands. These silver hands, provided by the therapist, help to show us that there is a healthier way to protect our self; one which will also allow us to live a more feeling, full and vibrant life. However, because these silver hands come from the therapist they are only of use for a limited period of time and eventually we have to risk giving them up in order to grow our own human hands. This transition is fraught with difficulties. The silver hands are not easily surrendered; the old self-care system will often try to hang onto them in order to keep us 'safely' away from our own unique life.

One way to hold on to the silver hands is for the protector/persecutor to seduce the therapist into its world. As a therapist, when you see the life-denying system in which a client is entangled you want to help, but it is all too easy to be pulled into an illusionary world and to keep feeding the silver hands, instead of encouraging the client to grow his or her own hands. For example, I had a client who would bring me either an archetypal dream or a profound piece of poetry every session. The material was so rich with images, and so full of apparent meaning, that I became bewitched and we spent hours exploring it. However, when I eventually noticed that despite all of our 'work' nothing was changing in my client's outer life, I began confronting her. All hell broke loose. She frequently flew into a rage; threw my books off shelves and hurled coffee cups against the walls of my office. Eventually, on my invitation, she called me at home at three in the morning, after a terrifying dream. She was in a suicidal state. We talked about her dream and she gradually calmed down, but when it looked as though our call might end, she returned to her suicidal state and threatened to kill herself. Having gone through this cycle several times, something in me eventually snapped. I said: *'Your life is a sacred gift as far as I am concerned, but what you do with it is your choice. I am not here to try to talk you into living!'* Then I hung up. Needless to say I had a sleepless night wondering whether to call her back or whether to call the police or an ambulance. I waited anxiously the next morning to see if she would be there for her appointment. But when she arrived she was much calmer and she thanked me for giving her power back. I had finally seen the illusion that her self-care system had woven around both of us to keep her 'safely' out of life, and I had refused to participate in it. That had then opened the door for her to start to grow her own hands, but it was not an easy process to be part of!

This transition from depending on the artificial silver hands to using our own human hands is a 'moment of urgency' and in this fairy story it begins when the king must go away on a long journey. Through a series of betrayals and misunderstandings, the Handless Maiden is now exiled to the forest for seven years where she and her son, named Sorrowful, live in genuine misery and poverty, cared for by angelic beings which symbolise the support that is available within our own imaginal psyches. All the while, the king is longing for her but cannot find her and all through these seven years she is attending to her child, and slowly growing her own hands.

Often, when working with trauma survivors, there are a series of crises like the one I have just described in which the patient feels deeply betrayed by the therapist. Feelings of betrayal can result from the therapist saying something that the patient does not want to hear, or they can be constellated when the apparent 'promise' of endless love and togetherness is ruptured. Perhaps the therapist leaves town like the king did. Perhaps the therapist is inattentive or does, or says, something that reveals the professional aspect of the relationship. Often this 'truth' about the relationship – that it is *both* loving and professional – is too much for the child in the patient to bear. Whatever the trigger, the patient then withdraws. This withdrawal is engineered by the self-care system. The protector/persecutor now fills the patient with '*I told you so!*' and '*How could you be so stupid? Why did you trust him?*' etc. If the bond between the therapeutic partners is strong enough these ruptures can be repaired, whereupon an increment of the previously unbearable pain held by the innocent part of the psyche is experienced and integrated into the patient's relational life. With each such rupture and repair, the patient develops a deeper connection to her inner child 'Sorrowful', grows her own hands back, and the previous dissociation is gradually bridged.

Daniela: You have said that not everybody who has suffered trauma can make this tortuous journey into life. What is the difference between those who can and those who cannot?

Don: I have often wondered that myself. Some people will never be able to surrender the world created by the self-care system. Giving up what has saved them in trauma, and reconnecting with the underlying pain, is too much for them to bear. They are happy with a partial healing and with the silver hands provided by an external support system, and who can blame them? Still others make the full journey into their own unique lives. Certainly one of the important factors is whether the therapist can engage in a relational process with the client and see it through. It is not easy and we are only just beginning to know how to do this.

As far as internal factors, there is something about will … something innate … a creative passion for life and desire to live all of it. There are also environmental factors in early development: has there been anybody on the side of life who could offer the child the love that was needed? You do not need many people to keep that possibility alive for a child – an uncle, or a good teacher who saw the vibrant, creative child who wanted to live. It does not even need to be a human being who keeps that spark alive; it can find sanctuary in a loved animal, or through music, art or nature. However, in order to make the tortuous journey into life, a person does need to have had some experience where that essential spark has been seen, received and valued.

Daniela: You use fairy stories to illuminate the creation and dissolution of the self-care system; however, fairy stories have 'happy-ever-after' endings. Surely they misleading? Even if I go through one crisis and successfully take on my protector/persecutor, I am very lucky if I can get through the following six months without coming face-to-face with it again!

Don: Fairy stories are a wonderful vehicle for talking about the struggle of the soul through life, and even though they may not be 'realistic' I think that we all need stories with happy endings. The happy ending is like the vanishing point in a painting which gives it perspective. We may never get there, but it is the goal and it helps to know where we are heading. The happy ending is peace where there was war ... freedom where there was imprisonment ... wakefulness where there was trance ... love where there was hate ... wholeness where there was fragmentation ... suffering where there was violence.

Sure, the protector/persecutor does keep returning if we are on a journey of growth, and the happy ending is misleading if it is understood in a superficial way or as a bypass of the struggle with darkness and evil. But every time we are successful in challenging the inner self-care system, our world expands, we take one more step towards wholeness, our experience becomes a little fuller, and another glimmer of the divine spark returns to animate our life.

2 Return from exile

Beyond self-alienation, shame and addiction to reconnect with ourselves

J. Bruce Lloyd and Daniela F. Sieff

Summary

In essence, emotional trauma occurs as a result of a discrepancy between an individual's inner and outer world. If our environment cannot give us what we need to grow, we have no choice but to dissociate parts of ourselves, and abandon aspects of our internal reality. In time, we become self-alienated. Out of such self-alienation flows shame: an all-pervasive, embodied sense of being fundamentally defective as a human being. Shame distorts and poisons our relationships with ourselves and others.

In a misguided attempt to alleviate the suffering born of dissociation, self-alienation and shame, we look *outside* of ourselves for healing. Whatever appears to offer us respite risks becoming the subject of an 'addiction'. However, the relief is an illusion. In our inner world, nothing has changed. Rather, our misguided attempt to heal exacerbates dissociation, deepens shame and intensifies self-alienation.

Real repair requires that we turn inwards and forge authentic, compassionate and responsible ways to reconnect to ourselves. We must come to know our shame from inside our embodied experience, engage with our pain and acknowledge our fear. We must discover how we abandoned ourselves, dismantle our old defences and build a life that is rooted in our internal reality – a reality that includes the legacy of our woundedness. The feelings involved in this process can be strong, deep and, at times, overwhelming. Frightened by those feelings, we look for easier options. However, if we aspire to recover from our trauma, and to embrace the life that is authentically and uniquely ours, then we have no choice but to undertake this challenging inner work.

Daniela Sieff: How do you understand emotional trauma and its consequences?

Bruce Lloyd: Put a plant in an environment that matches its needs, and it will develop healthily. Put a plant in an environment that does not match its needs and it will either die, or its growth will be stunted and distorted. Humans, similarly, require an environment that matches their needs to develop healthily. A child's environment can appear adequate, but it may not give that particular child what he or she needs to grow and develop.

In terms of psychological development, the salient component of a child's environment is his or her relationships with parents and caregivers. Did we, as children, get what we needed from our relational environment to develop our individual physical, mental, emotional, relational, sexual and spiritual potential? When some part of us is not adequately mirrored by our parents, caregivers or teachers, our development is stunted and distorted, and we enter the domain of trauma. We unconsciously disown the parts of ourselves which are unacceptable to those upon whom we depend, and begin to create a system that is inauthentic and false to who we really are: a 'false self system'. We abandon what we might have been, to become what we think we ought to be. We set out on a quiet pilgrimage of desperation and despair. We become refugees from our own being. We no longer feel real. We are physically alive, but we die inside. We have no choice. It is our only means of survival.

The creation of the false self system is a progressive process. It represents the first stages of a 'Lost Journey'. This journey takes place under the radar of awareness, so we do not know what is occurring.

Trauma is compounded when the pain of living in an environment that does not match our needs is unrecognised. As children, we do not have the psychological resources to process pain without support, so if our caregivers do not recognise our pain, it is left unprocessed. Unprocessed pain separates us further from ourselves. We separate head from heart. We separate thinking from feeling. We cut the internal lines of communication because it is too painful to stay connected. Unprocessed pain leads to the creation of a fault line which exiles us from our emotional selves. At the heart of emotional trauma is dissociation and self-alienation.

I grew up on a farm. I was outside from morning to night. Aged 12, my world changed and I no longer had that freedom. It broke my spirit. Additionally, I moved to a school that did not understand me because I am not a linear thinker. It was excruciatingly painful. One day, sat in a hall, I discovered I did not have to be there. I could not physically leave, but I could separate from my pain. In that moment I knew that I had stumbled across a way to survive. That discovery was so vivid I can remember where I was sat 50 years later. For many children, dissociating from pain happens surreptitiously, rather than in a vivid moment of realisation. However, the effect is the same; a fault line is created in our being.

Another consequence of trauma is that whenever we find ourselves in a situation which our unconscious perceives to be similar to the one in which we were wounded, a suite of knee-jerk reactions is automatically triggered. We are flooded with a terrible conviction that we are about to be retraumatised. Terrified, we may enter an acutely dissociated state in an attempt to protect ourselves. Depending on our personality, we may also freeze, run away, lash out or become submissive. Typically, our present situation is different to the traumatising one, and our reactions are not based in current reality. However, given our past, our terror is real, and for a traumatised psyche that is all that matters.

Daniela: You see shame as intrinsic to childhood trauma. What is shame and how is it formed?

Bruce: Shame is a deeply held, embodied and implicit belief that there is something wrong and defective with who we are. It sits as a black hole at the centre of our being, and, as John Bradshaw says,[1] is experienced as the all-pervasive feeling of being fundamentally flawed and inadequate as a human being. Shame weeps into the fault line created by trauma. It results in internal bleeding. Shame is excruciating because we become the object of our own contempt. It leaves us feeling profoundly empty, isolated and alone.

Shame is created through many different routes. The most obvious is when we are explicitly made to feel that there is something wrong with us by parents, caregivers, older siblings and teachers. In this case, being shamed is the traumatising wound. However, shame is also created surreptitiously in the wake of physical, sexual or emotional abuse, irrespective of whether shame is an explicit feature of the abuse or not. Similarly, it is created when we implicitly sense that our parents do not want or love us, or when they push us to be something other than what we are.

Shame is inevitable when we are set up for what might be called 'pathological failure'. When we are repeatedly given goals that are beyond our capabilities, we have no choice but to fail and to feel inadequate. The unreachable goals can relate to any sphere of life, including intellectual attainment, sporting prowess or physical appearance. When parents have unaddressed emotional trauma and unconsciously look to their children for healing, we are also set up for pathological failure because we are being asked to do the impossible.

At the other end of the spectrum, when our dreams are dismissed and belittled, we unconsciously conclude we must be flawed for having those dreams. Similarly, when we are told that what we are feeling and thinking is not what is actually happening, we grow up to believe there must be something wrong and untrustworthy with how we are put together.

All too often part of a child's emotional reality is inadvertently shamed. When parents are unable to express a particular emotion, they will unknowingly block that emotion in us. We then conclude that we are abnormal for feeling that way. Before long, that emotion becomes bound in shame, dissociated, denied and avoided at all costs. But emotions are like rivers; we need these rivers in the same way that dry land needs irrigation. Without emotions we become the living dead. We become human doings, rather than human beings.

Sometimes, shame comes to us covertly through the traumas of previous generations. Our identity, and implicit sense of who we are, is created through the mirror we receive from parents, siblings and significant others. If any of them carry unconscious and unprocessed shame they have no choice but to inadvertently pass it on. Psychologically, there are no secrets in families. Wounds that remain unconscious are furtively played out across generations.

1 Bradshaw, J. (1988) *Healing the Shame that Binds You*, Health Communications, Inc, Florida.

My grandfather, who had a small business, got into financial difficulties. His shame was immense. The trouble was never discussed; however, the implicit message passed to his descendants was that we must *never* do anything that might incur debt. In me that was expressed through the belief that I was incapable of running my financial affairs. I distorted my reality, and lived in fear, in order to avoid the risk of repeating what my family had experienced as unbearably shameful. It took me years in recovery to trust myself to manage my finances. As I became more conscious of my fear, and at the same time pieced together what had happened to my grandfather, I began to develop a sense of the inherited shame that I was dealing with. For many people it is impossible to discover the source of the trans-generational shame; then it is much harder to challenge the self-delusional beliefs and fears we have inherited to 'protect' us.

Irrespective of how shame enters our world, it is internalised and woven into our identity. We become 'shame-based'. There is no sense of an 'I' that is separate from our shame, and able to see it for the mistaken, trauma-derived belief that it is. Instead, at some deeply embodied and all-encompassing implicit level, we perceive that our defectiveness is an immutable part of us; something that cannot be rectified or repaired. As a result, the ways we relate to ourselves, others, and the world at large are distorted.

Daniela: How does being shame-based distort the ways we relate to ourselves?

Bruce: To be explicitly aware of our supposed defectiveness is unbearable, so we must, by necessity, escape from self. The false self system, which was created in response to our original trauma, evolves to fulfil this purpose. The greater our belief in our own inadequacy, the more we hide ourselves behind that system and the unreal guises which it creates. As a result, we become ever more disconnected from our own reality and self-alienated. We lack an authentic identity and a means of developing self-awareness and self-worth. And we struggle to find direction, purpose and meaning.

When we are shame-based we tend to criticise ourselves viciously for our perceived inadequacies, hoping to bully ourselves into becoming more than we believe ourselves to be. Typically, our goal is 'perfection'. Convinced that we are less than human, we strive to become more than human. But relating to ourselves this way creates escalating and self-perpetuating cycles of shame. When our attempts to achieve perfection fail, as they are doomed to do, we feel doubly flawed. When we belittle ourselves for our supposed inadequacies we become increasingly self-alienated, enter the territory of self-abuse, and compound our shame. Even when we achieve one of our goals, we are unable to truly integrate our success because of our shame.

Ultimately, the black hole of shame is bottomless. I have the image of millions of people with wheelbarrows carrying their contributions to the edge of a gigantic pit. With the best of intentions, they pour these contributions down the hole in the hope of filling it. This is a fruitless task. The hole cannot be filled; it has to be healed. Until the hole is healed, the bottomless pit of shame exists as an enormous drainage system in the emotional psyche, down which the fresh waters of life pass into the sludge and grime of the sewers. Unless shame is healed we will never be enough. At times, we will feel that we have managed to fill the hole, but like the egg timer, the sand will eventually drain out. Then, we are left with the mad scramble of trying to fill the hole again. This is shame. Constantly… constantly… desperately… desperately… trying to fill the hole that lies at our core with something, anything, rather than turn, face the hole, understand it, accept it, feel it and heal it.

Daniela: How does being shame-based distort the ways we relate to other people?

Bruce: Our relationships with other people are distorted by the hidden imperative to conceal our supposed defectiveness from both ourselves and others. Terrified that we might be exposed, the traumatised parts of our psyche see other people as dangerous. Genuine intimacy becomes impossible. We unwittingly put up barriers, push people away, or try to gain power over them, perhaps using force, or manipulation, or by adopting a victim or martyr stance. These behaviours also create self-perpetuating toxic cycles of shame. Shame begets shame.

At the same time, being shame-based and traumatised results in co-dependency. Being unable to turn to our compromised inner reality for our identity, meaning and self-esteem, we must depend on somebody or something outside of ourselves to give us those things. We do not consciously choose to become co-dependent; it is simply what happens when we are self-alienated.

There are greater and lesser degrees of co-dependency. The most extreme form is 'enmeshment'. We are so dependent on the external, and so out of touch with our self, that we cannot tell where we stop and another begins. We live through another's life. We walk in another's shoes. We feel everything that other does or says as a direct reflection on us. Enmeshment is defining ourselves through others because shame and trauma has prevented us from being able to define ourselves through our own reality.

Daniela: How does addiction fit into the system created by trauma?

Bruce: I do not like the word 'addiction' because it squeezes a fluid and multi-dimensional dynamic into a small and static box. However, as we have no better word, I will use it and place it within inverted commas. Many people drink, take drugs, overeat or whatever, but 'addiction' is not in the bottle or the drugs or the food. It is in our *relationship* to those things. When we are exiled from ourselves, shame-based and carrying buried pain, the psyche instinctively looks for healing. 'Addiction' is a misguided attempt to attain that healing through external means. It is driven by the need to find our way home from the Lost Journey, which we embarked upon as traumatised children.

'Addiction' is an attempt to use something outside of ourselves to overcome the pain of the original wounds, to leap across the fault line that was created when trauma left us disconnected from our reality, and to free ourselves of the mistaken belief in our own defectiveness.

'Addiction' is driven by the need to become who and what we really are; it is an attempt to overcome our thwarted drive to actualise our potential.

'Addiction' is an attempt to find unity; to return from exile. The greater our internal disconnection, the greater our need for something external to bridge the internal fault line. Whatever appears to restore that feeling of unity will become the object of obsession, and its attainment, the means of compulsion.

In short, from within the perspective of a traumatised psyche, 'addiction' is a genuine, if misdirected and divisive, attempt to heal our original wounds, and transform the systems set up in their wake.

People do not understand this, because 'addiction' is such a self-destructive process. What is more, the 'healing' provided by 'addiction' is an illusion precisely because it depends on something external. All the same, the experiences we have when mood-altered give us valuable information which can inform our eventual recovery. I started to use something to change how I felt when I was 15. Being in a mood-altered state offered me a taste of life beyond the cage of my shame-based identity. It gave me an apparent way to connect to the abandoned parts of myself. And it provided me with an experience of unity. My challenge during recovery was to achieve that same transformation without using something external. It took years.

Of course, the momentary sense of 'wellness' that we experience during our mood-altered state is countered by the horrendous feeling of inadequacy that typically occurs when we come down from the 'addictive high'. But tragically, this feeling of inadequacy can also provide us with a sense of unity, albeit a far more pernicious one. We need our internal and external worlds to match, and because shame is formed covertly we do not know why we feel flawed. Thus we are driven to find, or to create, a reason for our supposed defectiveness. 'Addiction' appears to be one way to achieve that: *'I am flawed because of my addiction.'* Finally, there is a fit between my internal and external world. This is not necessarily a conscious or chosen process, and such thinking is hugely destructive. It keeps us locked in a self-perpetuating prison of shame. But in the upside-down, back-to-front, inside-out world that is created in the wake of trauma, it has a logic that makes sense.

Daniela: If addiction is a misguided attempt to repair a psychological system organised around early trauma, what does that mean for working with addiction?

Bruce: Society's way to tackle 'addiction' is to focus on stopping the 'addictive' behaviour. This does not produce meaningful or lasting change. 'Addiction' is not the crux of the problem; it is the visible, external manifestation of an invisible, traumatised, internal state. 'Addiction' is not the issue in 'addiction'; the issue is being traumatised, disconnected from our selves and shame-based.

Thus, separating somebody from their 'addictive' behaviours is only the first part of a process. Without a committed effort to clean out the shame, reconnect to ourselves and heal the original traumatising wounds, the work is incomplete. The 'addict' is likely to 'recover' from 'addiction' by developing another 'addiction'.

'Addicts' have several means to bridge their dissociative splits and blot out shame. There is no such thing as a simple 'addict'. Every 'addict' has an 'addiction' profile. Treating the primary 'addiction' is the first step. But if the underlying trauma is not addressed, we will turn to something else. The new 'addiction' may be more socially acceptable, such as work, fitness or religion, but we will still be relying on something outside of ourselves for our identity and meaning, as well as to bridge our internal splits, and to escape our sense of being flawed. Thus, we will still be living in fear of having our supposed defectiveness exposed. We will still be disconnected from our true feelings and dissociated from aspects of ourselves. There will still be a fault line running through the core of our being.

'Addictions' are not the only avenue we explore when trying to heal our trauma. Some people move to a foreign country in a misguided and unconscious attempt to soothe pain, bridge inner splits and escape shame; others believe that a relationship or children will give them that. Some people unconsciously believe they will find healing in a PhD, an Olympic gold, or achieving partnership in a law firm; others pin their hopes to a face-lift, liposuction or steroids. Most people try several avenues simultaneously.

Whichever avenue we pursue, it cannot work. We are looking for healing in the external world, whereas healing is, by necessity, an inner experience, an inner restoration and an inner reconnection. Recovery is an inside job; a journey into the dark recesses of our being to find ourselves.

Daniela: What does that inner journey entail?

Bruce: When we are traumatised during childhood, we have *no choice* but to disconnect from aspects of ourselves, develop shame and set out on a Lost Journey. Recovery is different. It does not happen of its own accord; rather we have to *choose* to do the inner work. This requires a conscious decision. That said, recovery takes every ounce of courage, commitment and perseverance that we possess. Some people do not have the resources to make that choice; they are not to blame for that. For those who do have the resources, recovery consists of three interwoven processes (Figure 2.1).

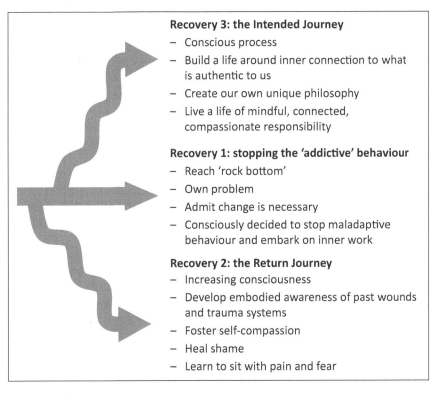

Recovery 3: the Intended Journey
– Conscious process
– Build a life around inner connection to what is authentic to us
– Create our own unique philosophy
– Live a life of mindful, connected, compassionate responsibility

Recovery 1: stopping the 'addictive' behaviour
– Reach 'rock bottom'
– Own problem
– Admit change is necessary
– Consciously decided to stop maladaptive behaviour and embark on inner work

Recovery 2: the Return Journey
– Increasing consciousness
– Develop embodied awareness of past wounds and trauma systems
– Foster self-compassion
– Heal shame
– Learn to sit with pain and fear

Figure 2.1 The three processes necessary for recovery.

Recovery 1: stopping the 'addictive' behaviour

This basically involves the awareness that the systems we created to protect ourselves from our traumatising wounds no longer work. We come to realise that we cannot continue like this. Typically we are brought to this realisation by hitting 'rock bottom'; the inescapable recognition that change is necessary. Genuine change is intrinsically frightening, and letting go of anything that has offered us a sense of protection or harmony is doubly hard. We only change when we are threatened with losing something we cannot live without; when we are more frightened of the consequences of not changing than we are of changing. What constitutes a rock bottom varies from person to person. Regardless of how it comes about, we are left with no choice but to finally admit that change is absolutely necessary.

The concept of 'hitting rock bottom' is relevant to a broader range of issues than 'addiction' – it applies to any problematic behaviour, belief or relationship that we developed in the shadow of trauma.

Recovery 2: the Return Journey

The Return Journey is essentially a process of becoming progressively more conscious of our misguided attempts at healing, dissociated feelings, hidden shame and original traumatising wounds.

We dig deep into our psyche to explore the systems which were constellated by our trauma. We work our way down to the core of our original wounds, and open to the associated feelings of pain and fear. We uncover what happened to us, not necessarily in terms of the factual details, but in terms of how our psyche and body were impacted. We develop an embodied consciousness of how we react when our present situation is perceived as similar to the traumatising situation. We come to know the false self system that we created in order to survive. We feel how we dissociated from parts of ourselves, as well as from our emotions. We discover how we abandoned ourselves, and how that self-abandonment brought us new layers of suffering.

As we engage in this process, we need to develop self-compassion. We need to realise that in the wake of being traumatised, we had no choice about the paths that we took and the psychological systems that were constellated. We need to grieve for who we had to become in order to survive, for what we have lost, and for the pain we have endured.

It is not only the original childhood trauma that we must revisit during the Return Journey. We must also revisit the trauma we inflicted upon ourselves during our misguided search for healing in the external world. We can be desperately damaged by our 'addictions', as well as by the other avenues we explore. These wounds must also be owned, grieved and faced with compassion and understanding.

A related, and non-negotiable, requirement of the Return Journey is the healing of our shame in all of its manifestations. So long as we remain shame-based in any way whatsoever, there can be no real recovery and no genuine healing.

Revisiting our past is a gateway to a new life only if we do not become stuck in our past and defined by it. Otherwise we assume the identity of the 'victim' and become 'trauma survivors'. That is not recovery. Recovery means knowing our past from the inside-out, becoming aware of how it affects our present, and then, most crucially, learning how to reconnect to ourselves, as well as having experiences of living from that more connected place, so that we can build more fulfilling and authentic lives. We are not to blame for our trauma, but we are responsible for its repair.

Equally essential to the Return Journey is an ability to contain pain and fear. When we have been traumatised we will not have that ability, and it takes time, perseverance and courage to learn that.

What is required of us during the Return Journey is very tough. It is tempting to look for easier options. But if we aspire to heal our trauma, move beyond our addictions and live authentic lives, then we have no choice but to undertake the monumental tasks involved in this deep-seated process of repair and change.

Recovery 3: the Intended Journey

The Intended Journey is a conscious process. We become tireless explorers of our internal world and forge a life that is built on an inner connection to our physical, mental, emotional, relational, sexual and spiritual selves. We take responsibility for the way of being that emerges as a result of this inner connection. And we piece together a bespoke philosophy that is rooted in our own uniqueness, values and experience, and stand by our philosophy.

When we embark on a process of recovery we often adopt a philosophy created by somebody else. Examples include joining a spiritual group, becoming dedicated to a 12-step programme or following a particular school of psychotherapy. These kinds of philosophies can help us to develop our awareness and understanding. They can also provide us with a structure within which we can learn to live in emotionally healthier ways. When our internal world is compromised by dissociation and shame that is often invaluable. It may literally save our lives. However, we are still depending on something outside of ourselves for our well-being. We are wearing clothes fashioned by another and inhabiting an off-the-shelf identity. Ultimately, if we are to be true to our own inner reality, there comes a point when we need to step out on our own, trust what is inside us and find our own route. *'To thine own self be true.'* Simple words – monumental task! Leaving a system that has saved us, to find our own unique path is a huge leap into the unknown. It is terrifying. It takes everything we have got.

Thus, although at first glance, the Intended Journey seems as though it should be easier than either the Lost or Return Journey, it can be equally frightening and painful. There is no hiding behind an established philosophy. There is no group to whom we can abdicate responsibility. Other people's discoveries can help us to formulate and validate what we are discovering within ourselves; however, this is, by definition, an individual path – a process that Jungians call 'individuation'. It is also a truly creative journey, in that we have to create it for ourselves. Despite how tough that is, if encountered with a connected, mindful, responsible and compassionate stance, the Intended Journey allows us to forge a meaningful, fulfilling and dignified life.

Daniela: You mentioned that during the Return Journey we need to develop an embodied consciousness of how we react when our present situation is perceived as similar to the original traumatising situation. Can you talk about this?

Bruce: As mentioned earlier, when something in our world is perceived as being similar to our original trauma, a suite of fear-based reactions is triggered. If these reactions run their course, they are likely to throw us into an intensely dissociated state, suck us down into a whirlpool of acute shame, and drive us into freeze, flight, fight or submission. As a result, we become alienated from ourselves and others, and will probably behave in ways that cause ourselves and others more pain.

If we have been traumatised, it is unlikely that we will ever be able to prevent these reactions from being triggered. However, if we can become conscious of how they operate within us, we may be able to prevent them from running their course. Becoming conscious of these reactions is easier said than done. These reactions are mediated through implicit and embodied emotional systems. Thus, the only way to become conscious of them is to relive them in an environment that is safe enough to allow us to develop an awareness of what we are living, while we are living it.

I rarely set out to activate a client's trauma, but when it is activated through real-life experiences, or during our work together, as it will inevitably be, I do not try to placate the situation. Instead I look at it as a learning opportunity. I think of such moments as 'healing crises'. If we can go *into* the old patterns in a way that allows us to maintain even a fraction of consciousness, we lay the foundations for being able to contain those reactions more healthily when they are triggered during daily life. If we avoid re-experiencing our reactive states, and merely talk about them from a safe distance, nothing changes. The principle is akin to that which underlies live vaccinations. We are given a shot of an attenuated and weakened strain of the virus which enables our immune system to learn how to respond if there is a genuine attack by a more virulent form of the virus.

But, and it is a huge 'but', there is a fundamental difference between 're-experiencing' our trauma reactions and 're-enacting' them. To 're-experience' trauma reactions, we must be held in a safe environment, and accompanied by an individual who can relate to us with compassion and consciousness. Thus, although the re-experiencing can be painful, and although we do not necessarily feel safe in the moment, we are neither abandoned in our trauma, nor totally overwhelmed by it, nor are we left in a dysregulated state. That allows us to learn from the re-experiencing. In contrast, when we 're-enact' our trauma, we are swamped by the emotional tsunami of our reactions and retraumatised. Then there is no learning; instead old patterns are reinforced.

The line between re-experiencing and re-enacting our trauma is terrifyingly thin. To keep on the healing side of that line, we need to be working with somebody who is very experienced and self-aware, and who has a deeply embodied consciousness of their own trauma, as well as a profound ability to remain connected to both themselves and us, irrespective of what is happening. When our trauma is triggered, we are likely to behave in ways that will trigger the trauma of the person trying to help us. Unless that individual can remain connected and self-contained at this time, we are not safe and risk being retraumatised.

Daniela: You emphasised that healing shame is central to the Return Journey. How do we do that?

Bruce: First we need to recognise its presence. Shame is an intrinsic part of emotional trauma, but because it disguises itself behind many walls it is very difficult to identify. Most people who carry shame do not know it. Therapists, and others who facilitate healing, also tend to overlook shame. As a result, shame is all too often the unseen, unspoken, unaddressed, ghost in the recovery process. However, it can be observed by the experienced eye of somebody who is conscious of their own shame. It is visible in body posture and gestures, facial expressions, and especially in eye movements.

Healing shame requires more than a cognitive recognition of its presence. To move beyond our shame, we must re-experience it, get to know it from the inside, and we must *feel* how it affects our lives. To achieve that, we must come out of hiding. We must make eye contact with another person and tell our stories from the heart and from the body, not from the head. We must tell the stories of our original wounding, of our Lost Journey and of our misguided attempts to find healing. And we must tell these stories from inside our emotional self, rather than from an intellectual viewpoint.

While telling our stories, we must also separate our being from our doing. Some of our behaviour will have been destructive, causing pain to both ourselves and others. We must take responsibility for that. Yet, at the same time, we must develop self-compassion. We must understand that we behaved in these ways, not because we are fundamentally flawed and inadequate, but because it was the best we could do at the time.

Shame is ultimately a phenomenon that can only be known and addressed through embodied experience; thus it is *how* we tell our stories, and what we *feel* as we are telling them, rather than the actual content that is crucial to healing shame.

This embodied, heart-felt, compassionate telling of our stories is a process, not a one-off. We will probably need to tell our stories more than once, each time feeling and exposing more of our shame, and our experiences. This process is not for the faint-hearted. Most people look for an easier route.

Daniela: Allan Schore (in his books and in this volume) offers us a scientific understanding of why shame can only be known through felt experience. Schore explains how the two hemispheres of the brain differ. The left hemisphere is the seat of thinking, cognition and concept-orientated verbal language. The right hemisphere is the seat of emotion, non-verbal language and our implicit, embodied sense of who we are. Schore tells us that shame is a product of the right hemisphere, and that it is expressed as non-verbal, implicit experience. Given that, we simply cannot get at shame through verbal language and left-hemisphere cognitive approaches. Rather, we have to go into the right hemisphere world of embodied feelings, lived experience and non-verbal communication (for example, eye contact) to heal shame.

Bruce: Absolutely! Schore's work has been hugely important in affirming why we have to work with our own shame in the way that we do. Schore's work has been equally important in explaining why so much is demanded of those who help us to do that inner work.

Emotional healing can be facilitated by a variety of people, including therapists, counsellors, spiritual teachers, sponsors in 12-step programmes and friends. We do not have a good word to describe this wide range of individuals. However, because I want to acknowledge the diversity of people who can facilitate our recovery, I will use the word 'healer' in this context.

Anybody who facilitates healing must know about shame, and the only way that knowledge can be attained is through personal, embodied, right-hemisphere, implicit experience. Moreover, those who help us heal must have come to know their own shame, not because it was a requirement of their training, but because it was utterly necessary to their lives, and their own emotional healing.

Those who are facilitating our healing also need to have done their own shame work, because being a right-hemisphere phenomenon, cleaning out shame ultimately depends on an implicit, non-verbal connection between the healer, and us, as somebody who is trying to heal. Individuals, who have not addressed their own hidden shame, will be unable to connect to us in a manner conducive to recovery. When working with shame, quantum principles of the observer and the observed are crucial; the eyes through which we are seen will determine how our recovery evolves. If a 'healer' has unaddressed shame, then she or he will look at us through tainted and contaminated eyes. If we are met with any level of unconscious shame on the part of the person who is supporting our healing journey, there is a danger that our original trauma will be compounded, and our shame exacerbated.

Another reason why those who support us must be doing their own shame work is because they need to be a living example of life beyond a shame-based identity. We may not consciously appreciate this, but our unconscious will learn from their example, so it is crucial that the 'healer' is authentically living the process.

To help us heal our shame, whoever we are working with has to be genuinely in-tune and connected to us. Rather than hiding behind a therapeutically passive and distant professional persona, she or he has to be *in* the healing relationship. Shame results from closed, non-communicative systems; traditional psychoanalysis can recreate those systems. The 'healer' and the person looking for healing must come together as two human beings, each with their own struggles, frailties, fallibilities and vulnerabilities. There must be mutuality and reciprocity. That does not necessarily need to be explicit, but there must be an implicit right-brain to right-brain communication of that reality.

Daniela: Can we heal enough of our shame to become shame-free?

Bruce: Sadly, no! A shame-free existence is the ideal, but a more realistic goal is to become as shame-free as possible. If childhood trauma left us dissociated and shame-based, we will always be at risk of heading into shame in the domain of our deepest wounds. That will be especially true when our resources are low, as they are during times of growth and change, or when we are tired and drained.

If we are unable to accept that reality, we inadvertently set ourselves up to compound our shame, because whenever we go into shame, we think of ourselves as inadequate. In contrast, when we accept that as a formerly shame-based person we will always be prone to shame, we take the shame out of shame. That is healing in and of itself.

That said, we can heal enough of our shame so that it no longer drives our daily lives. We can also get to the point that when shame does arise, we are more-or-less able to identify it, contain it, and prevent it from taking us into a devastating downward spiral.

Daniela: You said that learning to sit with pain is a crucial requirement of the Return Journey. However, Randy Nesse explains (in his papers and in this volume) that pain evolved to tell us that we are in danger and to motivate us to do whatever we need to do to get out of pain. So why do we need to learn to sit with pain?

Bruce: As you say, the desire to get away from pain is part of our biology. Most people walk through my door because they can no longer tolerate their pain and want it fixed as quickly as possible. Their over-riding question is *'How can I stop feeling like this? How can I get out of my pain?'* It is a natural question. However, if we are to recover from emotional trauma we have to go against our biology. During the Return Journey it is not our pain per se that is important, but how we relate to it.

If we are carrying unaddressed trauma, then we are likely to exist in a state of chronic, deadening pain. This pain is not caused directly by our original traumatising wounds; rather, it is a symptom of the dissociation, shame and self-alienation that characterises trauma. Thus, in the same way that we have to go beneath 'addictive' symptoms to move beyond our 'addictions', we have to go beneath this deadening pain to move beyond it. But beneath this deadening pain we encounter the acute pain of our original traumatising wounds. That is tough. Moreover, we do not encounter the acute pain just once and then purge ourselves of it. If we were emotionally traumatised, the imprint of this pain will be with us for life. We may not feel it on a daily basis, but when something presses on our old wounds, the pain will flare up.

We will also carry the imprint of the pain created by our misguided attempts to heal, and again there will be times when this pain is intense. Additionally, some of the dynamics involved in the Return Journey are painful, as are aspects of the Intended Journey.

Thus, if we cannot suffer pain, we are left forever trying to avoid anything that might trigger our trauma and cause pain. This is not necessarily conscious, but it drives us, and locks us into a small, contracted, trauma-limited world. Moreover, when pain does arise, as it invariably will, not only because we are wounded, but also because it is part of the human condition, we will automatically revert to old ways. We will dissociate our feelings, deny our reality and look to something in the external world to numb our pain.

Don't get me wrong, I do not like pain and I do not seek it out. However, when we are driven by the need to avoid pain, we inadvertently close down and sentence ourselves to a life of deadening, chronic pain.

There is a huge difference between the constructive, acute pain of healing and growth, and the destructive, chronic, gnawing pain invoked by living with the trauma system's status quo. Pain is there whether we like it or not. The issue is not the pain; the issue is: Do we say 'yes' to the pain and grow, or 'no', and wither?

Daniela: What does it mean to say 'Yes' to our pain? Is feeling our pain enough?

Bruce: Feeling our pain is an important first step, especially when we have dissociated, and are unaware of it; however, healing ultimately demands more from us. It requires us to both feel our pain, and to remain conscious of what is happening while we are feeling it. There is a profoundly important difference between being conscious *of* pain and being conscious *in* pain.

Many people are conscious *of* their pain. When we are conscious *of* pain, we feel it, and are aware of our feelings, rather than dissociated from them. However, there is no part of ourselves that can stand beside us in our pain, knowing that there is more to what we are experiencing than what we are feeling in the moment. There is no part of us that can see the larger context, find the meaning in our pain and learn from it. There is no part of us that trusts that our pain will pass. As a result we are flooded by pain, unable to function and frightened. We do not have our pain, rather it has us. Under these circumstances, we have little choice but to fight against our pain, try to escape from it, and feel victim of it and of what we perceive as having caused it.

When we are conscious *in* our pain we are open to its full intensity, while at the same time there is a part of us who stands beside us, remains conscious of what is happening and provides us with a sense of the larger context. This part of us knows that we are in pain, but that it will pass. It also knows that our pain has meaning and that if we stay with it, then we will grow. This part does not have to be big. So long as it exists in some small corner of our psyche, we can begin to let our pain run its course, rather than fighting against it and trying to escape from it. As a result, we have our pain, rather than our pain having us. Additionally, because we are containing our pain, we have more choice about how and when we express it. As importantly, we do not feel like a helpless victim of it, and of whatever we perceive as having caused it. Rather, we feel the dignity that comes from accompanying ourselves with compassion and responsibility, and from knowing that our pain is part of a larger process.

We might call the ability to be conscious *in* our pain the ability to 'suffer' pain. I see one of my most important therapeutic roles as helping people learn how to suffer their pain, so that they can relate to pain in a context of growth, and no longer have to try to escape from it.

Learning how to suffer pain is extremely difficult and takes time. If we were traumatised by childhood experiences, our parents, almost by definition, will not have taught us how to accompany ourselves in our pain, so we need to start from the beginning. It is even harder if our parents shamed us for our pain, because whenever we approach it, our shame will be triggered. In these circumstances we need tremendous courage, patience and perseverance to push onwards.

Daniela: My therapist used to encourage me to stop fighting my pain. I thought he was crazy. For many years, my pain left me wishing I had never been born and fantasising about suicide. I was terrified that if I opened to my pain, I might act on that fantasy.

Bruce: That fear is common, but we turn to suicide as a last-ditch attempt to escape from pain. Thus, if we accept our pain, and learn how to be conscious in it, we are less likely to commit suicide because we no longer need to escape.

Daniela: Why is it crucial that we learn to sit with fear? And what does that learning entail?

Bruce: Most people are equally determined to eliminate their fear as they are to fix their pain. Again, there are good biological reasons for this. However, unless we learn to sit with fear we shut the door to recovery, change and growth. Unless we learn to sit with fear, we can never fulfil our potential.

When fear strikes, it is natural to focus on whatever it is in the external world that is frightening us, and try to change the situation. But, if we are traumatised, we will have a dysregulated and oversensitive fear system, and may see danger where none exists. At these times, we need to sit with our fear, check with present-day reality, understand that our fear may be a trauma-reaction, and take responsibility for it. If we cannot do that, and instead try to change the external situation, we are likely to create problems for both ourselves and others. To begin with that check with present-day reality may only be momentary; but it is a start and we can build from there.

We also have to learn to sit with fear because the changes involved in the Return Journey are genuinely frightening. Our trauma-derived systems are all we know. Moreover, we owe our survival to them. We have no idea what will happen without them. Questions abound. What if the surrender of our old defences leaves us unable to survive? What if, having dismantled the false self system and reconnected to previously dissociated parts of ourselves, we do not like the person we find ourselves to be? What if we discover that our career, marriage and social world are part of the false self system, and inauthentic to who we really are? What if the new more authentic us is called to do work which takes us back into the domain of our trauma?

In short, when we let go of old ways, irrespective of whether we are on the Return or the Intended Journey, we cannot know what will emerge into the space we create. Encountering the unknown is always fearful. When we are unable to tolerate fear, our ability to effect meaningful change is compromised.

Ultimately, it is the physical manifestation of fear in our bodies that we have to learn to live with. When fear is constellated, despite 'knowing better', we have no choice but to feel that fear, and perceive our reality through the lens of those embodied feelings. To sit quietly with that physical experience goes against everything in our biological nature. We have to work at it. Just as we cannot run marathons without considerable training, nor become a quantum physicist without years of study, the emotional fitness required to stay with our fear is gradually built up through hard personal work and lived experience. There are no short-cuts. If we are going to say *'Yes!'* to change, and to growth, we have no choice but to do that work.

Daniela: Can you say more about the process of psychological change?

Bruce: Most of us do not really understand how psychological change happens. Real change occurs at implicit and embodied levels which lie beneath consciousness. Not being conscious of the dynamics involved in the process of change makes it all the more frightening. Developing a sense of the stages we need to negotiate can help us to contain ourselves as we work through this largely unconscious process. We can envision change as consisting of four stages (Figure 2.2).

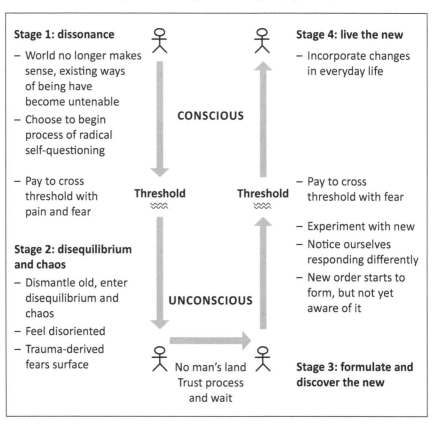

Figure 2.2 The process of change.

Stage 1: dissonance

Events occur in our lives which create dissonance between our inner and outer world. The impact of the dissonance means that it becomes impossible to avoid the awareness that our world no longer makes sense, and that our existing ways of being are no longer tenable. Maybe we have reached rock bottom, and our old ways of coping with our trauma have become unbearable and obsolete. Maybe we are being constrained by the philosophy that held us during the Return Journey, and need to leave it behind. Or maybe we have passed from one stage of life into a new one, and this new stage requires something different from us.

Irrespective of what causes the dissonance, we have a choice as to how we respond: we can deny the dissonance, shore up the obsolete status quo and contract back into our old life; or we can consciously decide to engage in a process of radical self-questioning, commit ourselves to change and begin the process of expanding into a larger and more authentic life.

The desire to deny the dissonance and shore up the status quo is driven by fear of what might be demanded of us: *'Do we really have to give up our old defences, beliefs and identity? Must we leave our job, our marriage, our church, our group? Surely there is an easier path? Perhaps we can tweak the old ways and patch them up.'*

If we aspire to heal our trauma and live authentically, then patching up old ways will not work. Instead, we must consciously choose to suffer our fear, while engaging in a process of radical self-questioning: *'Why is there a mismatch? What is no longer working for me? What is it that I don't yet know how to do? Where am I going? What do I need to change? What do I need to learn?'* At this stage we must hold our questions loosely, rather than actively look for answers. If the change is to be meaningful, the answers have to emerge from deep within us, and that happens in its own time. If we try to hurry the process and cognitively think our way into the answers, we are unlikely to create lasting change. Thus, we must live with *'I don't know'*, surrender to the process, and descend into our unconscious psyche.

During that descent we come to a threshold. To cross this threshold we have to pay with pain and fear. We need to let go of the old and leave it behind; that is painful. We have to walk forward not knowing what lies ahead; that is frightening. Any implication that meaningful change can be achieved without pain and fear is a deception. There are natural resistances to crossing the threshold.

Stage 2: disequilibrium and chaos

If we can work through these resistances, we start to dismantle our old ways of being and perceptual frameworks. As a result, we enter a period of disequilibrium and chaos. We feel we are falling apart. In truth there is a falling apart – the old ways have to be dismantled.

The danger is that we try to pull ourselves together. We might attempt to retrace our steps. We might embark on the types of therapy that are designed to take us out of chaos. Or we might latch onto a philosophy developed by somebody else.

However, the ability to fall apart and reconstruct our lives, as well as our perceptual frameworks, is fundamental to the process of growth. When we take ourselves out of chaos, we deny ourselves that opportunity. As Nietzsche wrote in *Thus Spoke Zarathustra*, 'one must still have chaos in oneself, to give birth to a dancing star'.

During this phase, the fears and vulnerabilities embedded in our original trauma often resurface. Having been deeply imprinted on our psyche, they are habitual. We fear that if we walk forward we will end up in a situation which is similar to the one that left us traumatised. We will be abandoned. We will be shamed. We will be misunderstood. We will lose our livelihood. We will fail. The force behind these fears is born out of an unconscious determination to protect ourselves from retraumatisation. This energy warns us against continuing with the process of change, and as Donald Kalsched has so powerfully described, will endeavour to sabotage our move forward, turning viciously self-persecutory if needs be.

If we can counter this misguided and retrograde protective instinct, and stay with the chaos and the trauma-derived fears, then the process of change moves deeper into the unconscious. At this point, we typically feel disoriented. We have left the old world behind, but have not yet reached the new. We are in no-man's land. This can feel similar to the dissociated and self-alienated states that follow trauma. Hence, we are in danger of being drawn towards anything that offers us a quick fix of unity, and of falling back into some kind of 'addictive' cycle. It takes much experience to differentiate between the feeling of dissociation that follows trauma, and the feeling of disorientation that is intrinsic to genuine change. It is important to be accompanied by somebody who can help us make that differentiation. We also need to be encouraged to trust that our unconscious will find a way through, and wait for our process to unfold.

Stage 3: formulate and discover the new

Eventually, a new order is formed in the depths of our unconscious; one which is more in keeping with our current world. To begin with we are unaware of the changes which have taken seed. However, if we can be patient, the new order will gradually emerge and we will start to notice that we are responding to old situations in new ways. It is important to give ourselves time to acclimatise to these new ways.

While acclimatising to the new order, there will be occasions when we revert to old ways. So long as we have healed enough shame, our regressive steps prompt us to ask ourselves the questions that bring increased consciousness: *'Why did I go back? What triggered it? How was it different to the new way?'* It is through exploring the contrast between old and new ways that change becomes rooted and secure.

Stage 4: live the new

In time, we reach another threshold. Once we have crossed it, we begin the serious business of integrating the newfound ways of being into our consciousness, and into our daily lives. Often this means reshaping aspects of our external world, so that they are more in tune with who we have become. Having got this far, passing through this threshold is pretty much inevitable. Intuitively knowing that often provides a sense of calm.

That said, we still have to pay to cross this threshold, and again the currency is fear. On the one hand, we are frightened that when push comes to shove, we will be unable to live the new. On the other hand, we are frightened that if we do manage to live the new, it could have serious implications for our lives. Respecting our fears, we may choose to re-enter the world in disguise, or we may experiment with living just a little of the new at a time. But ultimately, if we are going to live in accordance with our unfolding reality, we will integrate the new into our everyday life, and make it real.

Daniela: How long does change take?

Bruce: How long is a piece of string?! A change may take weeks, months or years. It really does depend upon the individual. We now know that childhood trauma affects the structure of brains and bodies. Changing that structure can feel as though we are moving a five ton pile of sand from one side of a see-saw to the other side, one grain at a time. Each time we move a grain of sand we go through the process of change, but at some point we move the grain that takes us across the tipping point.

We tend to focus on that last grain – the flash of insight which appears to change everything; however, we must remember that this flash is the culmination of a long and tough process. I recall somebody writing that it took the Buddha 35 years and 35 seconds to gain enlightenment. This is the same principle. In short, we must never be fooled by the simplicity of our insights, or dismiss how painful and arduous it was to attain them.

Daniela: Does the process of change get any easier over time?

Bruce: In essence, real change is an organic process, but that does not mean easy. It can cost us everything both internally and externally. It is difficult, painful, frightening and lonely. To stick with the feelings created during the process of change takes a great deal of trust. We need to trust that we will survive when we let go of the old ways of being. We need to trust that we will move through the chaos and disorientation. We need to trust that we will overcome the old misguided protective forces which are determined to sabotage change. We need to trust that the new ways of being will bring more vibrancy and creativity into our lives. The first few times we go through a process of change we have no experience on which to base that trust, so it is particularly difficult. As we gain experience, although the actual passage through change itself does not necessarily become easier, we do start to trust process as well as ourselves. This helps to facilitate change and makes it less frightening.

Daniela: When you talked about the Intended Journey you mentioned that we need to forge a life based on an inner connection to ourselves, and take responsibility for the way of being that emerges. What did you mean?

Bruce: When our life is defined by trauma we are disconnected, dissociated and alienated from ourselves. Being on the Intended Journey means living the life that is authentically ours, and that requires us to be rooted in our own internal reality. We have to open to our emotions, instead of looking for ways to change them, escape from them or cut them off. We have to be aware of our needs and respect them, rather than invalidate and dismiss them. We have to be able to remain connected with ourselves, regardless of what is happening in both our internal and external worlds. As important, we have to behave in a way that matches what is happening inside of us.

Forging a life built on this inner connection requires that we constantly question ourselves: *'Do I know what is going on inside? Am I in touch with my feelings? Am I conscious of my fear? Am I "suffering" my pain? Am I acknowledging my anger? Am I opening to my love? Am I behaving in accordance with my inner reality? Am I treating myself and others with honesty, compassion and respect? Am I consciously choosing to spend my time on things that matter to me? When I get into bed tonight, will I know that I turned up to the day, and that I did my best?'*

Forging a life based on an inner connection to ourselves is synonymous with living 'responsibly'. True responsibility demands more than the simple ownership of our feelings, thoughts and behaviours. It requires that we tirelessly explore our inner world to discover where our feelings, thoughts and behaviours originate. For example, we need to recognise that although our emotions may be triggered by something outside of us, they arise within us, and are ours alone. Our ability to take responsibility is limited by our ability to connect to what is happening within us. It is similarly limited by our level of awareness; we can only be as responsible as we are aware.

Part of the challenge with 'responsibility' is that if we were shame-based it is extremely difficult to differentiate between *'I am responsible'* and *'I am at fault'*. However, this difference is critical. Responsibility is being committed to our own internal reality, and has nothing to do with finding fault in ourselves, or indeed, in others.

Living our lives within a context of responsibility is an intensively personal experience. We must be prepared to stand or fall by the reality that emerges from our connection to ourselves, and to defend our values come what may. This can invoke deep loneliness and be very frightening. Many people look for an easier path. However, when our lives are built upon foundations of responsibility, we are genuinely accompanied because we are being meaningfully present to ourselves. We are also securely rooted in the ground of our own being.

Daniela: How are our relationships affected when we live this way?

Bruce: Although it might seem selfish to prioritise our connection to our inner reality, the reverse is true. Unless we are aware of what is happening inside of us, and able to take responsibility for it, we cannot give other people freedom to be themselves. Instead, we have to manoeuvre them into being what we need them to be. Our tactics are often subtle, and typically we are unaware of what we are doing. The other person may be similarly unaware of what is happening. All the same, there can be no real intimacy when these dynamics exist.

We can only create truly healthy relationships when we are able to connect to our own reality and stand by ourselves, and at the same time, connect to another person, who is standing by his or her reality. Meaningful relationships are formed at this interface. It is here that there is openness and communication, give-and-take, trust and respect. When people meet at this interface, it creates the dynamic out of which a genuine 'togetherness' can emerge – a togetherness that is fluid and which can grow and change with us and with time.

Daniela: I would like to conclude by asking what 'healing' means to you, particularly in regards to our original, traumatising wounds?

Bruce: Although I have used the word 'healing' throughout our conversation, I do not like it, and prefer to talk about 'wellness'. 'Healing' implies that we can repair our wounds, whereas that is rarely the case. The actual pain embedded in our original wounds does not change, irrespective of the inner work that we do. What does change is our relationship with that pain. For example, one of my deepest wounds occurred through being misunderstood as a child, which was incredibly painful. When I began recovery I imagined that I would learn how to express myself well enough to avoid that pain. But being misunderstood is an inevitable part of my job as a therapist who works with emotionally traumatised people, and it can be as painful for me today as it was when I was a child. Yet at the same time my pain is different, because I have a different relationship with it. These days I am aware of my pain, I know it for what it is, and I understand where it comes from. There are still times when I want to run away from it, but generally I do not. Occasionally I am even able to 'cherish' my pain, knowing that although I would have preferred my childhood to have been different, it laid the foundations for me to become the man I am today.

Sometimes our enduring wounds remain so raw that they prevent us from fulfilling certain aspects of our potential: it is simply too painful and frightening for us to go there. We are limited as human beings; even more so if we have been traumatised. Nobody likes to hear this, but in order to be 'well' we need to face this reality with honesty, responsibility, compassion and grace. We need to foster an identity which is expansive enough to hold our woundedness and limitations without feeling inadequate, or hard-done by.

If we aspire to wellness, then the big question is: *'Do we accept what has happened to us in the past, acknowledge our present reality and say a committed yes to our future growth?'* If we answer this question in the affirmative, then we experience the dignity that is inherent in knowing that we are embracing the life that is authentically and uniquely ours, and living it to the best of our ability.

3 Dances of psyche and soma

Re-inhabiting the body in the wake of emotional trauma

Tina Stromsted and Daniela F. Sieff

Summary

Our journey through life is encoded in our bodies just as the rings of a tree encode the life-story of that tree. If we grow up in an emotionally supportive environment our posture will be secure, our movements fluid and our speech expressive. We will also be at ease with our bodies, and enjoy an open connection between body and psyche.

If we grow up in the wake of emotional trauma, it is a different story. Our bodies take on the postures, movements and ways of speaking that seem to offer us protection: we may puff ourselves up or make ourselves small, overeat or starve, yell or stutter. Once established, these bodily defences limit our experience of ourselves and the world. Additionally, they often create painful physical symptoms.

Equally damaging is the disembodiment that accompanies childhood trauma. Emotions are primarily bodily responses, so by cutting off from our bodies we can distance ourselves from unbearable pain. We are not necessarily conscious of our disembodiment, but there are consequences. We cannot pick up the subtle feelings that reflect our bodies' emotional states and which could act as a compass during life. We have little access to the images that arise in our bodies which could help to guide our journey. We see our bodies as objects and tend to blame at least some of our pain on their imagined inadequacy.

Healing trauma requires that we work directly with our bodies to release what they hold, and forge the connections between body and psyche that will enable us to live an embodied life. There are many creative ways to do this work, including authentic movement, voice-work, yoga and working with masks.

Daniela Sieff: Why should we pay attention to the body when we work with trauma?

Tina Stromsted: Our journey through life is not simply psychological or spiritual; it is also *concretely* experienced and recorded in the body. As a result, trauma is written into our physical bodies as well as into our minds. It literally shapes our nervous and hormonal systems, our musculature, posture and our movements.

Trauma, which is often defined as deep and lasting wounding resulting from overwhelming pain, can also sever our connection with our bodies. Sensations and emotions arise in the body and then 'make their way' up through the ancient parts of the brain to the oldest part of the right hemisphere – which as Allan Schore tells us, is the side of the brain that is primarily responsible for our emotional life. From there, from what we understand at this time, information passes to the more recently evolved areas of the right brain, which is where we become conscious of emotions and can start to put words to them. However, when pain is too great for us to bear, we block its journey into consciousness and into words, dissociatively trapping it in our bodies and in the lower regions of the right brain, where the survival-oriented fight/flight/freeze defence mechanisms are organised. However, we still need to make sense of our experiences, so we create substitute narratives, often self-critical ones, to help us understand what is happening beneath our awareness. This is often our only option at the time, but it means that our pain cannot be metabolised. It also means that we end up living half a life, inhabiting our minds and the critical stories we were told or came to believe, but not our bodies. What is more, when we dissociate from our bodies, we have no access to the emotions that normally guide our actions, and so we find ourselves without a compass.

Unable to draw on our bodies' natural wisdom or to reach out for needed support from others, we may feel 'orphaned', deflated or mistreated; slow to trust, or powerless. Some may inflate their importance in an effort to make up for a profound sense of impotence and emptiness. Others may become abusers, repeating the crime in trauma cycles that are passed down from one generation to the next, often non-verbally, in the earliest phases of life.

Trauma also shapes the way we think about our bodies. All too often, we mistakenly see our bodies as the source of our wounding and consequently despise them.

Despite the impact of trauma on our bodies, Western culture has, until very recently, paid little attention to the body when working with emotional trauma. However, we only have to look at common metaphors to realise that we implicitly know that our emotional life is deeply connected to the life embodied in our flesh and bones: 'I need to get this off my chest', 'I've had to shoulder that secret for so long', 'I was beside myself', 'I felt torn in two directions' and 'the ground was pulled out from under my feet' are familiar examples.

Ancient healing practitioners saw the body as essential, but although the Greeks believed in developing the body, they split it off from abstract, cognitive, intelligence, which they elevated. Later, believing the body to be the repository of sin, Christianity encouraged people to strive to move beyond their 'animal flesh' and reside in spirit.

We will not heal trauma if we reside in spirit – quite the opposite. To heal trauma we must bridge the dissociation between body and psyche, pay careful attention to what our body holds and re-inhabit it. To achieve that we have to work directly with our bodies, rather than seeing them as second-class citizens compared to our psyches.

It was at our family dinner table that I first became aware of the existence of the split I had suffered between body and spirit. The world of the intellect was lived above the table through literary, cultural and political conversations, whereas the world of the body was lived below the table through frozen legs, kicking feet and hands that were twisting napkins. Growing up I found myself as interested in the world under the table and in what our bodies were expressing as I was in the world above it. My work as a healing practitioner has deepened that interest.

Daniela: What would a healthy relationship with our bodies entail?

Tina: First and foremost, we would treat our bodies with respect and love. We would foster appreciation for their natural shapes, listen to their needs, and develop a sense of their intrinsic rhythms. We would feed our bodies with wholesome food and find a nourishing and sustainable balance between activity and rest, stimulating experiences and soothing ones, social relating and inner time. We would give ourselves time to walk, swim, dance and sing, and to fill our senses with the sights, sounds, smells and textures of the natural world. We would create opportunities to experience ourselves as embodied creatures that are a vital part of the web of life.

We would be connected to our bodies and allow their feelings and sensations to flow freely through us. We would give just as much value to what our bodies feel as to what our minds know. We would inhabit our bodies just as much as we inhabit our minds.

Because emotions are primarily bodily states, a healthy relationship with our bodies also requires that we are able to regulate our emotions and soothe ourselves when distressed, so that our bodies do not have to suffer prolonged periods of either stressful hyper-arousal or flattened hypo-arousal. To do that we need to be able to tolerate strong emotions when they sweep through us, finding ways to express and/or contain them, depending on the situation. Otherwise we have no choice but to try to escape from those emotions by splitting mind from body, by entering a flattened depressive state or by turning to an addiction. Additionally, when we are unable to tolerate our emotions, our musculature, organs and nervous system are left carrying our emotions for us.

We are born with the potential to have a healthy relationship with our bodies, yet realising this potential is deeply impacted by our early relationships. Our parents' attitudes about and treatment of their bodies, and ours, makes a lasting impression. If there's trauma involved from a deeply troubled childhood, it will take patient, sensitive work to bring the dissociated parts – the split-off embodied sensations, emotions and memories – back together so we can experience a sense of wholeness and well-being.

Daniela: In terms of objectifying our bodies, it seems that in the Greco-Christian belief-system we needed to tame and shape our bodies in order to secure the love of God, whereas in today's world we believe we need to tame and shape our bodies to secure the love of other humans. That belief seems to be particularly strong in those who, as a result of troubled early relationships, grow up believing they are inadequate and unlovable.

Tina: Absolutely. As children, if our parents and caretakers mistreat, neglect or in other ways fail to attune to and love us in the way that we need to be loved, then we seek to understand why. The conclusion we invariably draw is that there is something wrong with us that makes us unlovable and it is all too easy to imagine that it is our bodies. This is partly because of our culture, and partly because it gives us hope that we can 'fix' or control what is 'wrong' with us. As a result we may resort to drastic measures: we may get caught in a spiral of fad diets; get our fat sucked out; take steroids; inject the toxin Botox into our face and have 'body-enhancing' implants – all in the hope that if only we can achieve a perfect body we will finally become acceptable and lovable.

A client who, as an adult, had surgery to reshape her nose, was about 12 years old when, looking at herself in a mirror, her mother happened to walk by. In a kindly tone, her mother said *'It's too bad about your nose, honey, but when you get older you could do something about that.'* The mother, unable to love her own body and wanting her daughter to be happy, sincerely believed her child would have more chance of happiness if her nose was a different shape. But unfortunately what this mother ultimately gave her daughter was not the opportunity for happiness, but a deeply held belief that she was unattractive and that only surgery could change that.

Some people take such beliefs to an extreme and are convinced that they will only be lovable if they get rid of parts of their body. I read about a man who, hating his perfectly healthy legs, tried to find a surgeon who would amputate them.[1] None would agree; however, his hatred ran so deep that he packed dry ice around his legs and caused himself such severe damage that both limbs had to be amputated. This man had grown up when polio was common, and as a child he noticed how kind and empathetic people were to those who had lost limbs. Having never been treated with kindness, he developed the unconscious belief that he would only become lovable if he did not have legs. Thus he grew to hate his legs because he believed that they stood between him and love.

Face-lifts and Botox bring different problems. During conversations we depend on non-verbal cues to help us understand what is happening in somebody's internal world. After cosmetic surgery those cues are less available so it is challenging for us to engage with a person who's undergone such work. However, our lack of engagement may leave the person feeling they are still not attractive enough, and that may drive them toward more cosmetic procedures. But more procedures will make their predicament worse; the only way through is to address the emotional issues that lie beneath the surface of the skin.

Daniela: It is not only our attitude about our bodies that can become distorted with childhood trauma, but the physical body itself can become distorted too.

Tina: Through posture, gait, gestures, movement and muscular tone, our bodies record how we have shaped ourselves in response to our emotional environment.

---

1 Orbach, S. (2009) *Bodies,* New York, NY: Picador Press pp. 24, 28–29.

If we were held with love and attuned attentiveness as infants, that memory will be embodied, allowing us to become adults who hold ourselves securely and move in a strong, lyrical, flexible, coherent way. If we were held with ambivalence or cold detachment, then there may be areas of our bodies that are stiff, frozen, rigid and deadened. If we were sometimes held with a grasping neediness, sometimes with anger, and at other times with detachment, then our bodies might move in disorganised and conflicting ways and when we reach for something or someone, our arms might stretch forward while our pelvis pulls back. Culture also has its impact on our embodied shapes and movement patterns, as does the zeitgeist we were born into; the spirit of the times or larger matrix in which we develop.

The forms that our bodies take encompass more than just a simple reflection of our experience; they can also be protective. In response to physical or emotional trauma, we learn to take up certain postures in an attempt to protect ourselves. Wilhelm Reich was one of the first people to articulate this in the 1930s, and he called the process 'body armouring'. For example, we might push our chest forward and puff it out, having learned that we can intimidate others into leaving us alone. Conversely, we might collapse our chest and make ourselves small, having discovered that the less threatening we appear, the more chance we have of averting attacks, or perhaps eliciting caretaking responses from others. Animals are experts at this, instinctually changing their shape to improve their chances for survival.

When we *repeatedly* have to take on a posture in order to protect our self, that posture becomes part of who we are, shaping how we move in the world and ultimately how we experience it. If a childhood need to disconnect from unbearable pain left us with a head position that is set apart from the body and angled upward, as adults we may find it easier to have lofty thoughts than to connect to our needs and our emotions. Others may also think we are aloof, rather than simply doing what we can to cope with vulnerability. When the helplessness of our childhood becomes enshrouded in sunken shoulders, a collapsed chest and withdrawn limbs, then it is incredibly hard to reach out into the world, and others tend to look like 'parents' who are going to be critical. Worse still, with such a posture we are more likely to behave in ways that *draw* that critical energy to us. So our body's early attempts to protect us unwittingly become a conduit for recreating our painful early experiences, eventually producing a belief that the world is an unkind or dangerous place.

In addition, body armouring can cause physical pain. A woman that I worked with, who I will call Kate, suffered childhood sexual abuse. Her terror and pain were held in her clenched and frozen pelvis and in her arms, which were permanently tensed in an unconscious attempt to 'keep a grip on herself' and in the hope that she might be able to push her abuser away. Kate also binged on food, because somewhere inside she believed that if she became large enough then she would no longer be subject to abusive sexual attention.

However, the costs were severe. Kate's frozen pelvis left her with chronic lower back pain and her tensed arms resulted in persistent pain in her shoulders and neck. Her binges left her feeling terrifyingly out of control, and that was an unconscious reminder of her childhood trauma, when as an abused child she had had no control over what happened to her. In addition, she hated herself for being fat because a part of Kate secretly hoped a prince would rescue her from her pain and take care of her, and that part believed that no man would be attracted to her. So, as a result of her physical response to early abuse, Kate was left in chronic pain, and at war with herself. Kate's situation is not unusual. Many who suffer some kind of childhood trauma end up with their own unique set of emotionally and physically painful embodied consequences.

It is not just 'body armouring' that can be problematic. Secondary effects of trauma often involve somatic symptoms such as anxiety, chronic depression, fibromyalgia, migraines, skin disorders, eating disorders, sleep disorders, chronic fatigue syndrome, mysterious 'allergies', developmental delays, hormonal imbalances, inhibited growth, sexual problems, flashbacks, nightmares, obsessions, muscles spasms, fear of intimacy, addictions aimed at self medicating, and more.

Daniela: Donald Kalsched (in his books and in this volume) describes how the defences that we develop to protect ourselves as wounded children become so determined to prevent us from being retraumatised that they become self-persecuting. Can the protector/persecutor be written into our bodies as well as into our psyches?

Tina: Very much so, and Don's work has made profound inroads in deepening our understanding of these internalised dynamics. Imagine that as a child, whenever we started to cry, our parent said something like *'If you don't stop I'll give you something to cry about.'* it would not be long before we learned to bite our lip or clench our jaw to inhibit our tears. In doing so, we would protect our self from overt criticism but also incorporate that inhibiting, critical parent into the musculature of our face.

I had a patient who grew up in a Calvinistic household where pleasure was severely frowned upon. As a result, whenever he planned something that might be enjoyable, his body did whatever was necessary to keep him away from that supposedly unacceptable emotion. By way of examples, three days before leaving for a holiday in Hawaii, he lifted something that was far too heavy and damaged his back so badly that he could not go; he signed up for music lessons, but fell and broke his wrist so that he could not play; the day before going on a weekend hike with friends, he sprained his ankle. In short, this man's intense fear of pleasure – instilled in his unconscious during his childhood – was played out through his body which was trying to protect him from going into forbidden territory.

It is not uncommon for our speaking voice to be physically constrained by an embodied 'protector/persecutor'. Growing up in a healthy emotional environment our voices become rooted in our bodies. But in the case of childhood trauma, that cannot happen because it is too dangerous to speak our truth – so we may stutter, or talk with the voice of an unthreatening little girl or speak with a restricted, thin sound. Although these ways of speaking may protect us as children, as adults they prevent us from expressing our truth, sticking up for our values and being heard.

Daniela: Does trauma affect our breathing?

Tina: It does. If we have had a secure childhood, then we are likely to breathe deeply and easily, taking in life in a natural, effortless way. However, if we have suffered emotional wounding and lived in fear, then we are likely to constrict our breath, keeping it high in our chest, with our diaphragm held tight. This not only perpetuates our state of fear; it also contributes to the process of separating us from our bodies and prevents our emotions from reaching awareness. Neurologically speaking, when we constrict our breath, the part of the brain that is able to reflect and process what is happening (the orbitofrontal cortex) is dampened down, whereas the emotional limbic brain, which mediates our defence system, takes over.

Daniela: Can you speak to the need to work directly with our bodies as part of the process of healing trauma?

Tina: As I mentioned, one of the common consequences of early trauma is that we become dissociated from our bodies. If we speak our trauma story without attending directly to our bodies, we are at risk of perpetuating that dissociation rather than healing it. We also need to work with our bodies because, as we have discussed, many of the consequences of trauma are lodged in our bodies, and we simply cannot get at them through words.

Equally important is what Allan Schore teaches us: early trauma is typically stored in the right hemisphere of our brains, and the primary language of the right brain is images, metaphor, sensations and bodily emotions rather than words. Thus to access what the right hemisphere holds and to rediscover the aspects of ourselves that lie dormant, injured or silenced, we need to work in its non-verbal vocabulary.

Daniela: How do we go about working with our bodies?

Tina: The 'animal body' is instinctual and loyal. It longs to communicate its inner truth but it will hold tight until it is safe enough to do so. Thus it is essential that we find an environment in which our body's truth can be received in an attuned, respectful and non-judgemental way. Generally that means finding a therapist who is attuned to his or her own body and who can be present to our emotional experiences, and resonate with them. Such an attitude helps us to cultivate acceptance and curiosity about the meaning of our bodily communications which are typically expressed through non-verbal channels, such as body posture, spontaneous gestures, breathing patterns, tone of voice, quality of eye contact, rhythm and more. A sense of natural embodiment on the part of the therapist also invites the aliveness of our body into the space.

Once a sense of safety is established, we (as clients) can start to tell our story while reconnecting to the embodied aspects of our experience. To do that we need to slow down and pay deliberate attention to the sensations, feelings, movements and postures that may be present. The very act of pausing and bringing our embodied reality into awareness can change the anatomy of our brains as this interrupts our habitual journey down well-established neural pathways, and begins to build new pathways that offer us different options.

The next step might involve exploring a particular movement or posture that has come into awareness. For instance, becoming aware that we are tapping our feet, we can explore what may be revealed if we exaggerate that movement. Maybe our foot-tapping is powered by an unconscious desire to kick away emotional attacks; and maybe we realise that we would have gotten into even more trouble if we had tried to kick away emotional attacks when we were younger so we have hidden that energy in our feet. But as an adult on a healing journey that kicking energy could be profoundly transformative, and allowing the kick to become as big as it wants could help us to integrate that energy and use it to fuel change.

I worked with a woman who I will call 'Lydia'. Lydia constantly pulled at her hang-nails, and scratched the back of her hands until they bled, but she was barely aware of what she was doing. When she slowed that movement down, noticed her sensations and feelings and gave voice to the words that came to her, she said things like *'raw... torn... hurt... wounded'*. In a safe environment which fostered curiosity rather than shame, Lydia realised that in order to protect herself during her childhood, she had split-off those feelings from consciousness and buried them in her body where she was able to express them only obliquely.

Descending to a deeper layer in her psyche Lydia was able to bring even more awareness to her hands and to the meaning of the ripping gestures. As a child she had been unable to use her hands to push away the people who were abusing her, consequently she had experienced her hands as useless and herself as having no agency. The fairy tale of the 'Handless Maiden' resonated with her, as did images of the limp and constrained wrists of women who were once placed in stocks, accused of being witches. In that context, ripping her hands was not only an expression of Lydia's pain, it was also her way of punishing her supposedly useless hands for being unable to stop the abuse.

Daniela: Once we discover what our bodies carry, how can we take the next step?

Tina: We need to work with our bodies to build the resources that will allow us to free our bodies of their burdens. This involves learning to do what was once too dangerous for us to do. For example, after Lydia had gained these insights into her relationship with her hands, we worked extensively with 'directed movements'. These were specifically designed to help Lydia establish ways of holding herself that would create the foundation for a greater sense of agency. To start with we worked on grounding. Placing both feet firmly on the floor, about shoulder-width apart and with knees gently bent, Lydia pushed each heel into the floor. Through this movement she began to experience her connection to the ground; she started to develop a sense of having her own legs to stand on; and she began to feel the support her legs provided for her whole skeletal muscular system.

Changing how we stand, or altering other aspects of our posture, does not magically bring psychological change, but unless we change our muscular patterning, we physically limit what we can experience and the changes that can be made. So the first step for Lydia was to develop her body's ability to take on the hitherto unknown way of standing, and through repetition and patience, build the new neural pathways that would enable her new posture to become part of who she was.

Drawing on the support offered by her new posture, I invited Lydia to experiment with voicing sounds like 'Haa' in a full-bellied, assertive and powerful way. For several weeks she played with that – making the 'Haa' softer and louder, stronger and faster, seeing how each variation felt. Once she could say a powerfully embodied 'Haa' with ease, Lydia started to explore how it felt to say 'No!' rather than 'Haa'. 'Haa' is a relatively safe sound to voice because it does not have to mean anything; however, saying 'No!' from a connected, powerful, full-bellied place can be terrifying for many traumatised individuals.

Having practised her 'No!' for many weeks, Lydia's hands, which had previously hung limply from her wrists, began to form fists. Lydia explored how that felt and began to play with her fists. Then she started pushing against my outstretched hands, while grounding her feet powerfully on the floor, and saying 'No'.

It is one thing to talk about needing to develop a sense of confidence by becoming more assertive and finding one's voice, but quite another to live that. Gradually, within the safety of our relationship, Lydia began to experience a stronger and more embodied sense of agency. And because that experience was rooted in her body, Lydia was eventually able to take her newly developed sense of competency out of the consulting room and into the world, where it was powerful enough to enable her to say 'No!', both to her abusive husband (whom she eventually left) and to her bullying workmates.

Daniela: Is there a role in healing trauma for movement practices that follow an established form such as yoga or Tai Chi?

Tina: Forms like yoga and Tai Chi can be fantastic when we are beginning to connect to our bodies in the wake of trauma. They ease the breath and offer us a safe and containing framework in which we can start to become aware of both bodily sensations and how we hold ourselves. They help us to develop mental discipline and to become more mindful of our bodies. Their repetitiveness can be wonderfully comforting, enabling us to hold our self together when the chaos feels too much. They teach us new movements, thus helping us to move beyond the physically embodied defences that we have developed. And they are often done in a class, which offers us a feeling of community.

However, in terms of healing embodied trauma there are limitations to these practices; because they are directed by someone else, we are manoeuvring our bodies into someone else's standardised movements, rather than finding our own reality. Free-form movement practices, in contrast, offer us the opportunity to open to movements that spontaneously emerge, often from a deeper unconscious source.

Jung called the material that emerges from deep within our unconscious minds and bodies 'shadow material'. By this he meant emotions or expressions that lie beneath our conditioning and beyond our conscious awareness. These unfamiliar, forgotten, rejected, despised, underdeveloped or as yet undiscovered aspects of ourselves seek expression through unplanned gestures (as well as through slips of speech, body symptoms, relationship issues, accidents and other phenomena). We need to welcome these shadow aspects into our lives if we are to find a sense of wholeness, and the freer forms of movement exploration can help us do that.

Ultimately, it is important to have a range of bodily practices so that we can use structured and predictable forms when we are feeling fragile, and freer forms when we are feeling strong enough to explore the unknowns that we hold in our bodies and in our unconscious minds.

Daniela: Can you describe some of the freer forms of body work?

Tina: One of the most potent practices that I have discovered is Authentic Movement, a form of dance therapy, originated by Mary Starks Whitehouse (1911–1979). Authentic Movement facilitates a descent into the body and into the inner world of the psyche through unstructured, natural movement. It encourages us to surrender our habitual reliance on the verbal, rational, linear, time-bound properties of the left hemisphere, and instead to inhabit the non-verbal, affective right hemisphere and the body itself. With practice, unconscious emotions and gestures find words, the left and right hemispheres become more integrated, and we experience a more spirited sense of embodied aliveness, coming home to the body in the context of a supportive relationship.

Authentic Movement can be practised with two people, or in a group. The process involves a mover, and a witness who sits to the side of the room and remains present to the mover. There is no music, no choreography, no performance, no agenda, no right or wrong way to move. As mover, we find a place in the room, close our eyes, listen inwardly and wait for an inner impulse to move. When an impulse forms, rather than trying to control the process and direct it, we surrender to it and follow it, discovering where it may lead us. As Mary Starks Whitehouse said:[2]

> Movement, to be experienced has to be found in the body, not put on like a dress or coat. There is that in us which has moved from the very beginning; it is that which can liberate us.
>
> (p. 51)

Learning how to surrender to and be guided by the life impulse in the body can be healing in and of itself. If our childhood environment does not support us, then we cannot take the risk of allowing what is inside of us to emerge. But when practising Authentic Movement in a safe environment, we have the freedom to follow what is spontaneously unfolding within us, perhaps for the first time in our lives.

Engaging in the practice with an attuned witness also offers us an opportunity to let down our dissociative defences and tune in to our inner landscape of sensations, noticing what happens to our breathing, where we clench muscles and restrict our movement, and where there is a feeling of life and softness. We pay attention to how the movement feels and the sensations we are experiencing in our body. We greet any images that form and any dreams that return to mind. We notice any emotions and memories that arise. And we acknowledge anything that our bodies might do to push those emotions and memories away.

---

2 Whitehouse, M.S. (1999) Physical Movement and Personality. In P. Pallaro (ed.), *Authentic Movement: Essays by Mary Starks Whitehouse, Janet Adler, and Joan Chodorow* (Vol. 1, pp. 51–57). Philadelphia, PA: Jessica Kingsley Publishers.

Through this process we create gateways to our unprocessed trauma. Often that will involve literal re-enactments of the movement patterns surrounding our wounds. These are the places where resources ran out and we had to cower, freeze or puff ourselves up to survive. If we can return to the site of the wound, with the additional resources of adulthood and embodied, depth-oriented therapeutic practices, we can heal ourselves. A man I was working with in an Authentic Movement group described it like this:

> Closing my eyes, I feel unsteady, like an infant. Then I sense myself moving into young adulthood and feel angry, restricted, inhibited. When asked to imagine ourselves in the context of our 'family's dance', I feel my family moving in tight dance steps in small circles, reflecting our strict Irish Catholic heritage, which inhibited freedom of expression. My movements are wild Dionysian lunges away from them.
>
> … Beginning with controlled Tai Chi movements, I immediately feel chills in my body. This makes me close up and drop to my knees – a closing up that seems to happen when I stop controlling my actions. As I give up control I don't know how to act; my natural instincts feel as if they have died of inactivity.
>
> On my knees, anger rises up in me. I get up and begin to walk across the room and then pace back and forth. I am very agitated and want to explode and let whatever is holding me so tight come pouring out.
>
> Then something happens so naturally that I am not even aware of the change. The anger and agitation give way to a sadness that feels as far away as it is present. I sit down and lean against the wall, feeling small and innocent, and begin rubbing my right leg. I am lost in this moment for a few minutes when all at once I realise what I am doing. Tears come into my eyes. Was I not being seen? Was my pain not valid? I remember looking at my mother in front of the doctor's office and saying, 'I hope something's wrong with me so Dad won't be mad.' There was something wrong, but it took the doctors two years to find the cancerous tumour in my right hip.
>
> When we gather together after the movement, I share what I experienced, feeling deeply touched, vulnerable and astounded that so much memory and feeling could be recovered in that simple gesture of rubbing my leg. It feels good to be heard and important to have my feelings and pain acknowledged. I feel a lost piece of myself return.

Authentic Movement does not just help us integrate our old trauma; it can also help us form a bridge to our unconscious. Through the practice we can discover and develop parts of our potential that we could not live when we were growing up, either because of trauma, or because we simply did not have any opportunities to do so. In Authentic Movement these hidden or less developed parts often emerge spontaneously through unconscious movements, gestures, voice tone, verbal expressions and breathing patterns. Paying attention to what emerges, we become conscious of these parts, and can explore, integrate and practise living them. In so doing we foster our growth, connect to our creativity and gain a deeper sense of wholeness.

What is more, because in Authentic Movement we listen to our bodies with non-judgemental acceptance and respect, we move into our bodies and begin to inhabit them more fully. Then, instead of thinking of our bodies as 'objects' to be tamed and perfected, we begin to think of them as partners and teachers, and we start to see how much we can learn from them.

Daniela: Can you talk more about the role of the witness?

Tina: The witness attends to the mover with an attitude of non-judgemental compassion. Witnessing is very different from 'observing' or 'looking at'; looking can be quite objectifying, but witnessing means being actively present to the mover. A witness is not only present to the mover but also to what is happening in her/his own body as she/he attends to the mover. As a mover, knowing we are witnessed allows us to descend deeper into our psyche, and open to the mysteries held in the body.

Moreover, in having a witness who is attending to us with non-judgemental presence, we can begin to heal some of the damage caused by troubled early relationships. As Allan Schore and others have shown, it is our caretakers' ability to attune to us in an empathetic and non-judgemental way that enables us to develop an awareness of our inner states and to experience, contain and express the full range of our emotions. If our caretakers cannot attune to us in that way, then our bodies are inhibited and our psychological development is impaired. The relationship between witness and mover can contribute to repair.

Typically, the witness' role goes beyond silent observation. When, as mover, our movement comes to its natural conclusion, we may speak to our witness about our experience in order to reflect on and begin integrating what has arisen in us. Then, if we wish, we can ask the witness to describe the movements that she has seen us make. That helps us to remember the movements, sensations, emotions and the memories that we have just lived. When a witness is invited to share her experience, the task is to stick to what she saw, taking care not to judge the mover in any way or to project her own feelings onto the mover.

That said, it can also be helpful for a witness to share what she experienced in her own body when being present to the mover, so long as she owns those experiences as her own. For example, if the witness is strongly affected when we wrap our arms around our body and let our head drop, the witness might say *'I see your arms wrap around your body and your head drop, and I feel comforted and contained.'* By owning her feelings the witness is not imposing her history on us but giving us the opportunity to experience somebody being with us in a way that is very different from the original critical watcher.

Mind you, things are not always what they seem and sometimes what happens in the witness' body can open up the hidden reality. I am remembering an analytic client I will call Sarah who cried a lot as she moved. However, whenever I witnessed Sarah's crying, I did not feel sadness in my own body as I often do when witnessing other movers who are in pain. Instead I felt itchy; I wanted to scratch and noticed that I was really irritated. When Sarah asked for my authentic response I shared my sensations and feelings with her, saying that I did not know what to make of them. Sarah's instant response was *'I'm not angry'* and she stormed off, slamming the door to my consulting room behind her. When Sarah turned up for her next therapy session she said *'I have been so mad at you; I wasn't angry and I don't know why you were suggesting that.'* I was interested in her reaction and asked Sarah what else she had felt. Eventually it emerged that in Sarah's family it was okay to cry but not to be angry – that was too threatening. And so Sarah had learned to substitute crying for anger. While witnessing Sarah, my body picked that up despite the words she was using to describe her experience.

Daniela: In my experience, we can learn just as much from witnessing as we can from moving.

Tina: That is true. In particular, witnessing can be very powerful in helping us to develop empathy. If we had a difficult childhood, we may have shut down our empathic self in an attempt to put distance between ourselves and the negativity that others were directing towards us. Witnessing encourages us to take the risk of opening to receive another's experience.

Additionally, empathy requires that we resonate with another's experience and resonance happens through the mirror neuron system of the brain and through the sensations and feelings that we experience in our bodies, so if we are cut off from our bodies as a result of trauma, then our capacity for empathy is limited. Witnessing, in encouraging us to pay attention to our own body's experience, helps us to connect to our bodies and so fosters empathy. At the same time, witnessing can help us to learn that there is a distinction between our own feelings and those that belong to another person, and it teaches us not to try to impose our reality on others, paving the way for us to create increasingly conscious and respectful relationships.

Thus, for both witness and mover, the process can help us move beyond our isolated sense of self and experience what it is like to meet with another from a place of authenticity, relatedness and compassion.

Additionally, through witnessing we often discover aspects of what we hold unconsciously in our bodies – the shadow material I mentioned earlier. As witness, we constantly need to ask, *'What body sensations am I becoming aware of as I open to the mover's experience? Do I feel my own grief, or my own shutting down, or my own joy?'* Witnessing will activate our own mirror neuron system, so that we too may begin to feel aspects of ourselves that have long been shut away.

Daniela: When you talk about Authentic Movement it sounds like a mindfulness meditation practice – do you see it in that way?

Tina: Authentic Movement is a form of mindfulness, when mindfulness is taken to mean paying attention to our emotions, our bodies, our hearts and our souls. However, the mindfulness of Authentic Movement is different from the mindfulness practices of traditions like Zen meditation that involve impartial observation of what is happening without entering the subjective feelings.

Authentic Movement invites us into our bodies and teaches us how to follow our body's impulses and work with them so we can bridge the split between psyche and body. In contrast, Zen meditation requires us to sit still and inhibit our bodies' impulses, and in some cases involving trauma that may reinforce the split between psyche and body.

Authentic Movement helps us to develop a body that is strong enough and flexible enough to experience sensations and express emotions in healthy ways so that we no longer have to dissociate. In my understanding, Zen meditation encourages us to notice the sensations and emotions that are happening in our inner world, without attachment or engagement. In some cases this can enhance a capacity for self-reflection, containment and emotional regulation, while in others it may exacerbate dissociative tendencies.

Crucial to Authentic Movement is the relationship between mover and witness, and that human connection offers us the opportunity to heal the relational part of ourselves that got damaged when we were children. With Zen meditation, we may sit in a room with other people but explicitly relating to them is generally not part of the practice, so there may be fewer opportunities to develop our relational capacity.

In other words, although becoming mindful of what is happening in body and psyche is at the core of Authentic Movement, it is a different type of mindfulness than what is fostered by some of the sitting meditation traditions, such as Zazen. The former helps heal attachment wounds and encompasses attunement to bodily experience, while the latter emphasises self-management and an attitude of 'non-attachment' to emotions that arise. Each practice can be good, depending on what we need at a given time. For example, I would not advise Authentic Movement practice for someone in crisis, whose ego is already being flooded with material from the unconscious. At such times more structured body/mind practices are best, until the person's ego is strong enough to contain and channel the upwelling of emotional energy.

Daniela: In Authentic Movement groups, when people stop moving you often encourage them to allow the energy to continue to unfold through painting, modelling clay, writing or coming into voice? Why?

Tina: If we go from Authentic Movement directly into spoken words, we risk imposing our old, familiar story onto our experience, so the new energy that is ready to emerge closes down. However, if we go from moving to painting or sculpting or writing, we create an open space in which the new energy can continue to unfold and be received. It also allows the mover to linger a bit longer in the non-verbal right brain, rather than attempt to make meaning prematurely.

That said, for drawing or sculpting to be effective, it is best not to think about how we want an image to look, but rather to let the body, in concert with the right brain, continue to move through its use of colours, the marks it puts on paper and the shape it moulds out of clay. Then, once the body has finished creating its image, we can sit back and see what comes to mind: we may notice a lot of black or red, or a rainbow of pastel colours; the lines may be jagged or geometrical, or they may be soft and voluptuous. Seeing those things with an attitude of open curiosity can help us become increasingly conscious of the energy that first started to emerge when we moved.

We can do something similar with other creative forms, one of which is 'free-writing'.[3] We put pen to paper and do not let up until ten minutes have passed; we do not cross out; we do not write complete sentences or worry about grammar; we are not polite and there is no censorship. We simply let the words tumble out, and do our best to get out of their way. Coming out of an experience of moving, or indeed out of witnessing, we might start with a question like *'How did I feel?'* or *'What touched me?'* or *'What moved me?'* (using body-based questions can be particularly potent). Once we have got our starting point, if we can keep our hand moving, then we will begin to express a little more of what is ready to come into consciousness.

Moving between modalities is not only relevant to Authentic Movement, it can be very valuable in more conventional therapeutic settings too. When working with a dream, if there is a character that we are drawn to, it can be very enlightening to ask: *'How does he stand? How does she hold herself?'* Taking that stance, we might see what movements or feelings emerge, or we might let a sound come out, noticing how it feels to make those kinds of sounds. Eventually, if this character speaks in words, we might see what comments it makes, again noticing how we feel when we hear ourselves say these things. Alternatively, we might do some free-writing, taking on the perspective of the dream figure. Our images and dreams spring from our unconscious, so we can learn much more about ourselves if we embody our images by imaginatively inhabiting them with awareness, rather than just talking about them from a place of intellectual curiosity.

Daniela: Working with masks is another medium through which we can become aware of what we carry. You and I have both done mask work in the context of BodySoul Rhythms® workshops led by Marion Woodman, Ann Skinner and Mary Hamilton, and now you teach it. Can you describe this work?

Tina: BodySoul Rhythms® work is profoundly creative and deeply integrative. It is generally done in residential workshops that take place over several days, and working with masks, which give form to 'shadow' energies, is an important part of the process.

Working silently, in groups of three, a mask is made on the face using strips of plaster of Paris. As we lie down and surrender to the process, and to the intimacy of others touching our face, we begin to descend into the unconscious. The following day we complete the shape of the mask and 'decorate' it. As with other forms of body work, it is not our ego that makes these choices – rather we see what shapes, colours and textures call to us. Maybe the mask wants to be painted black on one side and gold on the other. Maybe it wants a spiral of string circling its cheek and a zigzag of sequins across its forehead. Maybe the mask wants to be covered with dirt and twigs. We do not need to be an artist – the mask gets

---

3 Goldberg, N. (1986) *Writing Down the Bones: Freeing the Writer Within.* Boston, MA: Shambhala Publications, Inc.

made on our face and then finds its own way to express what is currently alive in our unconscious.

Once its form settles, guided by a facilitator, we start to wear the mask. We come to this with no preconceptions and simply explore how we feel in our mask, how we move and what kind of sounds we make. Maybe we are a needy baby. Maybe we are a child, petrified by the stare of an abuser. Maybe we are cat-like, curious, independent and playful. Maybe we are a young boy who wants to climb fences, steal apples and see the world. Maybe we are a sexy, sensual woman. Maybe a wise old woman, who says outrageous things and does not care what others think. Maybe we are a tree rooted deeply into the ground. Maybe we are a fish swimming deep in the ocean.

Wearing our mask, we meet other masks, and within the confines of what is safe, we have permission to engage with those other energies in whatever way is initiated by the energy of our own mask. That allows us to go beyond our normal ways of relating, maybe to be silly or playful, funny or angry, sexual or powerful. At the same time the other masks may relate to us in ways that nobody has treated us before.

One of the advantages of a mask is that it gives us explicit permission to be something other than our familiar, well-practised everyday self. When we wear our mask we step into an unfamiliar shadow aspect of ourselves and explore it freely. What is more, we live that previously unknown aspect in a fully embodied way. It can be a very powerful and transformative experience.

Jung called the use of creative methods to bring hitherto unlived parts of ourselves into consciousness 'active imagination'. The steps include relaxing the ego to allow the unconscious to take the lead; giving the unconscious form through creative expression; reflecting on what emerges; and gradually integrating what we have learned through practising it in our daily life.[4] Mask work is one form of active imagination; Authentic Movement is another.

Daniela: Body work can create powerfully intense experiences, whereas bringing the emerging energy into daily life is a tough process that takes perseverance and hard work. As a result, one danger is that we seek one intense experience after the next, instead of striving to live what we have discovered in these experiences.

Tina: Yes, this can be a danger. Insights that come though imaginative body work can be exciting, freeing and full of adrenalin. We can get habituated to the neuro-chemical rush evoked by intense experiences. That may set-off an addictive hunger for more such experiences, whereas the real work lies in integrating our insights.

What is more, in certain social worlds going into altered states and having sacred experiences garners praise, and leaves us feeling special. If we have been wounded during childhood, carry shame and do not feel good about ourselves, then the social cachet and feelings of being special can be addictive in and of themselves. When that happens, we are at risk of doing the work not to fuel the

---

4 Chodorow, J. (ed.) (1997) *Jung on Active Imagination.* Princeton, NJ: Princeton University Press.

hard, slow grind involved in change, but for the narcissistic reward. That does not bring healing; it is important not to identify with transpersonal energies but to relate to and integrate them.

Jung said that once we have been informed by the unconscious, we have an ethical obligation to live what we have learned. He was right, but making the changes that will allow us to live our insights is often easier said than done!

Daniela: Why is it so difficult to make those changes?

Tina: Change is frightening. People often prefer to live with the 'terrible familiars' than to navigate the 'possible unknowns'. When old defences are challenged, our knee-jerk reaction is to put ourselves back together in the old way because we do not know how to live the new. Sometimes, when previously forbidden feelings enter our lives, we are so scared that we try to numb them out by reverting to old addictions and toxic behaviours. Or even worse, the new way of living is attacked by our old defence system. An inner voice may say something like *'I don't take up space like this – this is NOT all right'* or *'My voice doesn't usually sound like that – speaking like this will get me into trouble'* and so on and so on.

It is particularly hard when the attack from our old defences comes not as an inner voice, but via the musculature of the body. Suppose we have been speaking from a more embodied place and saying things that we have never before allowed ourselves to say; we might start to get a stiff neck that physically prevents us from speaking in the new way. However, because there is no obvious voice that comes with our stiff neck, we will have to work patiently to discover what underlies it. We might dialogue with the stiffness to see if a voice emerges; at the same time we might work very gently with our neck to slowly loosen it up; or we might allow it to take the lead in Authentic Movement and see what emerges.

Nonetheless, there is often truth in what the defence system is telling us. It is one thing to live a new energy with a trusted therapist or in the safety of a workshop, but quite another to live it with family, parents and colleagues who have not witnessed our transition and might feel unsure about the new 'us'. After all, many of the people in our world – including family and friends – will expect us to behave in particular ways. Indeed, if they are wounded themselves, then they will need us to behave according to our shared script; when we depart from the script and respond in new ways, they are likely to feel lost and uncomfortable. As a consequence, they will try to push us back into the old shape, or may even walk away from the relationship. We have to be prepared for that, and we have to have a system of support that will hold us if it happens.

Daniela: You see body-oriented practices such as Authentic Movement as enriching our lives not only through helping us to heal our trauma, but also through what they can contribute to a life-long spiritual journey. Perhaps, to conclude, you could talk about what you mean by that.

Tina: Yes, the spiritual journey is an essential dimension, as the practice becomes part of our life. We follow the practice not just to heal our trauma, but so that we can continue to develop and grow. We practise it because we want to remain open to the unknown in ourselves and to deepen our relationship with our bodies, with our unconscious minds, with others and with life's mysteries. The body holds our vital essence, the divine animating spirit that gives us life! We practise because we long to feel that essence, the shimmer of spirit in the body, the life force at the centre that can inspire and nourish us. When this happens we feel 'at One' with the universe, reconnected to the larger life force that animates all living beings. It is that deeper intelligence that can guide us, and give purpose and meaning to our lives. Conscious embodiment practices can awaken us to our deepest values, and teach us how to embody them. In the process, we discover more creative and authentic ways of living: ways that unfold within us as we grow and change.

In addition, engaging with a practice that enables us to come home to our bodies inspires us to enter into a healthier relationship with the rest of the living world. Our bodies are a microcosm of the macrocosm; when we stop blaming them for our pain, starving them, shoving junk food into them, shutting them down in an effort to protect us from unbearable suffering, or extracting every last ounce of energy from them through over-doing, then we are also much more likely to change how we relate to our animal cousins and to the planet.

Body-oriented practices such as Authentic Movement are soul work; they allow us to contact the spirit in the body, the light in dark matter; they awaken an embodied consciousness that can guide our life's path and support the fulfilment of our destiny.

The body pulses with the oldest language and contains a deep historical memory. We strive for an intellectual understanding of its language through neuroscience, genetics, attachment theory, evolutionary anthropology, somatic psychology and quantum physics. That intellectual understanding needs to be matched with the understanding that comes from *lived* experience. We engage in body-oriented practices to reconnect with our instincts, affirm our feelings, heal childhood wounds and develop healthier relationships with our bodies, ourselves and other people. Along the way, we often form a more realistic body image. We come to know and love who we are, and connect with a life force that is deeper and more meaningful than we have previously known. We embrace life, and are embraced by it!

Raymond Carver spoke of this when he wrote:[5]

> And did you get what
> you wanted from this life, even so?
> I did.
> And what did you want?
> To call myself beloved, to feel myself beloved
> on the earth.

---

5 Carver, R. (1989) "Late Fragment" from *A New Path to the Waterfall*, copyright © 1989 by the Estate of Raymond Carver. Used by permission of Grove/Atlantic, Inc. Any third party use of this material, outside of this publication, is prohibited. Also published by Vintage Books/Random House, London, UK, and reprinted by permission of The Random House Group Ltd. Electronic rights © Tess Gallagher, 1996, used by permission of The Wylie Agency (UK) Limited.

4   Spiralling through the apocalypse

Facing the Death Mother to claim our lives

Marion Woodman and Daniela F. Sieff

Summary

Emotional trauma results from being unseen and unvalued as children. It compromises our ability to live a creative and authentic life, and forces us to construct a false persona and to develop inauthentic goals. It makes us determined to control our emotions and our bodies, and leaves us striving for perfection. It propels us towards addictions.

Worse than being unseen is growing up with a parent who wishes that we, or some part of us, did not exist. The energy manifest by such a parent is symbolised by the archetype of the 'Death Mother'. It is a deadening energy which permeates both psyche and body, turning us to stone. It stifles growth and imprints our cells with profound fear and hopelessness. In time, our vitality drains away and we find ourselves yearning for the oblivion of death. Ultimately, our body may turn against itself, as it does with cancer or auto-immune diseases. The Death Mother energy is vividly depicted in the myth of Medusa.

Having internalised the Death Mother energy, reclaiming our life requires a series of descents into the underworld of the unconscious mind and body. During each descent we meet the fierce and uncompromising energy symbolised by the archetype of the 'Apocalyptic Mother'. This energy challenges us to face our truth and to surrender our old ways so that something new and more authentic can be born. Each time we accept this challenge, we move further beyond the clutches of our internalised Death Mother to reclaim more of our lives.

Daniela Sieff: Your life-journey, and your teaching, centres on the idea of becoming ever-more conscious and authentic. What has inspired that?

Marion Woodman: When we are born, if our environment validates us, we are free to express who we are without fear of critical judgement and we grow up to live unique and authentic lives. If, however, we are born into an environment that cannot validate us, our lives never quite get onto an authentic and meaningful track, and our potential is curtailed. If our childhood leaves us wounded and off-track, then the only way to live our authentic lives is to become conscious of the fear, pain, and beliefs that we carry deep in our psyches. My journey, and thus my teaching, has been inspired both by the illness that suffused my early adult life, and by my fear of coming to my death bed and realising that I had never lived *my* life.

Daniela: What constitutes an environment that cannot validate us?

Marion: Any situation in which the child is not valued for who she is and not allowed to be herself. This can happen for several reasons. It could be that the child is a 'mistake', born amidst a certain amount of ambivalence. It may be that her parents wanted a boy, and so they cannot appreciate their child as a girl, or vice versa.

Alternatively, a child may be brought into the world to fill a gap in her parent's life. For example, a woman may want a child to secure her place in the family, a man may desire a son to carry on the family name, a couple may hope that a child will save their marriage. When this happens the child is unable to be herself – her intrinsic value is unrecognised.

Other parents look to their children to live their unlived lives, thereby negating the fact that children have their own lives to lead. The unspoken, yet insatiable, message received by such children from their parents is *'I have no life. I sacrificed it. You will live the life I never had.'* When the child complies – to gain the 'love' that goes with fulfilling her parent's dream – deep down she may feel that the achievement is not her own and resent it. Success can feel like psychic rape.

At the opposite end of the continuum, a parent who was unable to live an authentic life may extinguish any spark in the growing child which reminds the parent of what has not been lived. If this child can do it differently, then the very foundation upon which the parent's life has been built is threatened. Of course this is not conscious, but a parent who needed to renounce his or her truth in order to survive will typically invalidate the truth of their child. Teachers can have the same effect.

My inner child was put in jail in grade one. My father had taught me to read before I went to school. I loved it and was looking forward to reading at school. However, we spent the whole of the first day making windmills. It was the same on the second day. On the third day I told the teacher I would not run around with a windmill anymore. *'Well'*, she said, *'you will run around with a windmill, like the other children.'* I put my head down on the desk in an act of despair and defiance, and she hit my hands as hard as she could with the pointer. Later, when I was seven, in art class, we were told to paint a house and a lawn. That day I was drawn to the colour blue so I painted the lawn blue. The teacher was furious, saying, *'You will stay after school until you learn to paint the grass the right colour – green!'* I did not paint again for many years. My teachers' unlived creativity feared my vibrant imagination – it threatened them. Instead of encouraging it they unconsciously determined to destroy it. Such teachers (or parents) demand that a child be good. They claim that it is for the child's sake, but what they really mean is, *'Swallow your anger, initiative, and creativity so I do not have to face what I haven't lived.'*

In any of these situations the child learns to perform. Her unique, creative core is split off and buried in a hidden recess of her unconscious psyche. Somebody I was working with described her experience thus:

> I was too traumatised to let out the cry of my soul. I left her silent as a stone. I had to learn to ignore her and to be soul deaf in order to function at all. I learned to speak with a thin little voice that had no connection to who I was, no resonance that would betray my authentic feelings and sensitivity. My soul child said *'If I had come out you would have killed me.'*

Daniela: How does a childhood lacking in validation affect us as we grow into adults?

Marion: Performance continues into adulthood because that is all we know. Whether the original teachers and parents are still in our lives does not matter; we have internalised their judgemental voices, they are alive in our psyche and our authentic self has to remain in hiding. Our goals, being derived from a false self, are distorted, and our potential remains unfulfilled.

Striving to achieve that which is not authentic to us opens the door to addiction. When our achievements fail to satisfy us, we mistakenly believe that if only we could achieve a bit more we would be satisfied and happy. But more of what we never truly wanted can never be 'enough', so we end up on the path of insatiability. Emily Dickinson depicts this dynamic in her characteristically concise and poignant way:[1]

> To fill a Gap
> Insert the Thing that caused it –
> Block it up
> With Other – and 'twill yawn the more –
> You cannot solder an Abyss
> With Air –

Addictions may also result from distorted and desperate attempts to fulfil our genuine needs. Our authentic Self may be in exile in some dark recess of our unconscious, but we cannot kill its energy, and its unfulfilled needs will make themselves felt, one way or another. We may find ourselves craving food that brings no nurture, drink that brings no spirit or sex that brings no union. Our hunger *is* for food – but it is for *soul* food; we are crying out for the nourishment that will enable us to express our creative individuality, not for bread and pasta.

---

1 From: *The Poems of Emily Dickinson: Variorum Edition*, edited by Ralph W. Franklin, Cambridge, MA: The Belknap Press of Harvard University Press, Copyright © 1998 by the President and Fellows of Harvard College. Copyright © 1951, 1955, 1979, 1983 by the President and Fellows of Harvard College.

Chocolate provides a fleeting experience of the sweetness that we are so desperate for, but when our only route to sweetness is through sugar we end up feeling sick and disgusted with ourselves. The alcohol-fuelled rise into spirit crashes down to hell when we wake to find that we are lying in our own vomit. The moment of ecstatic union we feel during casual sex dissolves into abject loneliness when we realise we have no feelings for our lover, or him for us. When we are unable to fulfil our buried emotional and spiritual needs, we turn to concrete substitutes, which then poison us.

Daniela: So there are important messages in our addictions?

Marion: Yes – addictions are the unheard parts of us demanding to be brought to life. They point to what we exiled in order to become acceptable. If we listen carefully to the implicit messages we can discover what is missing in our lives.

But there is also an unconscious death-wish at the core of an addiction. At this more sinister level, addiction can be understood as an attempt to escape the hollowness, pain and suffering of an unlived life. Our culture does not allow for suffering; it tells us that there is not time for pain and encourages us to take pills. The ultimate escape from pain is through death, and addictions are a slow and gradual form of suicide.

The energy that tempts us with the ultimate escape from pain is archetypal and it is best personified by the image of the Demon Lover. The Demon Lover tempts us with a vision of an everlasting existence that is free from the inconvenience of our cumbersome, needy and pain-infused flesh. He offers an ascent into the luminosity of pure spirit, seducing us with the fantasy of eternal ecstasy. *'Come fly with me!'* he whispers to us, *'You do not have to stay on earth and suffer like this.'* He is the force behind the addictions that take us out of our bodies and up into spirit, such as anorexia. To follow his promises means to abandon our bodies, and ultimately our lives.

Daniela: When you say that we can be addicted to things other than concrete substances, what do you mean?

Marion: Addictions that involve tangible matter like food, alcohol or drugs are visible, but we can also become addicted to ideas and concepts. The drive for perfection is a very common addiction, as is the need for self-control. We believe that we will be happy and free of pain if we can manage to suppress our unruly emotions, control our appetite or secure a promotion. We push and cajole ourselves in an unending quest for that pain-free happiness.

What people call love is often an unconscious and addictive quest for power. How often are we nice to somebody – burying our anger and disappointment and professing our love for them – when we are actually trying to ensure they stay with us because we are terrified of abandonment and loneliness? Paradoxically, an overwhelming desire to please is rooted in an addictive quest for control – by pleasing others we are better able to manipulate them, albeit unconsciously.

Believing that we need to control our bodies, families and jobs if we are to avoid annihilation is a dangerous illusion. It leaves us split between head and body, intellect and emotion, fantasy and reality. We cannot reconcile our yearning to be perfect and god-like with the reality of being human and fallible. We mistakenly believe that the inner judgemental voices will shut up if only we can achieve our goals. Life turns into a prison from which we seek to escape by gaining yet more control and by becoming supposedly more perfect. As we misguidedly run as fast as we can towards the mirage of perfection, we eventually meet our own starving and abandoned self. During my analysis I had the following dream:

> I go to the attic of my childhood home to find a black box. I put my hand in and feel the quivering, warm body of my pet bird. I cry because I have forgotten him and left him alone to die. I am afraid of what I may see when I take him out of the box, but I do so. As my tears fall over his tiny skeletal body, he turns into a tiny baby, and says *'I only wanted to sing my song'*.

Our childhood experiences leave us terrified of annihilation and that terror blocks our throats. We cannot sing our song – often we do not even know that we have a song to sing.

Daniela: One of your concerns is how we make our bodies the scapegoat.

Marion: In trying to protect ourselves from the thought that there is something fundamentally unlovable about us, women, and increasingly men, blame their bodies. If only we were slimmer… had fuller breasts… a six-pack stomach… more defined biceps… a bigger penis… then we would be lovable. Our desperate struggle for control and perfection leaves us frightened of our bodies with their desire to eat, their cravings for drugs and their eruptive, unruly emotions. We turn to surgery in our quest for supposed bodily perfection. We employ brutal and punishing willpower in our attempt to gain control of our bodies' impulses and needs. We become terrified of letting our guard down, in case our abused body seizes its chance for freedom and runs amok. We see our bodies as objects to be perfected, rather than the very heart of our lives. Such an existence takes us into hopelessness and despair. A woman who was trying to bring this dynamic to consciousness wrote a journal entry in which she allowed her body to speak,

> I am your body. My mother did not want me. I huddled in her womb as still as I could be. I was terrified of being thrown out. I survived the rupture of birth. I was unwelcome when I got here. I was always afraid of being killed so I tried to do everything I could to be loved. I have always been hated. Whoever it is that hates me never ceases to punish me for a crime I know nothing about. It's as if my very existence is a crime. I am punished because I exist. When I am hungry I am not fed. When I am exhausted I am not allowed to rest. When I need to move, I am forced to stay still. Sometimes I go wild with freedom, but I know it won't last. Whoever is doing this to me must hate me. But I do not know why I am hated. The punishment would stop if I ceased to exist. I am tired of being punished for a crime I never committed.

I am not guilty. No one listens to me. I want to die because I have been sentenced to life imprisonment for a crime I never committed.

Daniela: You use the myth of Medusa to illustrate how we come to oppress our bodies.

Marion: Medusa was one of the beautiful gorgon sisters who lived under the sea. The myth begins when the gorgon makes love to Poseidon in Athena's temple. Athena, born from the head of Zeus, lives in her intellect rather than in her body, and when the gorgon makes love to Poseidon in Athena's temple, the gorgon exposes the embodied passion that Athena is not living. Athena does not want her shadow exposed so she transforms the beautiful gorgon into the Medusa, a monster with writhing, insatiable snakes instead of hair and a look that turns all to stone. It is the same for most of us. In our culture, with its emphasis on intellect, will-power, control and rationality, Athena's unlived life leads to the inevitable creation of Medusa – the two energies are chained to each other.

Daniela: So both Athena and Medusa symbolise insatiability, but the insatiability is expressed in different domains? With Athena it is expressed in the guise of perfectionism, the need for achievement and the drive for intellectual knowledge and control, whereas Medusa exemplifies the insatiability of an oppressed and objectified body and it is expressed through addictions.

Marion: Exactly! When we are ruled by Athena's energy, power takes the place of love. When we are driven by perfectionism we deny our humanity. Thus, the inner world cries out to be heard through the shadow side of our unheard body, that is, through our addictions.

Daniela: You see Medusa herself as exemplifying the archetypal energy you call Death Mother. What is Death Mother?

Marion: The energy of the archetypal Death Mother is epitomised in the stare of Medusa. Death Mother's gaze penetrates both psyche and body, turning us into stone. It kills hope. It cuts us dead. Somebody may say something that appears to be innocuous, but if Death Mother's energy underlies that comment, then our physical body is changed. We collapse. Our life-energy drains from us, and we find ourselves yearning for the oblivion of death.

Death Mother's energy is most destructive when it comes from somebody we love and trust, and who is supposed to love us. This is what happened in the original trauma; we trusted our beloved mother but suddenly realised that we were not acceptable to her. We realised that our mother wished that we, or some part of us, was dead.

I need to make it clear that when I talk about Death Mother I mean an unconscious archetypal energy that is most easily imagined in a personified form, rather than an actual human mother. Archetypes are ancient and universal elements in the human psyche. They become visible to us through images and ideas. An archetype can be imagined as a numinous sphere of energy in the unconscious that forms around some primordial aspect of our existence. It acts as a magnet, over time attracting a succession of associated images based on our daily experience. For example, every human has an archetypal image of 'Mother' in his or her psyche; this image holds more power and is larger than our image of our own particular mother. Like every archetype it has both a positive, light and nurturing side, and a negative, dark and destructive side. Archetypal Mother is a magnet for our childhood experiences with our own personal mothers, caregivers and teachers. When we are wounded by these experiences, the negative, dark and destructive side of the Mother Archetype tends to gain the upper hand, and we are at risk of being pulled into Death Mother's domain.

Daniela: You have said that if we experience Death Mother while growing up, we internalise the archetype, whereupon it can become incorporated in our physical body. Can you speak about this?

Marion: If, while growing up, we sense that we are unacceptable to our parents, carers or teachers, or if we intuit that we threaten them, then our nervous system becomes hyper-vigilant. Our cells are imprinted with a profound fear of abandonment; as a consequence our body numbs-out the moment we feel threatened. In short, the autonomic nervous system says *'NO!'* and the ego withdraws. We experience a collapse of both our psychological and physical energy. I call this 'possum mentality'; as soon as we sense a whiff of rejection we are paralysed with fear, close down and stay absolutely still in order to survive. Eventually, that possum becomes a permanent feature in our body and psyche; then life is experienced as a minefield in which we are knocked down by explosions that are inaudible to others. If there is unconscious hostility in the environment, the inner body, acting autonomously, retreats and falls over 'dead'.

At the same time we may develop defence mechanisms that manifest in an armour of fat, oedema, vomiting, anything to keep poison out. Ultimately, our body may turn against itself as it does with cancer or auto-immune diseases. Death Mother is now in our cells.

Last summer I developed cellulitis. It spread into my bloodstream and became life-threatening. While in intensive care, I had the following dream:

> There are two immense lobsters in a huge, long concrete drain-pipe. The lobsters have blood-red heads, and are trying to kill each other. I am also in the drain and I am terrified. There is a black door in the wall of the drain and I am trying to open it so I can escape. I can't open the door. I bang on it with all my might, hoping someone will hear me and come to help. Nobody comes. I am left with the killer lobsters.

To me the drain symbolised my blood vessels and the lobsters my blood. Thus the dream described what was happening to me; instead of supporting my life, my poisoned blood was taking me towards death. Moreover, being in the grip of Death Mother I wanted to escape through the black door, and disappear into darkness. On waking I knew that had I opened that door and walked through it, I would have died. Fortunately it did not open and I am still here!

Daniela: It seems that having internalised Death Mother while growing up, when we find ourselves doing something that we deem to be unacceptable, we silently direct our own Death Mother back on ourselves. At such times we are not aware of what is happening; all we know is that we have fallen into a self-created and private hell.

Marion: Exactly. If we face Death Mother while growing up, we will inevitably internalise her, and if we have internalised her, then we will either project our internal Death Mother onto others – seeing her in our boss, our lover or our children, or we will act her out by directing her energy onto others, and/or onto ourselves. Until we examine what we are carrying within our own psyche, we risk possession by the Death Mother archetype.

Daniela: Having internalised Death Mother, one danger is that we develop a propensity to see Death Mother when she is not there. For example, somebody may say something with compassion, but due to our wounds and what we have internalised, we perceive the comment as coming from Death Mother. Thus, if we are to grow, we have to become conscious enough of what we hold in our psyche to know whether Death Mother is coming at us from another person, or whether it is coming from ourselves.

Marion: The point that you make is important. Our conditioning may mean that we misinterpret somebody's comment or actions as coming from Death Mother, when that is not the case. Or we may have a teacher who has opened us to our deeper selves and helped us to find life, but who can no longer be there for us, whereupon we can experience that withdrawal as Death Mother, when it is nothing of the sort.

Daniela: How does an internalised Death Mother affect our lives?

Marion: Change is fundamental to being alive; to remain fixed is to rot. If the Death Mother archetype is part of our psyche and our body, profound fear means that we fight against anything that might precipitate meaningful change. Potentially vibrant energy is locked into a cold, rigid, unchanging, lifeless form. Our way of relating to the world is petrified into stone. We are Medusa's prisoners.

For example, I was in kindergarten, when one day I found myself being pushed out of the building through garlands of beautiful flowers. I wondered where I was going. People said *'You are leaving kindergarten and going to junior school.'* I replied, *'Why would I want to go to junior school? I love kindergarten and I don't want to go somewhere new!'* That has been the story of my life. I did love kindergarten, but my fear of change kicked in whenever I was faced with having to take the next stage in my life.

Daniela: And that trauma was so strong that you lived it time and time again…

Marion: Time and time again! During my training to become a teacher, we were assigned to a class. I would be in front of my class, speaking, but the room would be filled with a painful silence. I was making the motions with my lips but no sounds emerged. I could not understand it. After the class our supervisor asked,

'Marion, what is happening to you?' All I could reply was *'I don't know. I can't make any sound.'* At the end of that term I got 98 marks for my lesson plans, and zero for my teaching. The terror was too great.

Daniela: So every time you go into the new, there is terror?

Marion: Every time I am overcome with the terror of getting born into a new reality. In every case I was moving out of an area in which I could perform well into a new area, and I was sure that some terrible disaster would happen, so I wanted to stay put. Being born had taken me into a hostile and dangerous environment, and that seeded a bone-deep ambivalence about change and growth.

Daniela: The paradox is that the anticipated disaster, which for you was manifest in physical illness, occurred because you were fighting against the new, rather than stepping into it.

Marion: Exactly – but there is the trauma. In every one of those situations I was afraid there would not be love. I was certain that the new world would find me unacceptable. It was my own terror which permeated my cells and which came to the surface through illness. It was my self-generated fear that stressed my body and created hell.

Daniela: The danger is that when we are overwhelmed by that terror we give in to Death Mother, which can literally mean succumbing to death. A friend of mine was an intelligent and vibrant woman who was terrified of being alone. She was married to an older man and had said that when her husband died she would commit suicide. By the time she reached her sixties her husband had dementia. Then she was diagnosed with terminal cancer. Her immediate response was *'That is a relief'*!

Marion: Relief at the prospect of death comes straight out of trauma and it lies at the heart of Death Mother's domain. It is more common than we realise. However, it is rare for anybody to allow that dynamic into consciousness, let alone to speak it in the way that your friend did.

Daniela: In the myth of Medusa, Perseus, whose task it is to kill Medusa, is warned not to look Medusa in the eye; instead he guides his sword by looking at Medusa's reflection in his shield. Similarly, you've said that we cannot look Death Mother in the eye. Why?

Marion: It is too dangerous! If we look Death Mother in the eye, we may be overcome by our trauma and turned to stone. We may become ill. To protect ourselves we use a reflective shield. We write a journal. We record our dreams. We paint or sculpt the unconscious emotions that are held in our body. We 'dance' our feelings and take note of the images that come to us. As Emily Dickinson wrote:[2]

2 Reprinted by permission of the publishers and the Trustees of Amherst College from *The Poems of Emily Dickinson: Variorum Edition*, edited by Ralph W. Franklin, Cambridge, MA: The Belknap Press of Harvard University Press, Copyright © 1998 by the President and Fellows of Harvard College. Copyright © 1951, 1955, 1979, 1983 by the President and Fellows of Harvard College.

Tell all the Truth but tell it slant –
Success in Circuit lies
Too bright for our infirm Delight
The Truth's superb surprise

As Lightening to the Children eased
With explanation kind
The Truth must dazzle gradually
Or every man be blind –

Facing Death Mother directly leads to blindness – or worse.

Daniela: In the journey of healing we need to work our way toward the heart of our wounds, and when we do this we will eventually arrive at what is darkest in us. Unless we face that darkness, it is impossible to take responsibility for ourselves. Surely there comes a time when we need to meet Death Mother directly, if we are to reclaim our lives?

Marion: Ultimately we may have to face Death Mother head-on, but *not* before we are ready. I had no consciousness of what I was facing until my second encounter with cancer. In all my years of analysis I never linked my illnesses to the fact that deep in my cells I harboured the knowledge that as a girl, I was an unwanted child, and that consequently a part of me wanted to die. I knew it, but I could not open to that truth at a deep enough level to make a difference. Instead, I spiralled around that reality, each time seeing its reflection from a different angle.

When I was diagnosed with cancer for the second time I was ready to face it head-on because by then I had developed huge compassion for myself and for my mother and my father. My mother certainly did the very best she could for me, but deep in her heart she was a suffragette, and in marrying a minister of the church she lost her freedom. She could not love her own femininity because the consequences of being a woman meant that she had been unable to live her own life, and thus she struggled to love a female child. So I had several reflected encounters, each spiralling back round and gradually coming closer, until eventually I was ready to face it. It took years and had I tried to speed it up, it would have killed me.

Daniela: But ultimately we have to face Death Mother directly if we are going to claim our life!

Marion: Someday perhaps, but it is not a journey to be undertaken lightly. We need to be ready and we need guides. My guides were Jung, my dreams, the images that came through my body work, and poetry – especially the poems of Emily Dickinson. Dickinson's images enabled me to understand what was happening and reading her poems chronologically I saw that it was her compassion for her mother and her sister which got her through. I began to see my mother's struggle. I became immensely grateful to her for doing her best for me. I also saw how my father had done his best. I realised that the child I was had also done the best she could.

Daniela: What triggers an attempt to break free of Death Mother?

Marion: We attempt to break free only when the frozen state becomes too much for us to bear. We go round and round until something finally wakes us and we are forced to come face-to-face with ourselves. If we are to come out the other side the conscious ego must recognise what it has so long feared and rejected.

The turning point may involve an illness or crisis, but often it is less dramatic. The apparently super-adjusted may find that their perfect performances demand energy they no longer have. *'If this is life,'* they say, *'I don't want it!'* Responsibility, duty and excellence hang heavily about their necks. Their fires are out. Depression pulls them into the mire. An escape via suicide beckons. For others the impetus to bring what is in the unconscious to consciousness may be triggered by the prospect of losing a meaningful relationship.

My wake-up call has always come through my body. When fear chained me to an obsolete way of being, it was illness that invariably forced me onto a new path. My body's agony was a manifestation of my terror and an attempt to keep me in the old, but paradoxically, it gave me no choice except to change, expand my life and live more authentically. Ultimately it was illness that picked me up, dropped me on a new road, and made me walk despite my terror!

Daniela: What seems crucial is how we look at crises: are we prepared to dig deep and discover what lies beneath? Are we prepared to change?

Marion: We have to question ourselves time and again. Key is asking the right questions – the ones that will allow our hidden truths to emerge into consciousness. The answer is lying silently in the unconscious, waiting for the 'right' question to be asked. Unfortunately, our first port of call is usually to ask the wrong question. We are addicted to thinking of ourselves as victims, but if we ask *'Why me?'* we fall into self-pity, diminish ourselves and learn nothing of importance. To break through we need to ask a deep and profound *'Why?'* rather than the smaller *'Why me?'*

Despite my initial struggle to speak in front of a class, I qualified as a high-school teacher and spent the first 25 years of my adult life teaching English. I loved my students and my life, but during that time I gradually developed oedema and felt that I was being unfairly punished for some unknown crime. I had starved myself in an attempt to remain thin to no avail. In my eyes, my body had become bloated and ugly. However, I was responsible for what was happening because I was making the wrong choices. Unbeknownst to me I was allergic to a myriad of foods but I was too disconnected from my body to know what it needed. To find my way I had to let go of my vision of myself as a victim, and figure out what was wrong with *my* choices. I had to grow up.

But my condition had to deteriorate until I was sleeping for 2–3 full days a week before I was prepared to risk change. At that point I was utterly desperate and so I finally listened to my dreams which suggested that I would find the answers to my oedema through the training I would do in Zurich en route to becoming a Jungian analyst. I left the teaching job that I loved, and took leave of my husband, not knowing if our marriage would survive, and went to Zurich. It was a turning point. In Zurich I began to connect to my body and to listen to it. It was a crucial step towards living my own life, and paradoxically, I would not have taken that step without suffering oedema.

It takes courage and perseverance to go through this process. We have to be willing to let go of what is obsolete, to take responsibility for our lives and to face the darkness that is in us. As von Franz wrote:[3]

> Every dark thing one falls into can be called an initiation. To be initiated into a thing means to go into it. The first step is generally falling into the dark place and usually appears in a dubious or negative form – falling into something, or being possessed by something. The shamans say that being a medicine man begins by falling into the power of the demons; the one who pulls out of the dark place becomes the medicine man, and the one who stays in is the sick person. You can take every psychological illness as initiation. Even the worst things you fall into are an effort at initiation, for you are in something which belongs to you, and now you must get out of it.

So long as we are blind to our inner Death Mother, we blame the outer world when trouble strikes and we fall into darkness. The focus of our blame can be a person, a political system, a social system, or it can be our own body. In turning to blame we miss an opportunity and the initiation fails. Death Mother's grip tightens around our lives.

Daniela: Is it crucial that we bring what is in our unconscious to consciousness?

Marion: Dismissing the unconscious and focusing solely on the cognitive layers of consciousness is akin to weeding a garden by cutting off the shoots and flowers of the weeds. If we do not dig beneath the surface, we leave the roots in place to regenerate as soon as our backs are turned. Unconscious means unconscious, but collusion in denial does not change the situation. When we act unconsciously we literally do not know what we are doing, and it is a long, frightening and painful task to bring it to consciousness. This is the hardest work I know.

Daniela: How might we bring what is in the unconscious to consciousness?

Marion: We can look at our everyday lives. What are we struggling with? Where are we stuck? Where is there no energy? Where is there insatiability? Where do we give our power away?

Working with a trusted therapist is one of the most powerful ways to discover what is in our unconscious. The relationship pushes us to the edge where we have to challenge our protective but obsolete beliefs and behaviours, and holds us when we are there.

---

3 Von Franz, M. (1972) *The Feminine in Fairytales*, New York, NY: Spring Publications, p. 64.

For me, and many others, dreams are key. The language of the unconscious is image and metaphor; dreams are snap-shots of what is happening in the unconscious. Collecting dream images, and working to uncover the impact of the metaphors they contain, is a profound and effective way to explore what has been hidden in the unconscious.

Writing a journal is also a wonderful tool for becoming more conscious. A journal is like a mirror – it reflects our own face back to us, allowing us to glimpse parts of ourselves that we have hidden away. Through journaling we build a relationship with ourselves and the stronger that relationship the easier it is for what is in our unconscious to emerge.

Body work has been another cornerstone in my exploration of my unconscious. I take a dream image, visualise it in my body and see how it transforms and moves me. I focus on where my body is out-of-sorts, move from that place and notice what images emerge. I think of my muscles and ligaments as the strings of a cello; energy flows over them and sets up vibrations which carry their information to my brain, which then changes those vibrations into images. Body work enables me to experience my dreams in my body, and at the same time it enables the unconscious experiences held in my body to be translated to images in my mind.

Bringing what is in the unconscious to consciousness requires more than cognitive knowledge. In our society we believe that once we have the words to describe a phenomenon, we understand it, but although words are necessary, they are insufficient. Meaningful discovery becomes possible only when knowledge is enlivened by experience that is lived though the body. If an experience is not coming from the body, then it is now known. To know something in our head does not change our life. William Blake, one of the Romantic poets who explored this before Freud and Jung gave us the maps that we have today, said it in his own inimitable way:[4]

> Embraces are Cominglings: from Head even to the Feet;
> And not a pompous High Priest entering from a Secret Place.

Daniela: What does the journey towards consciousness entail?

Marion: Paradoxically, it starts with a descent. 'Descent' is a mythological term for what happens when the conscious ego loses control and we journey into the underworld of the unconscious. We feel we are tumbling into a bottomless abyss. We are disoriented. Life is a mess. We cannot continue as we are. We are ill, exhausted or overcome with depression.

To reap the benefits of a descent into the unconscious we have to stay with our confusion, fear, depression and pain, and turn inwards with our own microscopes of introspection. We do not know if there is another way to live, but our inner

---

4   Blake, W. (*c.*1821) *Jerusalem: The Emanation of the Giant Albion.* Plate 69, lines 44-45.

voice says *'If this is it, it's not worth living.'* This is the end of performance and the beginning of terrifying risks. Many of us have been performing since we were toddlers. Letting go of old ways of being is terrifying, and many seek an escape through psychiatric drugs, supposedly quick-fix therapy or through addictions. However, if we are going to escape from the clutches of Medusa and live more authentically, we have to surrender to the descent, allowing ourselves to fall into chaos. In her poem, 'Transcendental Etude',[5] Adrienne Rich captures the stark terror and loneliness of this journey:

> But there come times–perhaps this is one of them–
> when we have to take ourselves more seriously or die;
> when we have to pull back from the incantations,
> rhythms we've moved to thoughtlessly,
> and disenthrall ourselves, bestow
> ourselves to silence, or a severer listening, cleansed
> of oratory, formulas, choruses, laments, static
> crowding the wires. We cut the wires,
> find ourselves in free-fall, as if
> our true home were the undimensional
> solitudes, the rift
> in the Great Nebula.
> No one who survives to speak
> new language, has avoided this:
> the cutting-away of an old force that held her
> rooted to an old ground
> the pitch of utter loneliness
> where she herself and all creation
> seem equally dispersed, weightless, her being a cry
> to which no echo comes or can ever come.

Daniela: What happens if we can surrender to the descent into chaos?

Marion: Chaos creates a space that the unconscious can move into; this is where the starving soul-bird can emerge from the black box and begin to sing his song. This is where we eventually open to new possibilities. In this state, the stony automaton created by Medusa starts to fracture and life begins to flow through us. If we can stay with it we will discover a new way of being; one that is free of the wilfully imposed order that we created in an attempt to ensure our survival. This new way emerges organically from our unconscious depths, allowing us to live more creatively, authentically and in a more embodied fashion. But entering the

---

5 The lines from 'Transcendental Etude', from *The Dream of a Common Language: Poems 1974–1977* by Adrienne Rich. Copyright © 1978 by W.W. Norton & Company, Inc. Used by permission of W.W. Norton & Company, Inc.

chaos takes immense courage. When I, or one of my clients, is in this place, I turn to a passage from T.S. Eliot's *Four Quartets*:[6]

> I said to my soul, be still, and wait without hope
> For hope would be hope for the wrong thing; wait without love,
> For love would be love of the wrong thing; there is yet faith
> But the faith and the love and the hope are all in the waiting.
> Wait without thought, for you are not ready for thought:
> So the darkness shall be the light, and the stillness the dancing.

Daniela: At the depths of chaos is psychosis. What is the difference between psychosis and chaos? How can we protect ourselves from psychosis? How can we tolerate the terror?

Marion: To go beyond our own boundaries, and to let go of the familiar landscape of our own restrictions, is to risk madness. With psychosis we do not know that we have descended into the chaos of the unconscious. There is no observing ego that can hold a detached position. Detachment experiences suffering, but does not identify with it. It maintains a larger perspective, knowing that we have to go through the chaos to find new and more authentic ground. Jung wrote that at five o'clock on the afternoon when he split with Freud, he felt the rug pulled from under his feet. His inner observer made a conscious decision to go with it. That inner observer makes all the difference but it takes years of painstaking and gradual work to build an ego which can hold onto consciousness while suffering pain, fear and chaos. Thus, it is important that we drop into chaos one step at a time, and do not descend past the point where we can hold onto reality. On our next turn round the spiral, if we have learnt anything, we may descend a little deeper. I cannot over-emphasise just how slow and hard this work is, and the importance of having compassion for ourselves as we attempt it.

Working with a therapist who has been through his or her own repeated descents into chaos is crucial. We cannot do this alone. To be safe and to find healing we need another to witness our descent, encourage us and hold us. The other can only do that if she has been through the bowels of this journey herself, and not all therapists have what it takes to go there.

Trusting that there is something more authentic and vital at our core makes a difference. At first we jump, fall or are pushed into the abyss, not knowing if we will find anything except annihilation. The first time I found myself in chaos, I was at the Jung Institute, and I did not think I would survive. I feared that I would never return home from Zurich. I have now learnt that if I sit with it and listen, a

---

6 Excerpt from 'East Coker' from *Four Quartets* by T.S. Eliot. Copyright 1940 by Houghton Mifflin Harcourt Publishing Company; Copyright © renewed 1968 by T.S. Eliot. Reprinted by permission of Houghton Mifflin Harcourt Publishing Company. All rights reserved. And also from *T.S. Eliot Collected Poems 1909–1962* (Faber, 1974), by permission of the publisher, Faber & Faber Ltd.

way through will emerge, so although the pain and fear is still intense, it has never been as shattering as the first time.

Writing a journal can help, as can our dreams. When we listen to our dreams we realise that deep within our unconscious there is help for our lost, terrified and pain-ridden ego. The image of the starving soul-bird who only wanted to sing his song held me during one of my descents.

The attitude that we bring to our unconscious is critical. If we fear and reject the unconscious we will either be subsumed by it and fall into madness, or we will look to escape from it and thus get stuck in repetitive and fruitless cycles. If, on the other hand, we respect our unconscious, and treat it as a guide and companion by attending to our dreams, journaling and doing body work, then it will bring us comfort. We will no longer feel so alone and helpless.

Nature is a great container. Intellectual knowledge can also be valuable so long as it is not used as a substitute for embodied experience. The writings of Jung and Von Franz provided me with a precious map, which enabled me to navigate through my terror. The expanding field of neuroscience is adding exciting new layers to that map. For me poetry was key, especially, as I have already mentioned, the poetry of Emily Dickinson. To this day, whenever I am stuck, I revisit her poems and they give me the sustenance I need to take the next step.

Daniela: What happens in the depth of chaos? What is the turning point?

Marion: At some point we meet the energy of *Death in the Service of Life*. In the Hindu tradition this archetypal energy is symbolised by Kali, the goddess who wears a necklace that in one moment is made of blooming flowers, and in the next of skulls. She is usually depicted with four hands; one of her right hands says *'Do not be afraid'* and the other right hand offers a bowl of rice. However, one of her left hands holds a sword and in the other is a human head. Kali brings love, ecstasy and life, but also darkness, terror and death. She is the natural cycle of life and death. In the European tradition this energy is best represented by the Baba Yaga of Russian fairy stories. The Baba Yaga's hut lies deep in the forest, and her door always opens to the darkest part of that forest. Her hut rests on turning chicken legs; when we enter her domain our perception becomes dizzy. In many stories the fence that surrounds her hut is made of human bones, and interspersed along the fence are 12 stakes. There are human heads on 11 of them, leaving one empty for the next victim, who might be us. Traditionally, the Baba Yaga asks the 'difficult' questions. She eats naive people who think life should bring them only happiness. She gobbles up the uninitiated, to whom suffering is unacceptable. She devours those who see life in terms of dualistic categories such as white or black, good or evil, life or death.

Daniela: For those who are unfamiliar with Kali and Baba Yaga, could we call that energy 'Apocalyptic Mother'? The word 'apocalypse' derives from the Greek word meaning 'to reveal', or more specifically, 'to uncover that which has previously been hidden'. We also understand apocalypse to mean the coming of a day of judgement, after which the old will be destroyed and a new order will prevail. It seems to me that this is what a meeting with the Baba Yaga, or Kali, entails; a revelation of what has been hidden, death of the obsolete and birth of the new.

Marion: Yes! You have coined a phrase which does capture that archetypal energy.

Daniela: How do we differentiate between Death Mother and Apocalyptic Mother?

Marion: Death Mother prevents new life coming through. She turns life into stone. What you have called 'Apocalyptic Mother' shatters that stone. All change, all growth, presupposes the death of the old. Apocalyptic Mother precipitates the death of old values, rooted in fear and power. Her energy is impersonal. She does not care how painful and terrifying that process is. Her only purpose is to serve life by instigating change. She brings about what Death Mother strives to prevent.

The difference between Death Mother and Apocalyptic Mother is best depicted by the contrast between murder and sacrifice. Both kill energy, but the motives behind them are quite different. Murder, committed by Death Mother, derives from the ego's need for power, control, safety and domination. It aims to prevent us from living our reality for fear that we will be found lacking and annihilated. Sacrifice is rooted in the conscious ego's surrender to the guidance of the Self – the totality of our being which thus encompasses our potential. Such sacrifice transforms destructive, although perhaps comfortable, energy patterns into the creative flow of life. Sacrifice demands the life-affirming *'Yes!'*, which requires all our courage and faith and love to utter.

Daniela: What is required of us when we meet Apocalyptic Mother?

Marion: Change and healing depend on us staying awake and listening to whatever comes into consciousness. We have to stop the incessant chattering and really listen. Fear keeps us chattering; fear that wells up from the past and fear of future repercussions. This is the place where truth can set us free if we can hear it and if we then have the courage to act on it. Whether we grow or wither in this encounter depends on whether we cling to the rigid standpoint of our wounded ego, or whether we choose to trust the Self and leap into the unknown. If, on meeting the Apocalyptic Mother, we can face our truth, then we reclaim a little more of our authentic life. If not, we sink deeper into the mire of Death Mother.

I began to listen to the Apocalyptic Mother when working with my first analyst, Dr Bennet. Our work was going very well, but then I started turning up for my session and he was not there, or he was with another client. I concluded that I was not very important, and that he could not be bothered with me. After about four weeks of this I was walking away from yet another session that he had not bothered to turn up to, when his wife saw me on the street. She called out, *'You better come in'*, but feeling hurt and abandoned, I replied, *'No! I will not!'* and walked away. As I stepped through my front door, the phone rang. It was Dr Bennet. *'I want you to come over here at five o'clock for tea'*, he said. Ungraciously, I replied, *'I will think about it!'* He repeated himself, but with rather more force, *'You WILL be here for tea at five o'clock.'* When I arrived he said *'You claim that I missed your sessions. Let me see your diary. It is you that have written them down incorrectly!'* I did not believe him. He challenged me to look at my history, saying *'Can you see what you did to that relationship... and to that one...? As soon as the person truly loved you, you couldn't accept it and found a way to leave. Now you are trying to do that with me. By writing down the times incorrectly your unconscious has set you up to miss your sessions, while being able to blame me for the disintegration of our relationship. You will get rid of me before I get rid of you. You will not take the chance that I'll stay with you, because you are sure that I'll abandon you.'*

I immediately started to defend myself, becoming quite emphatic, *'I really do believe you got the times wrong, Dr Bennet, rather than me.'* I did not want to face my truth, and surrender my defence system. Dr Bennet implored me to hear him, becoming increasingly angry at my obstinacy. He said *'You are cutting off your life. You have come here so that I can try to do something for you, and I can do nothing because you set up walls that nobody can get through.'* Finally, after a couple of hours, he told me that I needed to go because he had another client. I said, *'I guess I won't see you again.' 'What do you mean, you won't see me again?'* he bellowed. *'Well,'* I replied, *'you are so angry with me that I can't imagine that you'd want to see me again.'* He shook his head, *'Do you think I'd spend all this rage on you if I didn't love you? Do you think I'd waste my time? I love you! Get that into your head and get here for your next session!'* Walking home across the park I thought, *'God – this is the story of my life. It really is. This IS what I have done in the past. As soon as my deepest love is involved, what comes up is my terror of being left and abandoned so I find a way to leave. My fear has sabotaged my life. I am doing it again with Dr Bennet.'*

Facing the Apocalyptic Mother can be excruciating. Early in our journey, when Death Mother's stranglehold is particularly ferocious, and when consciousness is afraid to open itself to the otherness of the unconscious, we experience ourselves as the victim of the apocalypse; in time, as we bring Death Mother to consciousness and begin to experience life beyond her clutches, we may come to see ourselves as partners in the apocalyptic process.

Daniela: I had a dream that described the ferocity of meeting Apocalyptic Mother:

> I have given birth to a radiant baby boy, but I am confused and surprised, because I had not known that I was pregnant. In fact, I am not entirely sure when I became pregnant. Then I realise that my son was born nine months after the gardener raped me.

When I had this dream, it was time for me to sacrifice old and toxic ways of being, but I was fighting against change with all my might. In the end my therapist had to kick me quite fiercely before I would let go of my old ways and allow new life to come in. In this dream my therapist was symbolised by a gardener; somebody who sows seeds and then protects and nurtures them as they grow. Being raped by the dream-gardener reflected the fact that my therapist had to be the conduit for the apocalyptic energy, and it also showed that I was not going to open myself to that energy unless I was forced to do so. At times, if Death Mother's energy is to be dissipated, Apocalyptic Mother has to challenge it in a fierce and unequivocal way.

Marion: I totally agree. Change means change. Stark honesty, however painful, is needed on this journey towards the Self; the unconscious will not tolerate anything less. We must be willing to face many cruel truths: those we keep hidden from other people, and those we keep hidden from ourselves.

Not only do we have to die to a false image of ourselves, but we have to change our outer life accordingly. We may have all the insights, but if we do not incarnate them, they are in vain. We may have to die to our job, to a particular relationship, to our religious faith. We may have to die to our addictions, to our striving for safety and security. Death is agonising and lonely. We have to be willing to suffer the loss of those things that have saved us in the past, but which have simultaneously stood in the way of our freedom. There comes a time when *'if only'* rings false and *'why me?'* is boring. Until we accept that change is up to us, we are stuck in infantile judge-and-blame games. If we are to be freed of our life-denying and (self) destructive behaviours, we must renounce our unconscious methods of getting our own way and take responsibility for ourselves by facing life more directly. When we cannot go there willingly, we need to be kicked, and being kicked by somebody who has our best interests at heart is a hell of a lot better than being kicked by illness or some other crisis!

This journey cannot be undertaken in kindergarten! Positive thinking will not get us there. There is no room for slushy sentimentality in this encounter. If we are lucky we have an analyst who has enough guts and compassion to get angry with us. Carl Jung described analysis as *'surgery without an anaesthetic'*. To think that we can meet the Apocalyptic Mother and find healing without suffering pain is wishful thinking.

Sooner or later, we all meet the Apocalyptic Mother. Do we respond as frightened children, push her back into our unconscious and strive to regain the illusionary security of a static but dead life? Or do we find the courage to ask, *'What is going on here? What is my responsibility?'* and thus open the door to becoming the vibrant, creative and unique adult that we were born to be?

Daniela: The meeting with the Apocalyptic Mother does not just happen once?

Marion: No – I am continually asking, right now, where are my ideas dead? Where is my understanding of the world obsolete? Where are my beliefs limiting me, making me smaller than I am, and strangling my life? Where do I need to expand? What needs to die for that expansion to take place? Where will the new root go?

In our goal-driven society, therapy is often seen as a way to solve a specific problem. That view is impoverished; it derives from our obsession with achievement and blinds us to the ever-unfolding process that is life. For me, the image that best describes this journey is that of a spiral. We keep turning around a central point, but because we work our way both up and down the spiral, we do not return to the same place. We come back to the same issue, the same wound, the same image, the same book, the same poem and we experience something new. With each circumambulation we move deeper into darkness and higher into light; both bring us consciousness. As Nietzsche said, *'The tree that would grow to heaven must send its roots to hell.'*

Eventually, the spiral may lead us down to the Apocalyptic Mother's ultimate question: *'Do I want to live?'* If the answer is *'Yes!'*, then it no longer matters what anybody else did to me. If the answer is *'Yes!'* we have to be prepared to take action.

Daniela: It seems that when the Apocalyptic Mother is asking *'Do you want to live, or do you want to die?'*, we are simultaneously meeting Death Mother head-on. At the deepest turn of the spiral the line between Death Mother and Apocalyptic Mother becomes imperceptibly thin. Thus, whether we meet Death Mother or Apocalyptic Mother may be unimportant. Instead what matters is whether, during that meeting, we say *'Yes!'* or *'No!'* to life.

Marion: Absolutely – how we respond to the encounter is crucial. When I was diagnosed with cancer for a second time I was initially caught in the despair of Death Mother. I saw cancer as a death sentence, cocooned myself in hopelessness and sank into darkness. Then something flipped. I met Death Mother head-on, which meant linking my childhood wounds to my unconscious death wish. With that I woke up.

Daniela: So ultimately cancer was neither Death Mother, nor was it Apocalyptic Mother – instead cancer was just cancer, and it was the energy that was constellated in you which swung between death and apocalypse.

Marion: Yes! My first reaction, as always, was, *'This can't be endured. This is so terrible I will surely die.'* I was terrified. Yet at the same time there was a spark in my unconscious which declared *'I will not give up! I WILL NOT!'* When that spark grew into a flame, I understood the origin of my unconscious death wish, whereupon I could work to combat it. Then I began to believe that I was going to live, despite what my doctors were telling me. Support came from my unconscious by way of a truly numinous dream. It was just before Christmas, and in the dream I was a shepherd standing on the hillside which overlooked the stable in which Christ was born, when I saw a heavenly host flying towards me. One of them, a great, big, blond, sexy angel took me in his arms and declared, *'Fear not, for I bring you glad tidings of great joy.'* That was powerful enough to shatter my terror. On waking, I knew that I finally had to trust my own path. I knew that I had to give up the remnants of my desire to control my life. I knew that I had to surrender the last vestiges of my perfectionism.

Daniela: So when we have the strength and compassion to look Death Mother in the eye she transforms into Apocalyptic Mother?

Marion: Despite years of analytical work, I was living my life as though it were a maze. A maze is a puzzle to be solved. It has dead ends. We may get lost forever. We may be killed by a minotaur. Before cancer, the wounded part of me was always looking for the traps, dead ends and minotaurs. Following that dream, despite being in the midst of a cancer diagnosis, my life opened as a labyrinth. A labyrinth looks superficially like a maze but it is different. It has no dead ends, no traps and no minotaurs. Its one path invariably takes us to the centre, albeit by a circuitous route. In cancer, in the deepest, darkest recess of Death Mother's domain, was the ultimate gift of trust and joy. I was finally able to surrender to life, because at long last I *knew* there was a centre. I trusted that if I kept listening, opening and walking forward, my path would lead me to that centre. Life had a different quality after that – there was no more fear. It fell off me like dirty rags. I thought, *'If I die, it's OK. If I live, that's OK too.'* So to return to your question – when I was eventually ready to meet Death Mother head-on, that energy did transform into Apocalyptic Mother and I entered a totally new world. In the heart of death, I found the gift of life.

Daniela: You say that surrender is essential to this journey; how does surrender differ from giving up?

Marion: Surrender is the conscious act of letting go. It is utterly different from giving up, which inevitably leads to the masochistic, repetitive suffering which reinforces our old patterns and identity as a victim. True surrender is experienced as a leap into an unknown. When we surrender, we let go of our old ways and say *'Yes!'* to something bigger – to our potential and our unique and authentic life.

Surrender is the only real way through an impasse, but it feels like madness, and I rarely went there willingly! I was inevitably brought to the point of surrender by an illness that left me desperate and without any other options. Looking back, I laugh because it was so obvious that some force other than my conscious ego was at work, but at the time I could not see it and it was hell. With cancer I finally surrendered my fears of annihilation, and in so doing I entered my own life. Nobody has described this more poignantly than T.S. Eliot in the closing of *Four Quartets*:[7]

> We shall not cease from exploration
> And the end of all our exploring
> Will be to arrive where we started
> And know the place for the first time.
> Through the unknown, unremembered gate
> When the last of earth left to discover
> Is that which was the beginning;
> At the source of the longest river
> The voice of the hidden waterfall
> And the children in the apple-tree
> Not known, because not looked for
> But heard, half-heard, in the stillness
> Between two waves of the sea.
> Quick now, here, now, always –
> A condition of complete simplicity
> (Costing not less than everything)

---

7 Excerpt from 'Little Gidding' from *Four Quartets* by T.S. Eliot. Copyright 1940 by Houghton Mifflin Harcourt Publishing Company; Copyright © renewed 1968 by T.S. Eliot. Reprinted by permission of Houghton Mifflin Harcourt Publishing Company. All rights reserved. And also from *T.S. Eliot Collected Poems 1909–1962* (Faber, 1974), by permission of the publisher, Faber & Faber Ltd.

'A condition of complete simplicity' is the ultimate outcome of surrender, but the cost is indeed 'not less than everything'.

Daniela: What does 'A condition of complete simplicity' mean to you?

Marion: It means we allow consciousness to move continually within ourselves. It means that we are perpetually letting go of what is obsolete in order to live what needs to be lived *now*! If we are truly alive, we are constantly burning away the veils of illusion and gradually revealing the ever-evolving essence of who we are. Simplicity is created by accepting this process. Whenever I think I am finally in balance and that I can relax, I find myself at the threshold of another gate which is guarded by the angels and demons of my unconscious, and yet again I am called to leap.

Daniela: So a condition of complete simplicity does not mean a life that is free from pain, although that is what many people seek when they begin therapy?

Marion: There is no path to a pain-free existence. The other night I was thinking that I have not got over the pain of myself as a very young child, but it's okay … it does not incapacitate me. It is what I carry. I have done everything I can to heal my wounds, but if early trauma is written into our cells we never get over it completely. When something knocks against that wound, the pain comes to the surface. I do not worry about it anymore. That is simply the way it is and I know that no amount of analysis will change that. Nearly everybody is carrying some wound, and at times our unhealed wounds may even enrich our lives. If I go to a Shakespearian play, my body responds from its wounds and I would not lose that resonance for anything. If we are incapacitated by pain it is a problem. Otherwise, it keeps us on an edge where we are alert and fully in life.

There are even times when addictive symptoms can return. A woman in her eighties, who as a teenager was so anorexic that her life was threatened, may have done the inner work that allowed her to live an authentic life, yet every once in a while she may be unable to swallow food, finding that it sticks in her throat like red hot molten metal. Somebody who was addicted to perfection may always struggle to discriminate between being all that he can be, and dropping back into the old toxic perfectionism. If we are on this journey, we strive to remain aware of what is going on and we work with that. Indeed, the fleeting return of addictive symptoms may be just what is needed to prevent us from stagnating. They keep us questioning and growing. But people do not want to hear that! They want more or less instant cures, which is a tragedy because they are robbing themselves of the process of living!

There is a vital difference between curing and healing. Curing implies that the pain disappears. Healing is a move towards wholeness, by which I mean connecting to different parts of ourselves, including our wounded and painful parts. *'A condition of complete simplicity'* means moving towards wholeness.

Daniela: What do we experience as we move towards wholeness?

Marion: We no longer live to please others; we do not even try to please ourselves. We are who we are because that is who we are. Our truth is rooted in the fact that we have faced our fears of aloneness and refused to listen to the voices of conformity that would smile pleasantly while laying us in eiderdown to suffocate.

We no longer see ourselves as victim of fate; instead we understand that we are partners in our destiny. We cooperate with our Self, taking responsibility for what is happening to us and for living our potential.

We have passion for what we are doing. We do it because it is authentic to who we are, not because others expect it of us. How many times have we told ourselves, *'I should be out there doing something useful'* when there is no authentic 'I' to do it? As we travel this spiral, the authentic 'I' is slowly revealed and we discover a profound meaning in what we are doing.

Our power comes from within us – from our connection to our core. We no longer have to affirm ourselves by dominating or manipulating others. Neither do we need to counteract the lack of passion in our own lives by usurping their lives. This is the point where love becomes possible. We can rejoice in the other, challenge the other and embrace the other without losing our own centre. We do not need to please others; we respect them enough to be who we are and let them like us or leave us.

We live with discipline, rather than willpower. Discipline is a beautiful word. Its root, which is shared with 'disciple', means devotion. Discipline emerges from love, not power. We work with loving discipline to hone the skills we need to fulfil our potential. We attend with loving discipline to our unconscious; recording our dreams, giving time to body work and writing a journal. We no longer see our bodies as objects to be rigidly controlled, rather we respect the wisdom they hold and listen with loving discipline to their messages. There is no freedom without discipline; there is only a prison with willpower.

We can hold apparently contradictory opposites. We no longer see things as either/or because we can contain both. We value paradox. There is good *and* bad, mind *and* body, support *and* opposition, masculine *and* feminine, sexuality *and* spirituality, choice *and* destiny, life *and* death. We can feel the pain of our wounding, *and* be grateful for the way that it has propelled us into finding consciousness. Death Mother is no longer solely Death Mother, but also an energy that has given us the gift of life because of what she demanded of us.

We do not have to project our dark side onto politicians, terrorists, our bosses, lovers, children or parents. We no longer project our dark side onto our bodies. Each time we circumambulate the spiral we see and accept a little more of our own darkness. As we do so we free both our bodies and fellow human beings from having to carry that burden for us. Owning our darkness also enables us to change it; true forgiveness is the transformation of what we would otherwise reject.

Driven by our hidden wounds, our fear of the future distorts the *Now* that could lead to a different future if we dared to be wholly in the present. As we move towards wholeness we start to live in the *Now*; present to ourselves, and present to whatever and whomever is in our environment. We open to what is, and muster the courage to let go of what has become obsolete. Imagine a sailing boat. The position of the sail in one moment is not the position in the next, and if we try to hold on in the new moment to what was appropriate in the old, the boat turns over.

As soon as we lock the sail or the rudder into a position we have ceased to listen, and we drown in our unconscious. If we relentlessly ask ourselves the right questions, *'Do I see what I am doing?'* – then we are alive in the moment. We need to work on maintaining an eternal dialogue between conscious and unconscious, ego and Self, light and dark, so we can discover what needs to live *now* – in *this* moment. As T.S. Eliot said in *Four Quartets*:[8]

> Except for the point, the still point,
> There would be no dance, and there is only the dance

We cannot live continually in this state. We experience it for a moment; we lose it. That is being human and imperfect. That is being a mortal rather than a god. However, if we are willing to face our inner selves and if we are prepared to walk the spiral that will repeatedly take us to the dark heart of the apocalypse, then we will be blessed with a glimpse of the still point which lies at our centre. We will be able to dance the unique life that each of us has the potential to live.

---

8 Excerpt from 'Burnt Norton' from *Four Quartets* by T.S. Eliot. Copyright 1940 by Houghton Mifflin Harcourt Publishing Company; Copyright © renewed 1968 by T.S. Eliot. Reprinted by permission of Houghton Mifflin Harcourt Publishing Company. All rights reserved. And also from *T.S. Eliot Collected Poems 1909–1962* (Faber, 1974), by permission of the publisher, Faber & Faber Ltd.

Part II
Neurobiological perspectives

5   The selves behind the self

Trauma and dissociation

Ellert R.S. Nijenhuis and Daniela F. Sieff

Summary

Under normal circumstances we take experiences that we deem to be significant to ourselves. As a result we feel they are our experiences, and weave them into our life-story. However, if we are chronically abused or neglected during childhood, or if we suffer overwhelming pain, we may be unable to integrate our experiences. As a result we become dissociated: our personality divides into two or more parts, each of which has its own feelings, reality, purpose and identity.

Some of these parts are fixed in the painful experiences. The traumatic past is their enduring reality and it frames their present. They are metaphorically called 'emotional parts of the personality'. Their purpose is to find safety, and they are typically guided by the mammalian defence system (freeze, fight, flight or collapse), or by the attachment system (which seeks protection from others).

Other parts are distanced from the painful experiences. The traumatic past has little, or perhaps no, place in their reality. They are metaphorically called 'apparently normal parts of the personality'. Their purpose is to navigate daily life. Because it is hard to do this when emotional parts are activated, apparently normal parts try to shut out emotional parts. They are rarely completely successful – the emotional parts, and the traumatic memories they encompass, intrude on daily life through highly charged flashbacks, nightmares and inner voices, behaviours, beliefs and bodily symptoms.

Healing requires the integration of trauma: apparently normal parts must realise that the traumatising events are part of their history, whereas emotional parts must realise that the traumatising events are over. Only then can the divided parts be integrated into a cohesive and coherent personality. It is a challenging process which requires patience, compassion and perseverance.

Daniela Sieff: What drew you to working with dissociation?

Ellert Nijenhuis: I trained as a behavioural therapist but was never happy working that way, and when I started seeing a patient called Anna, I knew I had to work differently. Anna had many symptoms and to begin with I tried behaviour therapy techniques. They did not work. I asked more experienced colleagues for advice. They said, *'Ellert, you have to learn that you can't help every patient – let her go.'* I could not accept that, and kept seeing her. One day Anna brought a powerful dream.

> It was winter and she had gone to her parents' house, but had left because it had not felt right. Walking home along the canal, she came across a body frozen in the ice.

Anna did not know what the dream meant, so having started training in hypnosis with Milton Erickson, I suggested that we explore it imaginatively. I asked whether Anna knew if the body was alive or dead. She did not. I asked if she had thoughts about why the body was there. She had none. Then I suggested that she take an imaginary saw, cut through the ice, get the corpse out of the canal and warm it. Anna was hesitant, but tried. A few moments later she screamed: the 'corpse' started to move. As Anna recounted what was happening her facial expression shifted and her body posture changed. Anna switched into a different part of her personality. With cold, icy eyes, she said, *'That took you a long time!'* Anna switched into three more parts of her personality before the session ended. Those parts had appeared before, but I had not picked them up because the switches had not been as dramatic, and because nothing in my training – which by then had taken seven years – had taught me about either trauma or dissociation. I treated Anna for 15 years and explored widely, learning all that I could. During that time I discovered the theory of dissociation outlined by Pierre Janet in the late nineteenth century – it allowed me to find more effective ways of helping Anna and other sufferers of dissociation, and became the basis for my ideas.

Daniela: How do you define dissociation?

Ellert: There are many definitions, but the one that Onno Van der Hart and I settled on as being most useful is the division of a personality into two or more parts, each of which has a unique sense of self, his or her own idea of the world, and own memories, bodily feelings, emotions, movements, behaviours, thoughts and perceptions. Although parts function in some regards rather independently, they are sub-systems within a larger system; they are part of a single human being.

There are no clear boundaries in nature, and we all lie on a continuum with regards to how integrated our personality is. Thus these ideas apply to many of us. However, because clinical and scientific concepts have to be specific, Van der Hart and I made our definition very tight.

Daniela: How do you define trauma?

Ellert: 'Trauma' means 'wound', 'injury' or 'shock', and although many people think of trauma as an event, whether an event is traumatising depends on the *effect* it has on the person, not on the event itself. An event can be described as adverse or potentially traumatising, but an experience is always *somebody's* experience, and that somebody comes to the experience with his or her (1) genetic endowment, (2) previous history and (3) currently available resources. It is the intrinsic relationship between the person and the event which causes trauma. That said, almost nobody survives severe and chronic childhood abuse or neglect by primary caretakers without becoming traumatised.

Daniela: What is the relationship between trauma and dissociation?

Ellert: Trauma implies dissociation. A healthy personality depends on our ability to integrate various aspects of our experience. In trauma, that integration fails. To integrate our experiences there are three distinct types of mental actions that we need to perform: synthesis, personification and presentification.

'Synthesis' describes the mental actions that bring different elements of our experience together. We believe that we register the world as it is, but that is an illusion. We are not the passive recipients of experiences and memories; rather we actively generate them, not in isolation of an outer reality, but in the context of our intrinsic relationship with our environment. To see, hear, smell, judge and remember something, we as brain and body must actively engage in the actions of seeing, hearing, judging and remembering. To feel a particular joy, sorrow or fear, our brain and body must generate these emotions. To create a coherent whole out of the separate elements that make up an experience, our brain needs to actively amalgamate the different components.

'Personification' describes the mental actions that result in experiencing and knowing that the event happened to '*me*'. It sounds obvious, but there are times when we have a cognitive knowledge of an experience, but do not truly feel that it happened to '*me*' because we are distanced from the emotions and bodily sensations that accompany it.

'Presentification' describes the mental actions that allow us to distinguish between our past and our present. When we engage in presentification, the present is more real to us than either past or future, and we can act in a way that is appropriate to now. While this again seems obvious, it can be challenging! How often does the past drive us in inappropriate ways? How often do we worry about the future more than is good for us?

The three integrative actions of synthesis, personification and presentification may happen more or less unconsciously, but they require energy and our ability to do them varies with circumstances. When we are tired, stressed or lack social support, integration becomes more difficult. Integration is also an ability that develops as we grow. A young child can integrate less than an adult, and an excessively stressed child struggles more than a child living in a safe, loving environment.

Chronically abused, maltreated and emotionally neglected children are caught in a terrible situation. Whereas they must integrate the terrors that happen to them if they are to function healthily, circumstances mean that it is almost impossible for them to do so. Furthermore, childhood traumatisation yields structurally impaired brains which make integration especially difficult. Dissociation follows. Different parts of their experience are held by different parts of their personality. Some parts know that the experience happened to 'me'; some do not. Some parts can live in the present; others are locked into the past. Dissociation does not arise to protect us from trauma; it arises because we are unable to integrate what has happened to us.

Daniela: Can dissociation have a protective function?

Ellert: Yes and no! Dissociation prevents us from functioning healthily in the long run and in that sense is not 'protective'; however, when a child is being traumatised at home and cannot escape, the only way to continue with daily life may be to act as though the horrors did not happen, and dissociation, in the sense of living as different parts of oneself, can help.

Oftentimes, the personality divides between one sub-system which attempts to shut out the traumatising event and gets on with daily life and a second which holds the traumatic experience. Marilyn Van Derbur, who became Miss America, was repeatedly raped by her father as a child, and describes this poignantly:[1]

> Because I had no way to escape and no one to turn to, I dissociated, or in my words, 'I split my mind.' ... In order to survive my mind created another separate self to stay and endure the invasions of my body.

Van Derbur called the part that experienced the abuse 'The Night Child' and the part that got on with daily life 'The Day Child':

> [I]n the morning, I was the happy, sparkly, respected, disciplined, highly moral young girl. That was real to me, the day child.... My mind had found a way to take the memories and feelings of terror, humiliation, rage, helplessness and hopelessness and compartmentalise them into a different part of my brain, body and soul.... How could I get through a day at school playing with my friends, answering the questions the teacher asked, riding my bike home – how could I survive a daily routine if I remembered what awaited me at night?
> (p. 24)

Building on the work of Charles Samuel Myers, a British First World War psychiatrist who described dissociation in 'shell-shocked' soldiers, my colleagues Onno Van der Hart, Kathy Steele and I use the term *'the apparently normal part of the personality'* (ANP) to describe the part that gets on with daily life, and *'the emotional part of the personality'* (EP) to describe the part that holds the traumatic experience.[2]

---

1 Van Derbur, Marilyn (2004) *Miss America by Day: Lessons Learnt from Ultimate Betrayal and Unconditional Love.* Denver, CO: Oak Hill Ridge Press, p. 22.
2 Van der Hart, O., Nijenhuis, E.R.S and Steele, K. (2006) *The Haunted Self: Structural Dissociation and the Treatment of Chronic Traumatization.* New York: W.W. Norton & Company.

Daniela: Are there degrees of dissociation?

Ellert: Yes! There is variation in (1) the number of divisions, (2) the elaboration of the EPs and (3) the ability of the EPs to impinge on the ANP.

In the simplest form there is one elaborate ANP and one, often rather rudimentary, EP. The classic example is post-traumatic stress disorder (PTSD), where the ANP gets on with life, until the EP, which holds the traumatic memory, bursts through, creating what are commonly known as flashbacks. More complex is when there is one ANP and two EPs. In this configuration one EP is typically organised around the emotional and bodily experience of the traumatising event(s), while the other appears to reside outside the body and observes the event(s) from afar. Even more complex is when there is one ANP and several EPs. In the most complex form of structural dissociation there is not only more than one EP, but also more than one ANP; one may be focused on a job, another on child-care and another on household chores.

Some EPs are not very elaborated – these contain only a small fragment of a traumatic memory, and have only a sketchy identity. Others are elaborated – they have a clear identity, which generally consists of a name, age, gender, preferences, etc. Sometimes the identity is modelled on TV characters. One patient had a group of EPs based on Star Trek characters. Mr Spock served as the intellectual, but emotionally devoid, observer-EP.

In terms of their ability to impinge on the ANP, in severe cases, elaborated EPs knockout the ANP, dominate consciousness and behaviour, and appear as fully functioning, independent personalities. A new patient, called Edith, missed her first session. She entered my waiting room, but found herself turning around, walking out and driving home. There had been a conflict between two subpersonalities. One wanted to get help. The other wanted to flee. In less extreme cases, an ANP appears to be in control, but an EP controls a particular area of the body. One patient, speaking as an ANP felt no anger, yet her hand, which was under the control of a fight-EP, was so tightly curled into a fist that her fingernails cut into her palms, drawing considerable amounts of blood – yet she had no idea of what was happening. Other times, instead of taking over a body part, an EP will intrude on the mental world of an ANP. Then the person experiences thoughts, feelings, voices and behaviours that seem to come from inside, but which feel alien. Not understanding what is happening, sufferers fear they are going mad. In other instances, EPs find their way to the surface in dreams. Charlotte Delbo, who survived Auschwitz, portrays how disturbing this can be:

> [I]n these dreams, there I see myself again, me, yes me, just as I know I was: scarcely able to stand … pierced with cold, filthy, gaunt, and the pain so unbearable, so exactly the pain I suffered there, that I feel it physically, I feel it through my whole body, which becomes a block of pain, and I feel death seizing me, I feel myself die.

Fortunately in my anguish, I cry out. The cry awakens me, and I emerge from the nightmare, exhausted. It takes days for everything to return to normal, for … the skin of my memory to mend itself.[3]

Daniela: Are there patterns in the type of EPs that are formed?

Ellert: Although, in theory, EPs could form along any lines, they tend to be organised around the basic actions that have evolved to facilitate survival. The commonest EPs are built around the five different action patterns that make up the mammalian defence system: (1) startle, (2) freeze, (3) flight, (4) fight and (5) submission.

The startle response kicks in the instant we notice something that we deem to be potentially dangerous. We lose interest in what we are doing, become hyper alert and scan our environment. Is there real danger? Where is it? Our heart rate and blood pressure increase. We start to breathe fast. We mobilise energy. If we discern a genuine threat all our attention focuses on it, and we jump into defensive action. How far away is the source of danger? What actions may save my skin?

Sometimes the most appropriate action may be to freeze. Our speech centres tend to shut down; we can hardly speak, if at all. Our muscles stiffen; our body becomes rigid. Like all physical defence-patterns, this psychobiological response is rooted in our evolutionary heritage. Under some circumstances freezing is adaptive for prey animals because predators struggle to detect immobile, silent animals, whereas movement triggers attack.

Other times, freezing is not the best option; instead we have more chance of surviving if we flee. Everything shifts when an animal starts to run – the danger remains in awareness, but we focus on where we are going and where we might find safety. Physiologically, oxygen is diverted away from the brain and into the large muscles of the legs; we can run faster and further, but we cannot think that well. We must act fast. No time for reflection!

If the threat is already within arms length, it is probably too late to flee. Then our best option may be to fight. Stopping the attacker – warding them off or hurting them so they cannot attack us – becomes everything.

In situations where neither flight nor fight will work, an animal may try to defend itself by playing dead. This is often confused with freezing, but it is different: muscles relax and heart rate, blood pressure and the speed of breathing drop to imperceptibly low levels. The individual may also urinate and defecate (to spoil the predator's meal). Mimicking death is evolutionarily adaptive because carnivores do not like to eat animals they have not killed in case the animal has been dead for a while and its flesh harbours disease. Playing dead is accompanied by a subjective feeling of physical and emotional numbness and of having left the body.

EPs are not only formed around these defences; they are also created around other action systems. All young mammals need to attach to an individual who can protect and nurture them, and EPs are often created around this need. Suicidal EPs

3 Delbo, C. (1985) *La mémoire et les jours (Days and Memory)*, Paris: Berg International.

are also fairly common, although generally their goal is to end the pain and to rest, rather than death itself. Perpetrator-like EPs are formed through the imitation and internalisation of abusers; they emerge from the urge for control in a world in which control was impossible. Hence, I refer to these parts as controlling EPs.

Daniela: What are the characteristics of the emotional parts of the personality?

Ellert: The emotional parts typically re-enact the past; their only reality is the time of traumatisation, which they live again and again. Their field of consciousness is so restricted that they cannot see the present; nor can they envision the future as anything but a repeat of the past. An angry face always means you are going to be hit. You will be abused by everybody with whom you have a close relationship.

The raison d'être of most EPs is to carry out one specific function, and EPs struggle to see anything beyond their domain. When a flight-EP is running the show, the world is filled with dangers from which we must flee. When an attachment-EP is in charge, we are focused on seeking out, and not being abandoned by, somebody we hope might protect us. When a suicidal-EP is dominant, killing oneself makes perfect sense. Because EPs struggle to understand the world view of other EPs, they often develop phobias of one another. A flight part will generally be phobic of a part that wants to attach, and vice versa. An intellectualised observer part may be phobic of all parts that hold feelings.

EPs act at a low level of sophistication; they behave in knee-jerk ways and find it hard to assess whether their actions will achieve their goals, and whether there might be a more productive response to the current situation. EPs also engage in 'substitute actions'. The belief, *'I am bad. It is my fault'* is a substitute for integrating the unbearable reality of parental abuse. Sometimes EPs find substitutes in physical outlets: one profoundly neglected patient learnt that if she binged and then threw up she felt at least some control over her life. Another cut himself to find calm when he was frightened – the resulting release of opiates soothed him and substituted for asking others for help. However, another patient cut herself not to create calm, but to feel alive, saying, *'It is as if I am only allowed to live when I feel physical pain.'*

Daniela: What are the characteristics of the apparently normal part of the personality?

Ellert: The ANPs only concern is to navigate daily life. To do that the ANP must disconnect from the traumatic experience – when we are threatened we are so focused on defence that we cannot eat, sleep, go to school, work, look after children, etc.

Sometimes disconnecting from the traumatic experience means that the ANP has no memory of the traumatising event, other times the ANP remembers what happened, but the memory has no depth or substance and feels as though it happened to somebody else. Charlotte Delbo describes this lack of personification:

> I have the feeling that the 'self' who was in the camp, isn't me, isn't the person who is here, opposite you. No, it's too unbelievable. And everything

that happened to this other 'self', the one from Auschwitz, doesn't touch me now, me, doesn't concern me.[4]

Keeping traumatic memories at bay requires an ANP to shut out the experience held in the EPs. ANPs use many strategies to achieve this, but at times an EP will break through; then the ANP, flooded with fear and pain, is unable to fulfil its daily tasks. As a result the ANP becomes phobic of the EP. Anything that might trigger its appearance is vehemently avoided. For Remarque, on returning from combat, that meant avoiding his father and other people:

> I cannot get along with the people. My mother is the only one who asks no questions. Not so my father. He wants me to tell him about the front; he is curious in a way that I find stupid and distressing; I no longer have any real contact with him.... I realize he does not know that a man cannot talk about such things; I would do it willingly but it is too dangerous for me to put these things into words. I am afraid they might become gigantic and I be no longer able to master them.[5]

Often the ANP is not only phobic of other people; it is also phobic of its own body, which holds the visceral experience of the trauma. That results in a feeling of disembodiment, and a propensity not to register tiredness, hunger or stress. It also means that survivors, as ANP, are cut-off from their emotions, as Nancy Raine poignantly describes:[6]

> The numbness ... seemed to spread out over the entire emotional landscape, like fog. Not only is pain blunted, but pleasure as well. Of all the consequences of the rape, this was the hardest to perceive and the hardest to endure. It was living with novocaine in the heart ... I felt cut off from everything, and as the years passed, even from the memory of emotional life as I had once experienced it.

When an ANP is desperately trying to avoid triggering an EP, life becomes increasingly restricted. But sometimes avoidance is not enough – then an ANP may turn to self-harm and substance abuse. These behaviours temporarily dampen emotional pain and block traumatic memories by stimulating the release of opiates, and by diverting attention.

Regardless of how an ANP blocks the EPs, because it is avoiding traumatic memories and trauma-associated experiences, it feels, knows and recalls too little. In the end, as an ANP, a person lives a shallow existence at the surface of consciousness, not knowing where it came from.

---

4 Delbo, *La mémoire et les jours (Days and Memory)*.
5 Remarque, E.M. (1929/1982) *All Quiet on the Western Front*, New York: Ballantine Books (original work published in 1929).
6 Raine, N.V. (1998) *After Silence: Rape and my Journey Back*. New York: Crown.

Daniela: How do EPs relate to the ANP?

Ellert: Just as the ANP is typically phobic of the EPs, EPs are typically phobic of the ANP. In most traumas neglect is part of the mix, so if an ANP responds to an EP with phobic avoidance, that neglect is recreated internally. The pain of that is so great for the EPs that they learn to keep away from the ANP.

That said, EPs have a potent need to be heard and sooner or later will turn to behaviours too powerful to be ignored. Van Derbur describes it thus:

> While extolling my father's virtues, my night child was screaming at my refusal to even acknowledge her, much less comfort and love her. She was like the child who goes into the kitchen and says, *'Mommy can you help me with this?'* And the mother replies perfunctorily, *'In a minute.' 'Please now, Mommy?'* *'I said in a minute.'* The child pulls on her mother's dress. The mother ignores her. The child pulls harder. Finally, the child pulls down the cookie jar, it splinters into hundreds of pieces. She now has her mother's attention.[7]

Pulling down the cookie jar can mean a myriad of debilitating behaviours. One adult patient had suffered all her life with fainting spells that began when she was two. Doctors thought she might have epilepsy but brain scans revealed that was unlikely. Instead, we discovered that her father had tried to suffocate her and that fainting resulted from an EP re-enacting that trauma with the aim of having it acknowledged. Another patient, whose father raped her with a loaded gun, haemorrhaged when she could not integrate that trauma, despite knowing it cognitively. It was as though her body was going to make sure she connected to its visceral experience.

Daniela: Is there evidence of biological differences between subpersonalities?

Ellert: Yes! Our research group has recently shown that a person's heart rate reacts differently to a potential threat, depending on which subpersonality is dominant. In one experiment pictures of an angry face were held some distance away from patients who had suffered physical abuse, and then the picture was slowly moved towards them. As the ANP their heart rate remained constant; as the flight-EP their heart rate increased significantly, but as the submissive-EP, although their heart rate rose initially, when the picture was brought within 70 centimetres it fell dramatically. Afterwards subjects said they had no memory of what happened past 70 centimetres – they had collapsed into a state of feigning death.

With regards to neuroimaging brain activity, our research group has compared ANPs to EPs, but have not yet had enough subjects to differentiate between EPs. Even so, ANP and EP have different patterns of brain activation when read scripts of a personal traumatic experience. For ANP, parts of the prefrontal cortex, which among its many functions regulates intense emotions, are activated. However, for

7   Van Derbur, *Miss America by Day.*

EPs, the prefrontal cortex is less activated, whereas the amygdala and other parts of the emotional brain that mediate defence are more activated. The sensory cortex – which is involved in bodily sensations – is also more active for an EP than for an ANP. We have also shown ANP and EP faces so briefly that they were not conscious of what they had 'seen'. It appeared that ANP and EP had different behavioural and neural reactions to angry as well as emotionally neutral facial expressions.

Some critics have argued that dissociation of the personality does not exist, and that it results from therapists implanting false memories into fantasy-prone patients through suggestion. Our group's neuroimaging studies showed that highly fantasy-prone women and actors, who were carefully instructed and motivated to enact ANP and EP, failed to generate the behavioural, physiological and neural reaction patterns of the authentic ANP and EP. This research demonstrates that the existence of dissociative parts of the personality relates to traumatisation, and not to suggestion, fantasy or role playing, as some theories proposed.

Daniela: What constitutes healing?

Ellert: Healing means that survivors integrate their trauma. It requires (1) synthesis – the elements of the traumatic experience must be brought together; (2) personification – the survivor must realise that the traumatising event happened to them; and (3) presentification – the survivor must realise that the trauma lies in their past and is over. Healing also requires the fusion of the different parts into an integrated personality. Healing can take many years of work in the case of chronic and severe traumatisation, and cannot be achieved without suffering pain. When the traumas are less profound, and result in a simple dissociative disorder like PTSD, treatment can proceed more quickly.

Daniela: You advocate that treatment is done in three phases – can you give an overview?

Ellert: In the first phase the symptoms need to be reduced so the patient can function better in daily life. Also, the dissociated parts need to be identified and learn of each other's existence. In the second phase the different parts share their traumatic memories and emotions. In the third phase the divided parts are (re)integrated into a single entity. The work cycles back and forth between these phases.

Daniela: Where do you start?

Ellert: I start with the belief that if somebody walks through my door, then they want to heal, while being aware that they do not have the tools to do that. And so I begin with whatever the patient brings. Behaviours, physical sensations, symptoms, stories, dreams and art-work all provide valuable information. Even a patient's 'resistance' contains information – it is the patient saying *'This is the wrong way, we need to go in a different direction'* or *'We need to do X, before I can do Y!'*

From the beginning I try to get into the world of the EPs and the ANPs. To help somebody redecorate their house you need to get through the door; standing outside is useless. It is the same with dissociation. The ANP and EPs are overly stable, rigid systems – meaning they are mostly closed to anything beyond themselves. My job is to 'destabilise' them. I call it 'throwing a bit of sand into the machine.' I cannot do that from the outside. The most effective way to get inside their world is through being genuinely respectful of them, and curious about what they are trying to do. By taking that approach, I also model the attitudes the parts need to develop towards each other.

From the outset I give the patient control. Traumatisation occurs when children have no control over their abusers, and if they then suffer from dissociation, they have no control over their symptoms. From day one I help patients find ways to signal 'stop', and when a patient tells me to stop, I do. Additionally, once somebody has been assessed as suffering from a dissociative disorder, I explain what it is. Factual understanding provides relief to patients who are frightened and ashamed of their behaviour.

Daniela: What is the role of the therapeutic relationship?

Ellert: It is crucial. Patients cannot do the work of integration alone. It is too much. They need a therapist to accompany them and guide them. However, those who were chronically traumatised as children have no experience of relationships as offering safety; instead the very people who should have protected them, caused pain. Thus some dissociative parts are phobic of relationships and will do what they can to sabotage the therapeutic relationship.

Creating a therapeutic relationship is made even more complex because in parallel to the parts that are phobic of relationship, there will nearly always be a part organised around the need to attach to somebody who will provide protection. This 'attachment-EP' is terrified of losing the therapist. It will be obsessively sensitive to possible abandonment, often misconstruing the therapist's actions and words. It will be greatly upset by absences. Craving constant reassurance, the patient as this EP will highlight distress, implicitly knowing that within a healthy attachment relationship it is the distress cry of an infant that brings the caretaker running. In a bid for more contact, the patient may make urgent phone calls, self-harm, threaten suicide or even attempt it. At times, controlling EPs are brought in for support; then behaviour is driven by a threat: *'If you leave me, I will make you sorry.'*

In other words, a secure therapeutic relationship – the environment which makes integration possible – is rarely achievable early in therapy; instead it is a work in progress and a major focus of therapy in itself.

Daniela: How can a therapist help a patient work with the phobia of attachment?

Ellert: The therapist must be empathetically attuned to the patient, present and authentic. At the same time, he must provide stable relational boundaries. What makes this balance particularly tricky is that different dissociative parts have different attitudes to the therapist, and different needs for closeness. The therapist must be alert to this and use 'multi-speak', by which I mean he must shape his language so that no part feels left out – whether it is actively present or not. Very early on, I will say something like *'As a whole person you might have mixed feelings about being in therapy and sharing things about yourself. It's not unusual for a part of us to want to share so that we can get help, while another part trusts nobody and wants to keep to ourselves. I am confident that we will find ways, at your own pace, to listen to and respect all parts of you.'*

Crucially, the therapist must be conscious of what is happening within himself. It is essential that the therapist has worked with his own attachment issues. Some therapists, with unhealed attachment issues, reify the child part who craves attachment. Treating it like an actual child, they try to parent it and rescue it. But reification bolsters the part's identity as a separate entity, while simultaneously causing the parts that are phobic of attachment to redouble their efforts to sabotage the relationship.

Daniela: You have said that it is sometimes more productive to work with the social engagement system rather than the attachment system. What is the difference?

Ellert: The attachment system motivates us to seek protection from another person; the social engagement system motivates us to collaborate with another person to achieve a shared goal. For many dissociative patients attachment is typically associated with trauma, whereas social engagement may not be implied so much and that makes it easier to work with.

Working with the social engagement system also provides a better model of what needs to happen in the client's internal world: ANP and EPs need to respect each other as equals and they need to collaborate. The attachment process, built on the need of a relatively helpless infant to secure nurturance and protection from an older and more powerful person, does not have mutual collaboration at its heart. Rather, the 'other' is conceived as an object that fulfils the infant's needs instead of a person with his or her own subjective perspective and needs.

Daniela: How do you start working with dissociated parts?

Ellert: The first task is to get a sense of the parts that exist and their functions. To reveal themselves, parts need to trust the therapist. That trust develops slowly. It depends on EPs learning that the therapist is genuinely curious and respectful about what they are trying to achieve.

However, it is not enough for EPs to reveal themselves to the therapist; ultimately the ANP needs to recognise their existence and listen to them. That can be incredibly hard for an ANP. The ANP will be phobic of the EPs because (1) it will be terrified that their pain and fear will prevent it from functioning, and (2) it will believe that if the needs of the EP are expressed, then retraumatisation will occur and it will have developed all kinds of beliefs to prevent that. One patient who was abused whenever she expressed any need took on the mantra *'I am a spoilt brat and always whining.'* Another who was savagely punished for expressing anger, suppressed it by believing *'If I feel angry then I am like my sadistic, violent father and I won't be like him.'* Challenging these beliefs is vital if the ANP is to recognise the EPs and needs to be done sensitively but firmly!

That said, in Phase 1, the aim is not to access traumatic memories and emotions, but to improve the functioning of the ANP in daily life. To that end, EPs must be given new, less problematic ways to achieve their goals and to make themselves heard.

Daniela: How is that done?

Ellert: With patience and perseverance! EPs are often resistant to letting go of old actions, frightened that they will be neglected, hurt or abused. And so the therapist should *not* try to take away the EPs' old methods, however harmful they may be in certain regards. Instead EPs must be assured that they are valued, and only then helped to learn new actions.

Learning new actions needs to happen in a structured sequence: (1) give the EP a choice of new actions, allowing it to decide which it wants to learn, (2) plan the new action, (3) begin it, (4) end it, (5) complete with an 'act of triumph'. Pierre Janet recognised that any action, either physical or mental, has a point at which it is completed and in that moment there is spontaneous joy – think of a footballer scoring a goal. He called such moments 'acts of triumph'. When an EP, which has rigidly stuck to a few actions for its entire existence, achieves something new, that must be celebrated irrespective of how simple the action is. The EP who made its presence felt by causing my patient to faint created huge problems, so I taught it to clench my patient's hand (that is, the ANP's hand) into a tight fist. That was inconvenient enough for the EP to trust it could still get noticed, but was a great improvement on fainting.

Daniela: Can an ANP's phobia of EPs be treated similarly to phobias pertaining to the external world?

Ellert: To a certain degree. When people are phobic of something in the external world, treatment involves exposing them in steps to whatever they are phobic of. Exposure has to be controlled because if it is too intense, the phobia is strengthened. It is the same with phobias between dissociated parts, only it is harder to control exposure because EPs tend to come in with full force. There are various techniques I use to protect a patient from that. I might ask an ANP *'How would you like the EP to tell you about itself? Should it speak in words? Should it show you images? Can you tolerate 1 per cent of what the EP knows? Can you listen to it for five seconds, for 30 seconds?'* If the patient replies *'five seconds'*, I will time it. For integration to progress the ANP must take huge risks so its trust is imperative. The therapist is responsible for fostering that trust. Patience is crucial to that process. Healing starts with what the person can do and builds slowly from there (just as when teaching a child to write, each step builds on the previous one). It is better to get five seconds of meeting between parts in one session, and 20 seconds in the next session, than to ask for too much and reinforce the phobia.

Another technique is to work with imagination. I may suggest that the EP shows itself on an imaginary TV while giving the remote control to the ANP. I tell the ANP she can fast forward through a section of film, slow it down, make the picture black and white, or even switch it off. Alternatively I may suggest that the patient imagine a meeting room which the ANP and EPs can enter and leave at will. For images to be effective they have to resonate with the patient and it may take time to find those images.

It is also important to realise that although integration depends on the ANP opening to the EPs (and the EPs to each other and to the ANP), an ANP may not be able to do this at the beginning. Then the therapist needs to work directly with the EPs. However, this is only a first step – with dissociative disorders the core problem is not the EPs, it is in an ANP's avoidance of the EPs. If the therapist looks after the EPs, the ANP can maintain its avoidance and go on an extended holiday, just as an agoraphobic person who has all his needs provided by a spouse never has to learn to leave the house.

Daniela: How would you approach what might seem to be particularly difficult EPs – the suicidal-EP, for example?

Ellert: Many therapists avoid the suicidal-EP because suicidality is high in those who suffer with dissociative disorders and therapists are frightened of that. However, avoidance backfires – every part is there for a good reason, and unless the therapist treats a suicidal part with respectful curiosity, it will remain split-off and garner ever more power.

That said, I have, on occasion, had to act in radical ways with a suicidal-EP. Recently, a patient said *'I've decided to end my life. I've had enough of this pain! I promised to tell you if I was going to commit suicide, and having kept my promise, I'm going.'* I knew that voice belonged to only one part of my patient, but I could not convince her. She claimed that she had had a meeting with all parts, and that each agreed on suicide. She headed towards the door. Without thinking, I jumped up, grabbed her arms and restrained her. She fought. I held tight and yelled *'You are not leaving like this!'* all the time wondering if my reaction was inappropriate – physically restraining a patient who had voluntarily walked into my consulting room, and yelling at her, contradicted everything in my training. Yet my heart was saying *'I will not allow you to die like this!'* Then the patient suddenly switched into a (subjectively) four-year-old EP, who appeared to be psychotic. I had her admitted. After three weeks she came out of her psychotic state and we talked. She said had I not acted as I did, she would probably be dead – and was very glad to have survived.

Daniela: How do you connect to EPs that formed before a young child has language?

Ellert: If other EPs exist, I may ask them to engage with the non-verbal EP and act as its ambassador. Other times I work at a non-verbal level. I will babble to the person as the pre-verbal EP with a rhythm and tone similar to motherese, and I will match their breathing patterns. Both help to modulate feelings. I will look in the same direction as the patient, and use simple, concrete words. I might say something like *'I can see you staring at the table ... that is fine.... There must be a very good reason why you aren't ready to talk yet...'* (the 'yet' suggests that the part, even if it has the identity of a pre-verbal child, will eventually be able to talk, and is a linguistic tool I use in a variety of situations).

Daniela: How can you reach a part based on submission and collapse?

Ellert: It can be hard, but it is not impossible. A patient called Elsie became extremely sleepy and unable to move whenever a particular traumatic memory was approached. This felt like the state of submission which Elsie had entered when her abuse was overwhelming. She described this EP as a little girl who did not believe that the trauma was over, who was convinced that nobody was coming to help her, and who was certain that she was dead.

There could be no healing unless this 'little girl' was included in our work, so I asked if the ANP could bring her into the session. The ANP tried, but could not wake her. Elsie then proposed that the ANP, along with her wise inner figure, go to the little girl. They told the little girl that she was alive and that the trauma was over. The girl did not respond. I suggested it might help to invite Elsie's fight-EP to help. Then the ANP suggested the image of breathing life into the little girl. The girl woke and saw herself surrounded by caring, supportive, protective people. I encouraged her to feel her heart-beat and breathing, and to make tiny movements such as blinking to help her realise that she was indeed alive. The ANP continued to assure the little girl that she was safe. The patient never had another episode of shutting down in session.

Daniela: Elsie was helped by 'a figure of inner wisdom' – what is this?

Ellert: Many dissociative patients have access to a figure of inner wisdom, which is often contained in an observer-EP. When such a figure exists I will suggest the patient asks it for advice. A therapist cannot delegate all responsibility to this figure, but by taking it seriously a patient's sense of autonomy and agency is nurtured.

Daniela: With Elsie there was collaboration between different parts; how do you work with EPs that are phobic of one another?

Ellert: I encourage the EPs to feel respect and compassion for each other. To do that I model a respectful and compassionate stance towards all parts equally. If the therapist favours one part it sends the wrong signals, but to be even-handed the therapist must be happy with all aspects of his own being. If he is more comfortable with submission than with aggression, he will unconsciously focus on the EP that mediates submission and avoid the fight-EP. If he is more comfortable with anger than with his need for attachment, he will pay more attention to the EP formed around anger. A therapist needs only a slight bias to become a part of the dissociated system and to perpetuate the division of the personality.

But a therapist's attitude is rarely enough; often the dissociated parts must be explicitly encouraged to see the value of one another. Controlling EPs that have identified with the perpetrator often turn their energy onto other parts. Consequently they are hated and avoided, so the therapist needs to explain that they are trying to do something valuable. One patient's controlling-EP was the internalisation of her viciously critical mother. Helping the other parts to understand that its aim was protective – it wanted to prevent the woman doing anything that might bring trouble – helped them to respect it.

Sometimes, the phobic parts have to be challenged, albeit in a playful and respectful way. One patient had a controlling-EP called Hans who was phobic of the submissive part that 'took' the repeated rape. Hans thought that the submissive-EP was 'a sissy' and 'pathetic'. To get Hans to listen to the EP, I played on his image of himself as brave and courageous, challenging him as to whether he was courageous enough to listen to the submissive part for just 30 seconds.

In such situations the language used is crucial. Thinking and speaking in verbs rather than nouns can make all the difference. Using nouns we remain stuck in old patterns, whereas verbs translate into what we can do differently. When Hans said *'Crying is dangerous'*, I replied *'Oh.... You perceive that crying is too dangerous for you to do ... what about if you tried a little crying? Thirty seconds, maybe? Would it be too dangerous for you to do that here with me?'*

Daniela: You encourage patients to eventually bring all parts together, why?

Ellert: They are all part of one system and need to recognise that. A group meeting is one way to achieve this. To ensure that no part is retraumatised I suggest that a patient creates an imaginary conference room, and insist on certain rules:

- All parts are equally important.
- Each part has one vote.
- One part speaks at a time.
- All parts must accept that all other parts have, at their core, a positive function even if they create suffering in trying to fulfil that.

Often some parts are too scared to enter the conference room. They should not be forced, but it can help to imagine a hole in a wall through which they can watch the meeting. As they gain confidence, they can communicate with those in the conference via an imaginary video link. Eventually, they risk entering the room.

Daniela: What gets shared in the meetings?

Ellert: To start with it's best to share only the existence of the different EPs and their function, but eventually each part needs to share its painful memories, emotions and bodily sensations. This is Phase 2. It sets the stage for Phase 3, fusion. When two parts have shared everything they know and feel there is no reason to remain separate.

Daniela: Can you talk more about sharing traumatic memories during Phase 2?

Ellert: At the heart of dissociation is (1) the division of the traumatic memory into one or more fragments, each of which may be held by a different EP, and (2) the ANP's phobia of these memories. In Phase 2 the traumatic memories have to be reassembled and shared across all parts. It cannot be done without pain. Just as we cannot learn to swim without getting into the water, patients have to 'get into' the physical and emotional aspects of their memories, not just address them cognitively. There is a danger of drowning – of being swamped by the memories and retraumatised – so a patient must be confident the therapist will help him to stay afloat and regulate overwhelming feelings.

Daniela: How do you help patients to synthesise divided memories?

Ellert: Because the pain can be overwhelming, synthesis has to be titrated. To do that, I work with patients to find the images which will allow the patient to determine how much, or how little, of the memory is presented at one time. With Katya, who loved to cook, I suggested that she remember no more and no less than 'just enough', like the amount of yeast needed to make bread rise. With Martin, a computer engineer, I suggested that ten bytes of a traumatic memory were downloaded at a time. Such images allow the person to make an intuitive assessment of 'just enough' or 'ten bytes', and so regulate their own experience.

When people recount a traumatic experience I will use language and non-verbal cues to keep the story moving; it is important that the patient does not get stuck. I will also help the patient avoid being swept away by the traumatic past, by reminding them of present reality and saying things like *'As you are speaking, notice that you are here in the room with me.'* If the patient is disappearing into the traumatic past, I will make more contact, perhaps by touching her hand and saying *'Notice my hand is supporting your hand.'* Consciousness starts with the body, so if the patient is okay with being touched it can be very valuable.

Sometimes memories have to be synthesised with only some EPs present, while others keep away until they are strong enough to cope. Anton had five EPs. One was terrified of recalling the brutal physical abuse he had suffered as a child and could not do so without being overwhelmed. I helped Anton to develop an imaginary soundproof space for that EP. The other four EPs, and Anton as ANP, then shared their painful memories while the vulnerable EP remained in the safe space until it was ready to take the trauma on board.

But the synthesis of memories is not enough. A person needs to feel that X happened to *me* (personification), but that it happened in my *past* and is over (presentification). A person also needs to understand that these things did not happen to me because I am bad, but because the world is unfair and I was subjected to people who abused and/or neglected me.

Daniela: What happens in Phase 3?

Ellert: Phase 3 involves both the unification of the personality, and (re)habilitation to 'normal' life. There is little written about Phase 3 and there is a stubbornly persistent myth that integrating traumatic memories is all that is needed to heal dissociation. It is not! Phase 3 can involve some of the hardest work. Parts often fear fusion, either because they still hold particularly traumatic fragments of memory, or because they are strongly invested in the idea of being separate persons and are terrified of ceasing to exist. Phase 3 is also a time of grieving for all that has been lost. It is a time of turmoil, as long-held substitute beliefs are relinquished and a new sense of self is forged. And it is a time of struggle as the person learns the skills needed to live a 'normal' life.

Daniela: How does fusion occur?

Ellert: Fusion is the final step in a long wave of changes. First, two parts have to get to know one another at a cognitive level. Then they have to learn to feel one another's emotions, and share experiences, including traumatic memories. Only then is the door open to realising: *'We are the same; that I am her and she is me.'*

There is often reluctance to take the final step so it helps for parts to come together for a short time, perhaps to feel a feeling or to think a thought, and then separate. In the next session they stay together a little longer, gradually getting used to this new state. Metaphors and images are also useful, such as suggesting that parts step into one another. Some patients are helped by formal fusion rituals; for others who were exposed to ritualised kinds of abuse rituals can be retraumatising.

Daniela: Can you talk more about the grieving that needs to occur?

Ellert: Grieving starts during Phase 2, when the patient realises that unmet childhood needs are not going to be met. In Phase 3 this grieving continues, but people also begin to grieve for the hopes and dreams that are no longer realistic because of what they suffered. Grief is tough; it is a task for the emotionally hardy. Its physical components mimic the sensations of traumatisation – anxiety, anger, dread, despair, loneliness, guilt, shame – and so grieving may retrigger traumatic memories, and even the dissociation that accompanies them.

To begin with grief is often accompanied by vehement rage; the person wants retribution. That is normal, but eventually that has to be put aside, or it will consume their life. That said, a therapist needs to help those who have suffered severe trauma to accept that grieving will never be over; rather waves of grief will ebb and flow through their entire life.

Daniela: What does becoming (re)habilitated to normal life involve?

Ellert: Prior to Phase 3 aspects of normal life are avoided because they reactivate traumatic memories; rehabilitation means learning to do these things. For example, one patient who before her trauma had loved running stopped because her raised heart rate triggered embodied memories of her trauma. She had to learn to tolerate an elevated heart rate, not only so she could exercise, but also so she could play with her lively young children.

Habilitating to normal life often includes doing things that were previously impossible, like making friends, going to university or getting a better job. One patient started his own business when, having brought his parts together, he realised that he had the skills to do so. But first, he needed to radically change how he related to the world, and how he thought about himself. That takes enormous courage.

Having an intimate relationship is a huge achievement for anybody who has suffered childhood trauma. First, beliefs and promises created to cope with trauma have to be dismantled. Typical beliefs include *'I promise myself that I will never trust a man'* or *'Love is a way to get hurt.'* Dismantling these beliefs is terrifying, because they were once protective, but while they remain in place, intimacy is impossible. Sexual intimacy is particularly hard for those who were sexually abused, because it may reactivate traumatic memories. A survivor wanting to explore their sexuality must go slowly and be in control. Once in a relationship, the survivor will need to learn to cope with the glitches that arise. The person is essentially protected from these in the therapeutic relationship, so it is new ground.

Finally, (re)habilitation means valuing the routines of a new life that is no longer chaotic and thus not always exciting. It also means accepting that normal life is not the golden fantasy that was dreamt of; rather, it is fraught with loss and disappointment and pain. Letting go of the fantasy can be incredibly hard.

Daniela: You say that traumatised patients are phobic of change and that this needs to be addressed. Why is change so charged?

Ellert: Although it is natural to resist change, most people can overcome their fears. For dissociated patients the onset of traumatisation was often associated with change, so change is linked to pain and is vehemently avoided. But avoiding change results in a restricted life, and helping patients to overcome their phobia of change is crucial.

Daniela: You describe how patients need to learn to deal with ambivalence – what do you mean?

Ellert: When somebody suffers from dissociation of the personality, different basic motivations and implied actions are held by different parts, so although there will be clashes between parts, within each part there is no ambivalence. With fusion, a person feels internal conflicts for the first time. Karl used to go to work as an ANP. In that state he had no distractions – neither tiredness nor hunger interfered with work because his ANP was cut-off from his body. That made him very successful. After fusion personal and physical needs entered his consciousness and Karl was terrified he would lose his edge. It took time for him to accept his fear and to learn to balance his conflicting needs.

Daniela: How far can healing go? Can somebody who has suffered from a dissociative identity disorder achieve a 'normal' and integrated personality?

Ellert: Yes, mental health is within reach of some patients, although it may take years of therapy. Others with dissociative identity disorder cannot get there. However, nearly every patient can establish a healthier ANP who will support the EPs and treat them with compassion.

Mind you, once traumatised, the world is always different. Danger becomes more real and more possible. Survivors are quicker to turn to their defences and have them shape their view of reality, sometimes inappropriately.

Daniela: You say that dissociation can occur at the level of families and societies. Can you conclude by talking about this?

Ellert: If a father abuses his child and the mother cannot deal with it, she will turn a blind eye, becoming the equivalent of an ANP. There are echoes of this in the way that society responds to trauma. Chronic child abuse and neglect results in attachment disorders as well as a propensity to long-term psychiatric problems, social dysfunction, sexual dysfunction, poor self-esteem, increased risk of violence and crime, lowered academic and occupational achievement, substance abuse, teenage pregnancy, self-harming and physical illnesses. The financial cost of childhood trauma is equivalent to that of HIV and cancer combined. Yet in the USA only one dollar is spent on the prevention of child abuse and neglect for every 100 dollars spent on cancer and HIV. I believe that is because we live in a predominantly 'apparently normal society' which is phobic of its traumatising strands.

Similarly, I would argue that those who suggest that dissociative identity disorders are created by therapists manipulating fantasy-prone individuals are in keeping with a society that is built in the image of an ANP, especially now we have got scientific data showing that patients diagnosed with dissociative disorders are not especially fantasy-prone, but that they do have very different psycho-physiological and neurobiological reaction patterns.

In short, I would argue that our ANP-like society wants to push childhood trauma, and its effect, under the carpet. It is profoundly damaging for all involved. However, recently there has been growing acceptance of the terrible consequences of chronic childhood abuse, maltreatment and neglect. We are on our way.

6   On the same wave-length

How our emotional brain is shaped by human relationships

Allan N. Schore and Daniela F. Sieff

Summary

Our earliest attachment relationships have long-lasting effects on the structure our emotional brain, our relationships with ourselves and others and our psychological well-being.

Good-enough early nurturing fosters the neural networks (located in the right hemisphere of the brain) which enable us to regulate our emotions healthily. We grow up trusting our emotions, be they painful of joyful, and capable of responding to our social world appropriately. As a result, we develop an embodied, deeply rooted and implicit sense of inner security.

In contrast, poor early environments compromise the development of the right hemisphere, leaving us struggling to respond to our social world appropriately and unable to regulate our emotions healthily. Unregulated emotions overload the system, and because we cannot tolerate being emotionally overloaded for long periods of time, we unconsciously learn to dissociate from our emotions and to prevent them from reaching awareness. If we turn to dissociation on a regular basis, dissociative neural pathways become engrained in our developing brains to create emotional instability, a nebulous sense of disconnection and an implicitly embodied feeling of fundamental insecurity. At this point, dissociation, which began as a defence, has become embedded in the structure of our developing personality and part of our character.

Repair is not achieved by making the unconscious conscious: rather it depends on restructuring the emotional brain itself through building new neural networks. Achieving this requires relationally based, emotionally focused psychotherapy with an empathic therapist who is an active participant in the process. Healing occurs primarily through the non-verbal, right brain, implicit connection between a therapist and patient.

Daniela Sieff: You emphasise the importance of feeling emotionally secure – why?

Allan Schore: Societies spend a huge amount on defence and on medical research in the hope that we will feel secure in our daily lives, but a feeling of security is a psychological state. All too often our emotional wounds, and the subsequent defences that we developed, prevent us from feeling secure. An internal sense of safety cannot be imposed upon a passive individual. To feel secure we need to know, at both a bodily and a psychological level, that we have the internal resources to cope with the stressors that accompany human existence. To that end, my work has focused on three questions:

- How do some children develop emotional security?
- What prevents other children from developing emotional security, and what are the consequences of that?
- What is required of therapy if it is to help those who failed to develop emotional security as children, develop it later in life?

I do not just look at these questions psychologically. A fundamental principle of my work is that no theory of emotional development can be restricted to only a description of psychological processes; it must also be consonant with what we now know about the biological structure of the brain. Moreover, by integrating what we know about the brain into our understanding, we gain hugely important insights into the dynamics of emotional trauma and what therapists need to do to work with it.

Daniela: Can you expand on what we need to be able to do if we are to feel emotionally secure?

Allan: We need to trust that we can appraise what is happening in our social environment and that we can respond adaptively. Emotions are the medium through which information about interpersonal relationships is transmitted, received and appraised. At the crudest level, feeling good tells us we are in a propitious situation; feeling bad warns us of possible trouble and prepares us to deal with it. But human relationships are complex and layered, so we need to develop several bodily based skills if our appraisals of our social world are to be valid:

- *We need to become sensitive to subtly differentiated emotions.* When we are born our emotions are relatively crude – we are happy or we are upset. As we develop, our emotions become increasingly differentiated, shaded and refined, yet also integrated. We learn to create blends of different emotions simultaneously. Things are no longer wholly good, or wholly bad. We can feel anger and compassion with somebody simultaneously. This greater differentiation of our emotional repertoire enables us to respond to interpersonal situations more appropriately.
- *We need to learn to tolerate intense emotions.* We each have what can be envisioned as a window of tolerance with regards to each of our emotions.

Within this window we can respond healthily to what we are feeling; beyond it we lose that ability. We begin life with a very small window of tolerance for intense emotions, but during healthy development the window expands and we become increasingly tolerant of intense positive and negative emotions.

- *We need to acquire the ability to differentiate what is happening outside us from what is happening inside.* As children we cannot do this, but we need to learn what is mine, and what is coming from another person.

Collecting and appraising relational information happens unconsciously. When we implicitly know that we can tolerate intense emotions, accurately perceive what is happening in the external and internal world and respond in a nuanced and appropriate way, we feel fundamentally safe. But when we are cut-off from some of our emotions, when we cannot tolerate intense emotions, or when past events colour current emotional responses, then our unconscious appraisals will be distorted and our ability to respond adaptively compromised.

Daniela: What shapes the unconscious processing and regulation of emotion?

Allan: We do not come into the world with these unconscious processes in place; rather they develop through attuned and nurturing early relationships. Our emotions, which include both the subjective experience of our feelings and what is happening in our body, are initially regulated by our caregivers.[1] If our caregivers do a reasonable job, then as our brain develops, we internalise that experience and begin to do it for ourselves. Moreover, upon finding ourselves distressed, we can either turn to somebody else to help us recover, or we can rely on ourselves, depending on the particulars of the situation.

In contrast, if our earliest years are emotionally impoverished, then our emotional development is compromised and we are left at the mercy of a simplified, unadaptive, rigid and restricted set of emotional responses. We may over-react to stress and our response may endure long after the danger has passed. Or we may struggle to regulate any of the intense emotions, including shame, rage, disgust, panic, terror, hopelessness, despair, excitement and elation. Moreover, a lack of early nurturing means we do not trust others enough to turn to them for help in achieving that regulation. Then our only option may be to dissociate from those emotions or to use drugs or to self-harm in an attempt to regulate them. When we intuitively sense that we cannot regulate our emotions healthily, a feeling of emotional security is beyond our reach.

Daniela: What features of the brain are most relevant to understanding emotional regulation?

---

1 Editorial note: We have used 'caregiver' and 'mother' interchangeably, because for the majority of infants, the primary caregiver is the mother.

Allan: It is crucial that we understand the differences between the right hemisphere of the brain and the left. There has been a paradigm shift – instead of thinking of right and left halves of one brain, we now understand that we effectively have two brains, each of which processes information in different ways, and each of which matures in a different rhythm.

Broadly speaking, the left brain is the thinking brain. It is highly verbal and analytical. It operates a conscious emotional regulation system that can modulate low to medium arousal. It is the domain of cognitive strategies. It processes highly verbal emotions such as guilt and worrisome anxiety. It constructs linear explanations. It provides us with a close-up and narrow view of details. The left brain does not begin its first period of concentrated development and growth until the second year of life, and so it plays little part in the early relationships which shape our capacity to regulate our emotions and to feel emotionally secure.

In contrast the right hemisphere is the emotional brain. It processes all of our intense emotions, regardless of whether they are negative such as rage, fear, terror, disgust, shame, hopeless despair, or positive, such as excitement, happiness and joy. When our level of emotional arousal becomes intense the left hemisphere goes off-line and the right hemisphere dominates. Our window of tolerance for intense emotions depends on the functioning of the right brain.

Our right brain enables us to read the subjective states of others through its appraisal of subtle facial (visual and auditory) expressions and other forms of non-verbal communication. The right brain makes these appraisals so quickly that our body and mental state is altered before we become conscious of what we are feeling.

Because of its ability to read the subjective states of others, the right brain is the seat of emotional empathy – it depends on us feeling what another person is feeling in an embodied way. In contrast, the left brain is the seat of cognitive empathy – it depends on us working out what the other is feeling in a less embodied and colder way.

The autonomic nervous system is the part of the nervous system that functions largely below the level of consciousness to control visceral functions such as heart rate, respiratory rate, digestion, pupil dilation, etc. It has two branches: the sympathetic branch which mediates energised arousal and approach, and the parasympathetic branch which mediates withdrawal, rest, relaxation and repair. The right brain mediates the balance between these two branches of the autonomic nervous system, and through that determines the somatic aspects of emotion as well as the subjective ones.

Connections between the right brain and the hormonal system are another channel through which the somatic aspects of emotion are mediated.

The right brain mediates our emotional and bodily-based response to danger, environmental challenges, pain and stress. It mediates fight, flight and freeze through its connections with the autonomic nervous system and hormonal system. Emotionality is the right brain's 'red phone', compelling the mind to handle urgent matters without delay.

The right brain has some limited capacity for language. Highly emotive words such as swear words or our own names are processed by the right brain, as are metaphors.

The right brain is more holistic than the left, holding many different possibilities simultaneously. It captures the gist of the situation and the big picture. Dreams, music, poetry, art, metaphor and other creative processes originate in the right brain. Importantly, and with direct relevance to psychotherapy, the right brain specialises in processing new information.

The first critical period of development for the right brain begins during the third trimester of pregnancy and this growth spurt continues into the second year of life. It is primarily the right brain which is shaped by our early relational environment and which is crucial to the development of emotional security.

Daniela: Can you talk about the trajectory of early right brain development, in terms of the development of emotional regulation?

Allan: Brains are modular; different areas specialise in different functions, but not all areas are operative at birth. With the emotional brain (also known as the limbic brain) there are three key 'regulatory hubs': (1) the right amygdala, (2) the right anterior cingulate (also known as medial frontal cortex), and (3) the right orbital prefrontal (shortened to orbitofrontal) cortex. These regions come on-line sequentially.

The amygdala begins a critical period of growth during the last trimester of pregnancy, so it is essentially functional at birth. The right amygdala is the brain's alarm centre, mediating the fight and flight responses. It is also the first port of call for processing both the non-verbal facial expressions of others, and our own internal bodily states. The amygdala is relatively primitive; information from the external environment is imprinted with a positive or negative charge depending on whether the situation is deemed to be nurturing or threatening. This occurs very rapidly and below the level of consciousness. The resulting actions appear as autonomic, innate reflexes. Such speedy responses are crucial for survival, but they are crude, which is why infants tend to swing back-and-forth between positive and negative emotional states.

Around two months after birth the right anterior cingulate begins to come on-line. It allows for more complex processing of social-emotional information than the amygdala. It is responsible for developing attachment behaviour.

Starting from about ten months after birth, the highest level of the emotional brain, the right orbitofrontal cortex, becomes active. It continues developing for the next 20 years and remains exceptionally plastic throughout our entire lifespan. The right orbitofrontal cortex gives rise to conscious emotions and is capable of much finer-grained (albeit slower) information processing than the earlier developing parts of the emotional brain. It is also the area of the brain that enables us to maintain a sense of continuity and to create an integrated and stable sense of who we are, which in turn forms the platform for self-reflection.

It is not until the second year of life that the right orbitofrontal cortex establishes strong, bidirectional connections with the rest of the limbic system. Once these connections are established it then monitors, refines and regulates amygdala-driven responses. We can begin to correct over- or under-reactions, allowing our emotional responses to be more appropriate to the circumstances. It is the healthy development of the right orbitofrontal cortex and its links to the amygdala that enables us to have a wide window of tolerance for intense emotions, and to respond flexibly and adaptively to our interpersonal world.

Daniela: How does the relationship between an infant and its caregiver shape the development of the emotional right brain?

Allan: Genes code for when the various components of the emotional brain come on-line, but how each area develops depends on the infant's epigenetically shaped emotional experiences with his primary caregiver. Those experiences, as John Bowlby first described, are circumscribed by the infant's innate drive to become attached (emotionally bonded) to his or her primary caregiver.

The attachment drive evolved partly because infants needed to remain close to their mothers for protection from predators and partly because infants cannot regulate either their bodily functions or their emotional states and need a caregiver to do this for them. The role of regulation is so important that I now see attachment theory primarily as a theory of emotional and bodily regulation. Typically an attuned caregiver will minimise her infant's discomfort, fear and pain, and, as importantly, create opportunities for the child to feel joy and excitement. She will also mediate the transitions between these emotional states.

The infant's experiences with his[2] caregiver are then internalised through changes in the brain. Experience activates specific neural circuits and the more frequently a circuit fires, the more established it becomes, whereupon it is more easily activated in the future. Over time, the infant's emotional core becomes biased towards certain emotional responses, thus creating a particular type of personality organisation. In short, brains develop as self-organising systems, but their self-organisation occurs not in isolation, but in the context of another self, another brain.

Daniela: Can you give us a feel for the types of interactions that typically occur between an attuned mother and her infant?

Allan: An infant who is between three and six months old mainly uses sight to gauge his mother's emotional responses. He will track his mother's face and if she is attuned enough to meet his emotional state with an appropriate response, then when eye contact is established both mother and infant implicitly know that the feedback loop between them is closed. The mother's face reflects her infant's reality and aliveness back to him and he learns to be with whatever it is that he is feeling.

Sometimes mirroring by an attuned mother amplifies her infant's emotional state. In physics when two systems match it creates what is called 'resonance', whereby the amplitude of each system is increased. Face-to-face play between an infant and an attuned mother creates emotional resonance and amplifies joy.

---

2 Editorial note: throughout this interview we have used the masculine pronoun to describe the infant, the feminine pronoun to describe the caregiver, because the primary caregiver is typically the mother and it was stylistically clearer if the infant is of a different sex. We have kept this convention when later talking about therapist and client – assuming the therapist is female and the client male, in order to be consistent and in an attempt to foster clarity.

Together infant and mother move from low arousal to high positive arousal, which helps the infant to expand his window of tolerance for intense positive emotions, a key developmental task.

Other times, the emotional intensity becomes more than the infant can tolerate, then he will avert his gaze. When this happens an attuned mother backs-off and reduces her stimulation. She then waits for her baby to signal his readiness to re-engage. The more the mother tunes her activity level to the infant during periods of engagement, the more she allows him to recover quietly in periods of disengagement, and the more she responds to his signals for re-engagement, the more synchronised their interactions. At times emotional mirroring between mother and infant can be synchronised within milliseconds. '*On the same wave-length*' becomes more than a metaphor, as the subjective internal state of both mother and infant converge, and his emotional reality is both validated and held safely through his mother's ability to be with his feelings.

During this process a mother inevitably makes mistakes, then the interaction becomes asynchronous. However, when asynchrony arises, a good-enough mother is quick to shift her state so that she can then help to re-regulate her infant, who is likely to be stressed and upset by their mis-match. Rupture and repair allows the child to tolerate negative affect.

Eventually, the face of an attuned mother will be written into her infant's right orbitofrontal cortex. This then acts as an emotionally containing and comforting neurobiological guidance system when she is not physically present.

Daniela: Could you talk about the internal models that are created as a result of interactions between a mother and her infant?

Allan: In response to their caregivers, infants create unconscious working models of what to expect, and these models are then generalised and applied not only to 'mother' but also to other people. For example, if the caregiver is mostly attuned, then the infant creates an expectation of being matched by, and being able to match, another human. The child is likely to develop what is known as 'secure attachment'.

Similarly, moments of misattunement, if repaired in a sensitive and timely manner, lead to the infant believing that others will help calm him when he is upset. Additionally, experiencing his mother's nurturing response to his distress the infant begins to develop a sense that others will attend to him and that his own activity can influence the effect that his environment has on him. This is the first step towards developing a sense of agency. The timely repair of misattunement also teaches an infant that instances of discord and negative emotions are tolerable. From such learning an infant develops emotional resilience, defined as the capacity to transition from positive emotions to negative emotions and back to positive emotions. Emotional resilience is key to creating an inner feeling of security and trust.

However, if caregivers are not attuned an infant will create an internal model that says that other people are not trustworthy, that he cannot really connect to them, and that he is unworthy of being loved. This way of seeing the world is typical of 'insecure attachment' and these unconscious emotional biases will guide life-long behaviour, especially when under relational stress.

What is more, the infant of a misattuned mother will frequently be presented with an aggressive expression on his mother's face, implying he is a threat, or with an expression of fear-terror, implying that he is a source of alarm. Images of his mother's aggressive and/or fearful face, and the resultant chaotic alterations in his bodily state, are internalised. They are imprinted on his developing right brain (emotional brain) as an implicit memory, and although they lie below consciousness, they will haunt him for his entire life unless he finds a way to work with them.

Early interactions also create the internal models which affect how the developing infant (and later the adult) approaches novelty. Between ten and twelve months infants start to walk. The toddler can now separate from his caregiver, begin to explore his physical environment, and learn new things. This ability is fundamental to development, but it can be dangerous so an exploring toddler needs direction and support from his caregiver. He gets that from referring to his mother's facial expressions, which either encourage or discourage his exploration. However, the infant does not only learn how he should feel about the specific objects in his social and physical environment that he is encountering through his mother's reactions, he also learns how to feel about novelty per se. The internal working models formed as a result of this learning will shape the way that he approaches the world for the duration of his life, either facilitating a capacity to grow from new social-emotional experiences, or inhibiting it.

Daniela: What is happening neurobiologically during attuned early mother–infant interactions?

Allan: The caregiver's more mature nervous system is regulating the infant's neurochemistry. This, in turn, has a profound influence on the structural organisation of the developing brain. For example, the hormone oxytocin is an antidote to stress and promotes bonding and trust. Its release is triggered by sensory stimuli such as a warm tone of voice and friendly facial expressions. If this system is primed by early attachment experiences, the infant grows into a person capable of trust and of establishing social bonds. Similarly, the face of an attuned mother triggers the production endorphins in the infant's growing brain, whereupon the infant's developing neural system learns to associate social interactions with feeling good. Additionally, in the presence of an attuned caregiver, an infant's brain experiences relatively high levels of dopamine, serotonin and noradrenalin. When levels of these molecules are sufficient, an infant's growing brain builds more receptors for them, whereas when levels are very low, fewer receptors are created. This difference in the number of receptors is retained in adulthood, and a deficit can increase the risk of psychiatric disorders, such as depression or PTSD.

Critical to postnatal brain development is the formation of connections between nerve cells. A single neuron will have between 10,000 and 100,000 branches, each of which connects to another neuron through a structure called a synapse. In the first year of life it is estimated that 40,000 new synapses are created every second. This takes an enormous amount of energy. The brain accounts for only 2 per cent of our body mass but it uses 20 per cent of the calories that an adult consumes, and 50 per cent of the calories consumed by a young child. However, a brain does not only need calories to build synapses; it also needs to be in an excited and activated state. Think of a car – it is not enough that there is fuel in the tank, the engine needs to be fired-up and running before it will move. It is the positive arousal created by the resonant interactions between an attuned mother and an infant that fires-up the infant's brain and which creates the conditions necessary for building neural connections.

At the same time the mother–infant relationship is responsible for the selective death of neurons and for pruning synaptic connections. This is a natural part of development: there is a genetically programmed over-production of neurons and synapses early in development, and those that are activated by the environment become established, whereas those that are not used atrophy and die. Maternal behaviour is the environment in which some neurons and synapses are selected as relevant to the infant's life, whereas others are discarded as surplus to needs. This shapes the trajectory of the infant's emerging self. For example, if a mother does not mirror her infant in a way to generate positive arousal, the positive arousal circuits are at risk of atrophying, making it harder in later life for that person to feel joy and excitement. On the other hand, if a mother is attuned and does create positive arousal in her infant, the neurons that are pre-programmed to respond to positive arousal will be fortified.

Daniela: How robust is the developmental process that leads to a healthy self-regulating emotional system?

Allan: The development of a healthy emotional system depends on growing up in a 'good-enough' emotional environment. Once the critical growth period for a particular brain area has passed, the structure of that area is more-or-less set and subsequent development is built on top of that platform. Thus early adverse environmental factors such as nutritional deficits, or dysregulating attachment relationships, can have a profound growth-inhibiting effect upon the right brain, and prohibit the development of a healthy self-regulating emotional system. The effects can last a lifetime.

Daniela: What happens to the developing brain in an adverse environment?

Allan: There are two ways that the developing brain can be compromised by an inadequate early environment.

1   Unused brain cells die naturally during the process of development, but early trauma can lead to excessive cell death.
2   The building of new synapses is reduced, and existing synapses that could be useful are destroyed. The ability to create functional and integrated brain circuits is compromised.

Daniela: Does the timing of relational trauma affect what impact it has?

Allan: Yes! Emotional trauma will negatively impact the parts of the brain which are developing at the time of the trauma. For example, if high levels of stress hormones are circulating in a pregnant mother, it upregulates the foetus' developing stress response – the hypothalmic-pituitary-adrenalin (HPA) system – making the child, and then the adult, hyper-sensitive to stress. In contrast, relational trauma that occurs around the time of birth has a negative impact on both the developing micro-architecture of the amygdala itself, and on how the amygdala connects to the HPA system and other parts of the limbic system. Such damage has a profoundly harmful effect on the ability to form social bonds, and on temperament. Suffering unrepaired and frequent emotional stress after about ten months interferes with experience-dependent maturation of the highest-level regulatory systems in the right orbitofrontal cortex. This opens the door to an impaired emotional regulation system, a limited facility for empathy, and problems in distinguish present reality from irrelevant memories. In the long term there is an increased risk of developing psychopathologies.

Cell death and over-pruning is equally damaging when it interferes with the connectivity between different brain regions. Relational trauma that occurs in the second year is likely to jeopardise not only the development of the right orbitofrontal cortex itself, but also its connection to the right amygdala, whereupon it becomes much harder to modify the amygdala's crude responses in accordance with reality. Over-reaction becomes the norm, leading to severe problems with intimacy and affection, as well as problems with the control of fear and aggression. Borderline personality disorder is one of the psychopathologies that can arise from this.

Daniela: What kind of parenting causes damage?

Allan: There are obvious forms of abuse such as physical and sexual abuse, but emotional abuse can be equally damaging. Emotional abuse can result from inconsistent, erratic and contradictory interactions, from over-powering and over-arousing interactions, or from neglect. In any of these circumstances the infant will suffer long bouts of unregulated stressful negative affects, and, too frequently, no interactive repair.

Neglect, which is proving to be the most severe threat to the development of the emotional brain, generally leads to what is called 'avoidant attachment'. The mother may be averse to physical contact and block her child's attempts to get close to her. She may be ambivalent about being a mother. She may be depressed. The neglect need not be overt – profound psychological harm can occur with a mother who is emotionally unavailable when her infant is distressed, even if she remains in physical contact with her child. Such an infant will learn to recoil from contact in an attempt to avoid the painful emotions roused in him by his rejecting mother. Over time withdrawal becomes entrenched. For the rest of his life he will tend to convey an unconscious, non-verbal message that says, *'Stay away ... I don't need you ... don't connect.'*

Neurobiologically, the lack of positive mirroring that characterises neglect means that not enough energy is generated for an infant's brain to grow all its interconnections. Moreover, because there is limited positive arousal, the growth of these brain areas is especially compromised. Such infants develop a bias towards a withdrawn state mediated by the parasympathetic branch of the autonomic nervous system. This is physiologically characterised by a low heart rate and low heart-rate variability.[3] Temperamentally, these infants tend to grow up feeling helpless and they have an increased risk of suffering from depression. They often have minimal emotional expression and a limited capacity to experience and to regulate intense emotional states, be they positive or negative. They are susceptible to over-controlled, over-regulated internalising pathologies.

Not only is a neglected child denied the interpersonal matrix upon which brain development depends, but without access to interactive repair, intense affect dysregulation endures as long-lasting stress states. These are psychobiologically toxic. Early maternal neglect significantly increases the process of programmed cell death in the cortex compared to healthy development.

Unpredictable and intrusive mothering often leads to what is called ambivalent-anxious attachment. Infants can only cope with a certain intensity of emotional arousal before they move beyond their window of tolerance into a state of stressful emotional dysregulation. To avoid this, an infant will signal his need to temporarily disengage by looking away. However, if the caregiver suffered early relational trauma herself, she may feel abandoned by her infant's move to disengage, and in order to annul her own anxiety she may redouble her efforts to get her infant to re-engage with her. This exacerbates the infant's hyperarousal; excitatory neurotransmitters and stress hormones flood the brain, causing profound damage, including neuronal death and the destruction of synapses. Such children appear to have a difficult temperament. Their autonomic nervous system tends to be biased towards the sympathetic nervous system. They express emotions in an excessive way and suffer intense negative moods. They are overly dependent on their attachment figure (presumably to make her feel more secure), but also angry with her and rejecting of her.

The most severe forms of both abuse and neglect create what is called 'disorganised attachment'. It occurs when an infant has no strategy that will help him to cope with his caregiver and so he ends up profoundly confused. An infant typically seeks his parents when alarmed, so when a parent actually causes alarm the infant is in an impossible situation. There is simultaneous and uncoupled hyper-activation of the sympathetic and the parasympathetic circuit. This is subjectively experienced as a sudden transition into emotional chaos. It represents a highly neurotoxic state that leads to death of neurons and the destruction of synaptic connections within both circuits.

Daniela: What might cause a mother to behave in such a harmful way?

Allan: Typically, women who cannot mother their children in an attuned way are suffering from the consequences of unresolved early emotional trauma themselves.

---

3 When our nervous system has developed in a healthy way, our heart rate varies on a moment-by-moment basis. In contrast, if the development of our nervous system has been compromised then heart variability is low, and low variability is a marker of high risk to both cancer and cardiac disease later in life.

The experience of a female infant with her mother influences how she will mother her own infants. Thus if early childhood trauma remains unconscious and unresolved it will inevitably be passed down the generations. To put it bluntly, a mother's untreated early relational trauma is burnt into the developing right brain of her infant's brain, leaving behind neurological scars.

Daniela: What role does the father play in a child's emotional development?

Allan: Subsequent to a child's relationship to the mother during his first year, the child forms a second attachment relationship to his father in the second year. The quality of a toddler's attachment to his father is independent to that of his mother. At 18 months there are two separate attachment dynamics in operation. Those who experience being protected, cared for and loved by their father will internalise that relationship as a lifelong sense of safety. It also seems that the father is critically involved in the development of a toddler's regulation of aggression. This is true of both sexes, but particularly of boys who are born with a greater aggressive endowment than girls.

Daniela: You highlight the damaging effects of long bouts of unregulated shame – what is shame and why is it so damaging?

Allan: Shame is the emotion elicited during a rapid transition from an excited positive state to a deflated negative one, typically when an interpersonal bond is broken through misattunement. When shame hits, usually unexpectedly, we feel that a spot-light is focused on us, revealing all that is wrong with who we are. We want to bury our head and disappear from view. We feel as if we could die. Shame is always associated with the subjective experience of inner collapse.

Shame becomes part of the emotional palette around the end of the first year. When an infant is ten months old, 90 per cent of maternal behaviour consists of affection, play and caregiving, but between the ages of 13 and 17 months this changes – a mother will express a prohibition once every nine minutes! That is because she needs to let her toddler know when his exploration is unsafe. Also, around this time a mother starts to become an agent of socialisation and must persuade the toddler to inhibit socially unacceptable behaviours. Shame, which has been described as the primary social emotion, is the means through which this is achieved.

Shame is not caused by the child's movement away from the mother, or even by the mother's movement away from the child, but by the active blockage of the child's return to, and emotional reconnection with, the mother. By this age, the securely attached toddler of an attuned mother will have an internalised expectation of being matched by her, so when he returns to his mother full of joy and she fails to match his emotional state, he will experience shock-induced deflation. In such a moment it is as though his mother becomes a stranger. The toddler's emotionally fragile, nascent self rapidly implodes and collapses. Shame is experienced as spiralling downward – a leakage in the middle of one's being.

Shame induces an intense emotional state which lies beyond the infant's window of tolerance, so the mother needs to instigate interactive repair. How speedily she does this is crucially important. A brief descent into shame is a necessary part of development, teaching the infant to avoid what is socially unacceptable or physically dangerous. However, long periods of unrepaired shame are physiologically toxic to the developing brain. They also have negative long-term consequences for the personality, resulting in chronic difficulties with self-esteem.

Daniela: What is the difference between shame and guilt?

Allan: The two emotions, through often confused, are separate and have distinct neurobiological pathways. Shame appears between the ages of 12 and 18 months. At 12 months the average toddler has three words and at 18 months about 20 words. Shame is therefore intrinsically non-verbal and a product of the early developing right brain. It is experienced implicitly as what Kaufman[4] described as *'a total experience that forbids communication with words'*. In contrast, guilt develops between three and six years – a three-year-old child has an average vocabulary of 900 words, and uses three- to five-word sentences. Guilt is a product of the later developing verbal, left brain.

The verbal nature of guilt makes it easier to recognise and articulate than pre-verbal shame, so psychotherapy tends to focus on guilt rather than shame. However, excessive unregulated shame creates far greater emotional damage than guilt does, and we do need to learn to recognise it, bring it to consciousness, regulate it and heal it.

Daniela: How do infants respond to being left with dysregulated emotions?

Allan: Infants respond through two separate and sequential processes: (1) hyperarousal and (2) hypoarousal.

Hyperarousal occurs when a perceived threat – either imagined or real – is detected by the amygdala, which then activates both the HPA system and the sympathetic branch of the autonomic nervous system. The activation of the HPA system culminates in the release of cortisol. The activation of the sympathetic nervous system releases adrenalin. Both cortisol and adrenalin play key roles in mobilising our bodily resources into the service of immediate survival by preparing us for fight or flight. Energy that was being used for non-emergency processes such as digestion or fighting disease is redirected towards survival. The level of glucose in our blood is raised to increase fuel availability. Oxygen intake is increased as the surface of our lungs expands and our breathing quickens. Our heart beats faster and more powerfully in order to speed up the circulation of blood which is carrying oxygen and glucose to our muscles. Pupils dilate, sweating increases, mental activity speeds up. In children, hyperarousal is accompanied by crying and then screaming – calls for help.

---

4 Kaufman, G. (1974) 'The Meaning of Shame: Toward a Self-affirming Identity'. *Journal of Counseling Psychology,* 21, 568–574.

Hyperarousal can save our lives, but it is a toxic state, so when a caregiver cannot help the infant return to a calmer state, or – worse – when the caregiver escalates the infant's distress, the infant has no choice but to get away from this state of hyperarousal by the only means possible – that is inwards, through collapse, hypoarousal. Energy leaves the system and the individual shuts-off input from the external world and from his own dysregulated and hyperaroused emotions. This is dissociation. In a connected emotional system, messages about the body's state move up from the body, through the lower levels of the limbic brain and into the right orbitofrontal cortex, where they are experienced as a conscious emotion. With dissociation this chain is broken. In a state of hypoaroused dissociation all pain is stilled; a soothing (but deadening) numbness ensues. The numbness is due to the massive elevation of endogenous opioids which instantly trigger pain-reducing analgesia and immobility, and which inhibit cries for help.

Dissociation, which appears in the first two months of life, is a last-resort survival strategy. It represents detachment from an unbearable situation. It is the escape when there is no escape. The infant withdraws into an inner world, avoids eye contact and stares into space. Dissociation caused by a hypoaroused state brings a constricted state of consciousness, a void of subjectivity.

This state of passive rather than active withdrawal is rooted in our animal heritage. Predators are attracted by movement, so if the potential prey cannot outrun the predator, it tries to reduce its chance of being detected by lying absolutely still. Additionally, predators do not like eating animals that they have not killed themselves, because the animal could have been dead for some time and its rotting flesh may be carrying disease. The immobility of dissociation mimics death.

Daniela: The Jungian analyst Marion Woodman described the collapsed state of dissociation as 'possum psychology';[5] what is happening neurobiologically?

Allan: Dissociation is achieved when the parasympathetic branch of the autonomic nervous system comes in over the top of the sympathetic system. This is akin to driving a car with one foot flat on the gas (sympathetic), and the other flat on the breaks (parasympathetic). The simultaneous yet uncoupled activation of the sympathetic and parasympathetic nervous system is highly toxic and exaggerates the normal processes of cell death and synaptic pruning. That, in turn, means that the capacity for healthy emotional regulation recedes ever-further into the distance.

Within the parasympathetic nervous system, dissociation is mediated by the dorsal, or reptilian, branch of the vagus nerve. The work of Stephen Porges tells us that the vagus nerve has two branches, each originating in a different area of the brainstem. The branch that originates in the dorsal part of the brainstem evolved with the reptiles, and in humans it comes on-line early during development, even prenatally. In contrast, the branch that originates in the ventral brain stem evolved

---

5 Sieff: see Marion Woodman (Chapter 4) in this volume.

with mammals, and comes on-line later during postnatal development. Activation of the ventral, or 'mammalian' vagus, facilitates communication via facial expressions, vocalisations and gestures. It alters heart rate in a finely tuned, flexible, beat-by-beat manner and allows for the subtle shifts of engagement and disengagement required by social relationships. In contrast, when the 'reptilian' vagus is activated, dissociation follows. The metabolism is speedily shut down, the heart rate drops rapidly, hiding behaviour and passive withdrawal are initiated and a hypoaroused physical collapse may be triggered.

Daniela: Once an infant starts to turn to dissociation as a defence, how does the dynamic develop?

Allan: As the child learns that his caregiver is unable to help him to regulate either a specific emotion, or intense emotions in general, or – worse – that she exacerbates the dysregulation, he will start to go into a state of hypoaroused dissociation as soon as the threat of dysregulation arises. Neurons that fire together wire together, so each time an infant has to revert to dissociation, the right-brain circuitry that instigates dissociation is strengthened, meaning that next time it is triggered even more easily. This is useful for a child, who is living with chronic trauma, but those who initially use dissociation to cope with highly traumatic events subsequently dissociate to defend against both daily stressors and the stress caused when implicitly held memories of trauma are triggered.

In the developing brain, repeated neurological states become traits, so dissociative defences are embedded into the core structure of the evolving personality, and become a part of who a person is, rather than what a person does.

Daniela: How does dissociation impact on our relationship with our emotions and with ourselves?

Allan: Emotions are processed hierarchically in the right brain; first reaching the subcortical amygdala and cingulate, and then the orbitofrontal cortex. It is the orbitofrontal cortex that enables us to become conscious of what we are feeling and to modify the responses of the amygdala. Pathological dissociation severs the connections between the right orbitofrontal cortex and the subcortical limbic brain. We are left at the mercy of the amygdala's crude, rigid, survival-oriented, black-and-white, emotional repertory. The finesse and flexibility required to respond to novel socioemotional experiences is missing. As a consequence, we avoid anything new, especially in intimate contexts that may release attachment needs. Emotional learning stagnates and the ongoing experience-dependent growth of the right brain is truncated.

At the same time, because the right orbitofrontal cortex is responsible for bringing our emotions into consciousness, we never really know what we are feeling. Then we lose the capacity for genuine self-reflection because although our left brain will be telling us what we think, knowing what we think is not enough if we are to engage in meaningful self-reflection. What is more, being cut-off from our emotions, we have dead spots in our consciousness so our experience of ourselves becomes riddled with discontinuities. We feel fragmented.

Being cut off from our emotions impacts on our sense of who we are more generally; our subjective sense of self derives from our unconscious experiences of bodily based emotions and is constructed in the right brain. If we cannot connect to our bodily emotions then our sense of self is built on fragile foundations. At times we may even lose our sense of physical presence. Many who suffered early relational trauma have a distorted sense of their bodies and of what is happening within them.

Daniela: How does the reliance on dissociative defences affect our relationships with others?

Allan: Throughout our evolutionary history the ability to maintain personally meaningful bonds has been vital for our survival, so when danger, rather than safety, emanates from the early attachment relationship, there are significant consequences for the relational unconscious. For example, we learn to isolate the deeper parts of ourselves in order to protect them from others who are seen primarily as sources of pain rather than comfort. Similarly, having developed a working model of dysregulated-self-in-interaction-with-a-misattuned-other, when we are in trouble, we turn away from others, instead of approaching them for help.

Another right brain function, affective empathy, our ability to feel what another person is feeling, depends on us connecting to our body's response to that other person. This is compromised when dissociation becomes characterological. Individuals with early relational trauma struggle to feel the empathy which is so vital in meaningful human relationships.

Daniela: What are the implications of characterological dissociation for the way that we interact with our environment and our ability to feel emotionally secure?

Allan: Feeling secure depends on the implicit knowledge that our emotional responses to our social and physical environment are appropriate. While dissociated, we are cut-off from at least some aspects of our environment so we are unable to respond appropriately.

Daniela: What does hypoaroused dissociation do to our experience of pain?

Allan: Dissociation, the escape when there is no escape, is a response to overwhelming stress and intolerable pain, and it triggers the release of massive amounts of endogenous opiates – our natural painkillers. But chronically high levels of opiates during the neonatal period influence the wiring of the pain circuits and the infant grows into an individual who appears not to experience pain as acutely as others. However, this higher pain threshold does not derive from a capacity to tolerate pain – quite the reverse – it derives from the fact that as soon as emotional pain is experienced, dissociation blocks awareness of it. Thus the pain which is still lived by the body and limbic system does not come to consciousness, it is never truly experienced and its messages go unheeded.

In time, such methods of pain relief may come to be experienced as an inability to feel anything – a loss of aliveness. Then we look for ways to escape this deadness. For example, self-cutting, which is associated with early relational trauma, may represent an attempt to get out of the numbed and lifeless state associated with a chronic elevation of endogenous opioids.

Daniela: You argue that the early development of dissociative defences may increase the risk of aggression, rage and violence.

Allan: Violence is aggression that has extreme harm as its goal, and when somebody commits a violent act it means that his or her developmental trajectory has gone astray. Despite overall decreases in violent crimes in the USA, juvenile homicide rates have increased and now surpass those of adults, so we have to look at early childhood for the causes. We already know that early relational trauma leads to the dysregulation of emotions such as fear and pain. I suggest that rage and aggression can also become dysregulated by early relational trauma. Under relational stress a developmentally impaired, right orbitofrontal cortex cannot regulate the amygdala's response to threatening stimuli, thus it is easy to over-react to what is perceived to be a threatening and humiliating stance in another with unmediated rage or violence. All of this is processed very rapidly, beneath levels of consciousness awareness.

Daniela: Could a dysregulated aggression system, coupled with internalised shame, lead to self-harm?

Allan: Definitely – people can suffer from either externalising psychopathologies where aggression is directed outwards, or from internalising psychopathologies, where aggression is turned in onto oneself, as it is with self-harm. Donald Kalsched's work on the self-care system[6] is a powerful description of how violence can be internalised, and directed from one part of the self to another part.

At the most extreme level, internalised violence, accompanied by a collapse in the right brain, seems to increase the risk of suicide. I am impressed by the work of Weinberg. He says when a right hemisphere, which has been compromised by early relational trauma, suffers extreme pain it may collapse, whereupon it is unable to regulate negative emotions such as loneliness, self-contempt and murderous rage.[7]

A collapsed right hemisphere also leaves the left brain in control. The left hemisphere is intolerant of ambiguity, thinks in terms of either/or, remains within the box, works with what is already known and is oriented to simple, linear solutions. Thus it is nearly impossible to find a creative way out of pain. As a consequence, suicide would feel (to the left brain) like the obvious, logical and only, solution.

Weinberg also suggests that the extreme dissociation caused by right hemisphere collapse opens the door to suicide because our sense of who we are is completely cut-off from our body, and this would appease our fear of death.

Daniela: If we have suffered early relational trauma can we do anything?

6 Sieff: see Donald Kalsched (Chapter 1) in this volume.
7 Weinberg, I. (2000) 'The Prisoners of Despair: Right Hemisphere Deficiency and Suicide'. *Neuroscience and Biobehavioural Reviews* 24: 799–815.

Allan: Yes! Although early relationships shape the developing brain, the human brain remains plastic and capable of learning throughout the entire lifespan, and with the right therapeutic help we can move beyond dissociation as our primary defence mechanism, and begin to regulate our emotions more appropriately.

Daniela: What kind of psychotherapy does it take to heal early relational trauma?

Allan: It takes painstaking, relational, embodied, long-term psychotherapy. Emotional regulation, attachment patterns and dissociative defensives are mediated by the right brain so healing requires the kind of therapy that can work with the right brain. Because what is held by the right brain is not immediately available to consciousness, and because that which is dissociated is doubly difficult to access, it is a slow process.

Moreover, right brain change depends on corrective emotional *experience*. In early life the human brain develops within the context of an emotion-regulating relationship with another human being – typically the mother. If we missed out on this as a child, then the therapist–patient relationship needs to facilitate the resumption of the blocked developmental processes. The relationship between therapist and client is called the 'therapeutic alliance' and unless it is strong enough, it will not be able to provide a growth-facilitating environment for the patient's under-developed right brain.

Daniela: What creates a 'strong enough' therapeutic alliance?

Allan: The patient has to trust that the therapist is benevolent and that the therapist understands him in a deep way which incorporates both mind and body. That means that the patient's right brain needs to know that it is seen, so although a therapist's left brain must listen to the words created by the patient's left brain in order to form an objective assessment of the patient's problem, the therapist must be sensitive enough to pick up, and empathise with, what is going on implicitly within the client's right brain and within his body. All therapeutic techniques sit on top of the therapist's ability to access the implicit realm via the right brain and body. A strong therapeutic alliance depends on the therapist knowing the patient from the inside-out, rather than from the top-down.

Another way to express this is to say that the therapist must develop her 'intuition'. Intuition is defined as 'the ability to understand or know something immediately without conscious reasoning'. Intuition is implicit knowledge gained through embodied, right brain learning. Intuition takes time to develop, but it lies at the core of clinical expertise. A therapist's bodily based intuition picks up what is held by the patient's unconscious mind and body, and it is this psychobiological connection that forms the foundation of the therapeutic alliance and which facilitates growth. Shotter writes that implicit knowledge relates to how '*people are able to influence each other in their being, rather than just in their intellects; that is, to actually "move" them rather than just "giving them ideas"*'.[8] A patient's

---

8   Shotter, J. (1993) *Conversational Realities*. London: Sage.

emotional growth depends on the therapist's ability to move, and to be moved by, those that come to him for help.

Daniela: What are the processes by which the therapeutic relationship helps a patient to resume the blocked development of their emotional system?

Allan: The therapist needs to help her patient to re-experience the trauma in affectively tolerable doses. Equally important is that the therapist helps her patient to learn how to regulate the feelings associated with that trauma so that the patient can integrate them into his emotional life, rather than having to dissociate when they arise. That requires the therapist's right brain to become the external regulator for the patient's right brain – helping it to tolerate what was once intolerable. In time the patient internalises the regulatory capacity of the therapist, learning to do this for himself.

Paradoxically, the greatest opportunity for such learning arises when something in the therapeutic relationship triggers the implicit working models that were formed during the patient's emotionally traumatic childhood, and he automatically begins to activate his old defences. A fleeting change in the therapist's tone of voice, a momentary facial expression, a subtle gesture or a single word may set unconscious alarm bells ringing and activate the patient's implicit working model of dysregulated-self-with-a-dysregulating-other. In these moments past history becomes present reality. The patient is catapulted out of his window of tolerance, becomes emotionally dysregulated and turns towards his old, unhealthy ways of regulating his emotions. He is at risk of either exploding into a state of dysregulated hyperaroused, or of imploding into a dysregulated state of hypoaroused, dissociation.

When a patient is catapulted into a hyperaroused state and subjectively experiences the therapist through the lens of the old internal working models, it is called 'negative transference'. When dysregulation takes the form of passive, collapsed hypoarousal it is called 'projective identification'. Projective identification occurs when the emotions and unconscious memories associated with early attachment trauma are intolerable. The patient unconsciously communicates his traumatic experiences to the therapist via non-verbal right brain channels, but immediately dissociates so that he is no longer overtly expressing or subjectively experiencing them. At that point it seems that only the therapist is experiencing the emotion. In neurobiological terms, the patient's right orbitofrontal cortex shuts down and the negative emotion is instantly driven beneath conscious awareness into the right amygdala. The patient's dysregulated hyperarousal still exists, but it is buried beneath conscious awareness.

For a patient who is in the midst of either negative transference or projective identification, there is no therapeutic alliance. However, if the therapist can maintain an attuned connection to her client, then the door opens to working with what got laid down early in the patient's life. I will begin by describing what happens if the therapist can stay connected to a patient who is in the midst of negative transference and then talk about working with projective identification.

When the patient is in a state of negative transference, the therapist's empathetic right brain will implicitly pick up the old fears and pain and dysregulation which have come alive in the patient, and will struggle to tolerate the resultant negative emotions flowing through her own body, whereupon her patient's right brain will unconsciously pick up on the therapist's distress. However, if the therapist has done her own work, then she will be able to metabolise those negative emotions whereupon her voice will become calmer and her facial expressions less tense. This, in turn, will be unconsciously picked up by the patient's right brain. At this point, three types of learning that are intrinsic to healing occur:

1   The patient's right brain, noticing the process that the therapist has been through, will observe that dysregulating emotions can be tolerated, metabolised and integrated after all.
2   The regulation occurring in the therapist's right brain will be actually mirrored by the patient's right brain, thus the therapist acts as an external emotional regulator for the patient. This dynamic happens under the radar of explicit awareness, but it is crucial because it gives the patient a living experience of what was missing during development.
3   The patient can begin to create new working models about the intersubjective world. The unconscious working model of a person who suffered early relational trauma predicts that in times of emotional stress others will exacerbate stress, rather than help to regulate it. Concurrently, the patient will have deduced that when he is emotionally dysregulated he is unworthy of help. If the therapist stays with him when he becomes dysregulated, the expectations of these unconscious, insecure working models are challenged. The patient begins to learn, again from lived experience, that there is nothing defective in him for feeling as he does, and that he is indeed worthy of help when in an emotionally dysregulated state.

In time, as new neural circuits are built, the patient can achieve what is called 'earned security'. Some of these new circuits connect the right amygdala to the right orbitofrontal cortex, allowing for a greater tolerance and regulation of intense emotions. Other circuits are responsible for the creation of new unconscious working models that embody a healthier way of seeing other people and oneself. The result is a growing sense of well-being and characterological change.

This process is considerably more difficult if the patient is in the midst of projective identification, because the emotions, working models and memories are dissociated, they need to be retrieved before they can be regulated and integrated. However, the therapeutic skills needed to work with projective identification are similar to those required to work with negative transference, in that it again requires that the therapist remain linked to the patient, when the patient has left the relational field. This allows the patient's right brain unconscious to perceive, in real time, enough of a sense of safety to begin to lift the dissociative defences. The therapist who waits patiently in the presence of the not yet speakable, being receptive to the not yet formed, sends out a lived message that the dissociated emotion is neither unacceptable nor intolerable. The therapist's resonance with the patient's dissociated emotion also acts as an amplifying mirror and in a genuine right brain-to-right brain non-verbal dialogue with the therapist, the patient gradually raises to awareness what he needs to be able to consciously feel and articulate, but which, until now, he has had to dissociate from. In doing so, links between the right amygdala and the right orbitofrontal cortex are forged.

Daniela: What is the importance of raising dissociated emotions to a place where they can become conscious and verbalised?

Allan: We experience and cope with life both explicitly through words and conscious thoughts and implicitly through our non-conscious visceral bodily based emotions. When these two domains come together it allows for a new and more complex sense of our emotional self. Consciously experiencing and naming an emotional experience while living it enables our emotions to develop from their crude early forms when they are experienced only as bodily sensations, into finely differentiated states.

Becoming conscious of our emotions also allows for emergence of a 'reflective self' that is capable of 'in-sight', a metaphor which speaks to our awareness of both our hidden thoughts, and as importantly, the rhythm of our inner emotional states.

Daniela: What happens if the therapist cannot contain the negative emotions created in negative transference and projective identification?

Allan: When a patient's traumatic emotions and memories are communicated through negative transference or projective identification, they may hit a therapist's sore spots created by her own attachment history. If the therapist cannot regulate the resultant negative emotions, she will try to escape through a verbal interpretation, too hasty an intervention or by labelling the patient's behaviour as something negative such as 'resistance'. When this happens the therapist becomes a co-participant in recreating her patient's trauma and the patient will be catapulted further into a dysregulated state of fear, shame and dissociation. The patient's old trauma-derived neural circuitry and defensive working models will be reinforced and strengthened.

There is an old adage in therapy that no patient can achieve a greater level of healing than their therapist has achieved – with modern scientific knowledge we can be more specific: the patient's unconscious right brain can develop only as far as the therapist's right brain can take them. Thus the central questions are: when a therapist's wounds are hit, can she regulate her own bodily based emotions and shame dynamics well enough to be able to stay connected to her patient? Can the therapist tolerate what is happening in her own body when it mirrors her patient's terror, rage and physiological hyperarousal? Can she tolerate what is happening in her own body when it mirrors her patient's shame, dissociation and hypoarousal? Herein lies the art of psychotherapy. For a therapist to stay with a dissociating patient who is projecting his trauma onto her takes many years of experience. More importantly, the therapist needs to have worked deeply with her own trauma, and has to keep working with it. A successful therapeutic relationship precipitates emotional growth not only in the patient, but also in the therapist.

That said, every therapist will have times when she is unable to contain her own negative emotions and when both patient and therapist are triggered the term that is used is 'enactment'. I explore the dynamics of enactment at length in my most recent book, *The Science of the Art of Psychotherapy*, but there is not space to go into it here. Suffice to say that periods of mutual misattunement will not cause damage so long as (1) they are temporary, (2) the therapist honestly owns her role in creating the enactment and (3) the therapist is able to instigate repair. In fact, cycles of misattunement and reattunement provide opportunities for corrective emotional experiences in that they show the patient that not every instance of misattunement is a precursor to abandonment or neglect, and that even when there is a stressful rupture of the bond, the interactive regulation of a caring other is available for genuine repair.

Daniela: It seems that a certain amount of emotional dysregulation is necessary to effective therapy. Is that right?

Allan: Yes! The therapist must strive to prevent the patient from being catapulted too far beyond his window of tolerance, because this will simply lead to the repetition of old patterns and to the strengthening of old trauma-derived neural circuits. But if it is to be effective, therapy must help to increase a person's tolerance to emotional stress and if therapy is too safe this will not happen. You have to be *in* an emotion to learn how to regulate it in a new way – talking about it is not enough.

The simplest way to describe this is through Figure 6.1, adapted from my colleague Pat Ogden. Within the central band we are working with what we can already tolerate and so there is no growth. Once we get into the outer areas – the danger areas – we are in such a dysregulated state of either hyperarousal or hypoarousal that we can learn nothing new. It is only by working at the edges of what we can tolerate – depicted by the thick, irregular, oscillating lines – that we can grow. Working along these safe-but-not-too-safe edges is how we learn to be with intense emotions and how to regulate them. That learning is embodied through forging neural connections between the right amygdala and the right orbitofrontal cortex.

Working at these edges is not easy! Chaos theory tells us that it is here that the system becomes unstable. However, chaos theory also tells us that it is this instability that creates the potential for the system to head in a totally new direction. In therapy, there are two possible responses to the instability. If the therapeutic alliance is not strong enough then the patient may fall back onto his long-established dissociative path. However, if the therapist can remain attuned, contain the chaos and provide a model of a different way to respond, then the patient has an opportunity to open up new neural pathways – ones that are at a more complex and adaptive level of organisation and which enable the different parts of the emotional right brain to become more integrated.

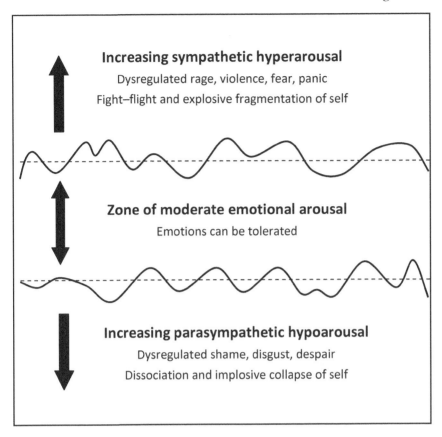

Figure 6.1 Working at the edges of the windows of affect tolerance.
Adapted from Ogden, P., Minton, K. and Pain, C. (2006) *Trauma and the Body: A Sensorimotor Approach to Psychotherapy.* New York: Norton .

Daniela: Short-term cognitive behavioural therapy is currently very popular – can it help with healing relational trauma?

Allan: In the academic discipline of psychology, the cognitive paradigm (which came to dominate the 1980s and 1990s) envisioned human brains as machines, and its research focused on cognitive processes such as explicit memory, rational thought, language and consciousness. Cognitively based therapy came out of this paradigm; its basic assumption is that we can change how we feel by consciously changing how we think and what we believe. That means that cognitive therapy focuses on language and thought, both of which are located in the left brain. That is rarely effective for patients who struggle with the consequences of early relational trauma, because such trauma impacts on the development of the emotional system of the right brain.

In fact, cognitive therapy – when applied to the emotional realm – uses linguistic, rational thought-based strategies to help the left brain gain more control over the right brain and its emotions. In other words, rather than fostering the growth of the right brain, cognitive therapy helps to shore up dissociation and keep our emotions out of mind.

Similarly, people who have trouble regulating their emotions typically have a left brain that is already more developed than their right brain, and they may well have learnt to use rational thinking and words to obscure the deeper emotional experiences and to keep them dissociated. Again, cognitive therapy risks strengthening the very strategies that keep the dissociation in place.

Even if the left brain becomes better able to control the emotions of the right brain, it can only dampen down emotional arousal that is of low or moderate intensity. Regardless of our childhoods, when emotional arousal reaches a certain level of intensity the left brain goes off-line and the right brain becomes dominant. Changes made in the cognitive strategies of the left brain are unavailable when this happens. At these times the only thing that helps is to have created the neural connections between the right amygdala and the right orbitofrontal cortex which allow us to tolerate and regulate intense emotions. Cognitive therapy, because it works with the left brain, simply cannot do this.

Another problem with cognitive therapy is that it often misses the real issues. 'Anger management' is a well-known cognitive treatment, but underlying a person's anger may be dissociated fear and shame and these cannot be accessed through the verbal language of the left brain. Cognitive therapy has no way to work with deeply embodied, underlying dissociated affects.

The final problem of cognitive therapy is that it is generally a short-term treatment so it is unable to build a strong enough therapeutic alliance to allow the patient to experience the corrective emotional experiences. Change does not happen when a patient is consciously reflecting on an emotion; it happens when a patient is *in* the emotion and when a resonating and actively involved therapist shows the patient a different way to be with what he is feeling. There is no room for that to happen with cognitive therapy.

In short, relational trauma cannot be addressed through the development of left brain cognitive strategies, rather its healing depends on working directly with the right brain to build an expanded, more tolerant, more interconnected and better regulated right brain. Psychotherapy that makes the right brain the focus requires much, much more from both therapist and patient, but it is the only route to genuine growth. We know that not only through the lived experience of therapists and patients, but also through all that we have learnt about the brain in the last two decades. In fact, I argue that we are in the middle of a paradigm shift in terms of how we understand ourselves. We are moving away from the cognitive paradigm that gave primacy to left brain conscious thinking, interpretations and verbal language, to one that gives primacy to right brain affect, bodily based emotions and what is held implicitly in the relational unconscious.

Daniela: Given that compromised neural circuits cause emotional dysregulation, some people argue that the cure lies in psychotherapeutic drugs. What are your thoughts?

Allan: There is no doubt that with certain psychopathologies, emotional dysregulation can be modified by bioaminergic drugs that directly impact the neurochemistry of subcortical brain circuits, but one of the main problems with psychotherapeutic drugs is that they are not site-specific. You may give somebody a selective serotonin reuptake inhibitor like Prozac, but there are serotonin receptors throughout the entire brain and body. It is a shot-gun approach so you get side-effects.

What is more a drug will not provide a growth-facilitating environment, and thus the patient will not necessarily develop the more connected and expanded right brain which then allows for more complex and adaptive emotional coping mechanisms. In other words, although levels of arousal will be altered, there may be no lasting improvement in processing social cues, no rewriting of the trauma-created internal working models and no development of the ability to turn to another for help in regulating emotional stress. The change may be limited to returning the individual to a more stable personality, rather than enabling the personality to tolerate more novelty and to structurally change and expand. If only pharmacology is used, the patient is denied the right brain growth and development that emerges from a psychotherapeutic process.

Daniela: What message would you like people to take home from this interview?

Allan: The earliest stages of life are critical because they form the foundation of all that follows. Our early attachment relationships, for better or worse, shape our right brain unconscious system and have life-long consequences.

An attuned early attachment relationship enables us to grow an inter-connected, well-developed right brain and sets us up to become emotionally secure. A traumatic early attachment relationship impairs the development of a healthy right brain and locks us into an emotionally dysregulated, amygdala-driven emotional world. Then our only way to defend against intense unregulated emotions is through dissociation. Over time, dissociation becomes characterological. Faced with relational stress, we cut-off from the world, from other people, from our emotions, from our bodies and from our sense of self. We cannot respond adaptively to what is happening in our environment. We cannot develop or grow emotionally. Instead we are stuck with a limited, crude and rigid emotional repertoire; a left brain that is desperately trying to keep control; and a deep-seated feeling of disconnection and insecurity. Too many people live like this. Too many people suffer desperate pain because of the emotional insecurity that results from early relational trauma.

For somebody struggling with this, the way to emotional security, and to a more vital, alive and fulfilling life, does not come from making the unconscious conscious – which is essentially a left brain process; rather, it arises through physically restructuring, growing and expanding the emotional unconscious itself. That is, it arises through changing the physical substrate of the right brain. Eric Kandel, the recent Nobel Prize winner, stated: *'There is no longer any doubt that psychotherapy can result in detectable changes in the brain.'* The most effective way to achieve these changes is through relationally based, emotionally focused psychotherapy with an empathic and psychobiologically attuned therapist who is willing and able to be an active participant in the process. It is the attuned interaction between the non-verbal right brain of the involved therapist and the non-verbal right brain of the patient, which enables the patient to tolerate emotions that previously had to be dissociated, to grow as an emotional being, and ultimately to develop the emotional security that was previously beyond reach.

7 Beyond the prison of implicit memory

The mindful path to well-being

Daniel J. Siegel and Daniela F. Sieff

Summary

People who enjoy psychological well-being are typically emotionally secure, compassionate, open-minded and curious. Underlying these qualities is neurobiological integration. Growing up in an emotionally nurturing environment fosters the development of neural integration, whereas an emotionally inadequate environment stifles it.

Our early emotional environment also plays a vital role in creating the unconscious models that contribute to our 'attachment status.' If our caregivers are attentive, compassionate and loving, we become 'securely attached' and learn to experience ourselves as lovable, others as trustworthy and the world as safe. However, if our caregivers are neglectful, intrusive or abusive we develop 'insecure attachment', whereby we come to experience ourselves as unlovable, others as untrustworthy and the world as unsafe.

These unconscious models are encoded in 'implicit memory'. Rather than returning as a conscious memory of a past event, implicit memory returns as a way of seeing the world, a suite of emotions and a set of behavioural reactions. Over time these ways of being become part of our character and we mistakenly believe this is who we are, rather than what we have learnt.

If our childhood emotional environment prevented us from developing emotional well-being, we can do so later in life. The human brain evolved to be shaped by interpersonal relationships, so working with an attuned and empathetic therapist can be powerfully reparative. Mindfulness practices can also make an important contribution. Not only do they foster neural integration and help us to become aware of our implicit memories, they also teach us to attune to ourselves with compassion and love, thereby enabling us to develop secure attachment through our relationship to ourselves.

Daniela Sieff: How do you define mental-well being?

Dan Siegel: That is an important question! Most mental health professionals have little sense of what constitutes mental well-being; in fact, few have even a single lecture on mental health during their training! Instead they are taught only about the symptoms and treatments for mental illness. But how can we help people with their mental suffering without a clear vision of what constitutes a healthy mind? Is it simply the absence of symptoms and dysfunctions, or is there more to it?

We now know that contented people – those who could be said to enjoy mental well-being – are compassionate, open-minded, curious and that they feel gratitude for their lives. I propose that underlying these qualities is 'integration'. Integration is the result of two processes: first, parts of a system are differentiated; second, the differentiated parts are linked together. The linked parts retain their individual characteristics and functions, but the whole is bigger than the parts. For example, the integration of the two sides of the brain, or the lower and upper parts of the nervous system, makes our mental lives more flexible, resilient and adaptive.

Imagine a choir: each singer has a unique voice, yet each singer is also linked into a complex and harmonious whole. Some sing the main tune while others may sing a descant, or a bass line. When their individual voices are coordinated they typify integration, and the result is exhilarating. However, if every singer sings exactly the same notes there is no differentiation and the audience is likely to get bored. Alternatively, if the singers all wear earmuffs and sing different songs, there would be no 'linkage' but only a chaotic and discordant jumble that would leave the audience running for the exit.

Daniela: You write about how integration fosters complexity; what are the benefits of complexity?

Dan: Complex systems are both flexible and stable. Their flexibility means that they can respond to novel situations quickly and learn easily; their stability means that they do not become a disorganised, chaotic mess. In terms of mental health, stability provides us with a secure sense of who we are, whereas flexibility allows us to live at the threshold of the unknown, take on new challenges and open ourselves to change.

The opposite of flexibility is rigidity and the opposite of stability is chaos; complexity cannot develop if either is present. Rigidity closes us down to change and prevents us from adapting to new situations. Chaos leaves us out of control, perhaps swept up in a rage or paralysed by old memories. All the syndromes in the *Diagnostic and Statistical Manual of Mental Disorders* (the psychiatric bible) describe either excess rigidity or chaos.

Daniela: What are the neural correlates of well-being?

Dan: Neural integration underlies our subjective sense of mental well-being. Our brain sits at the top of an extensive nervous system that runs throughout the body. Hormones, together with chemicals from the food and drugs we ingest, affect the signals sent along neural routes. Neural integration means that each part of our nervous system performs its assigned function efficiently, and in addition, the different parts coordinate their activities.

One area of the brain which is particularly important to well-being is the middle prefrontal cortex, located behind the forehead. Having extensive neural connections to many other brain regions, it performs a crucial role in many aspects of integration. These include:

1 *Bodily regulation.* It mediates between the sympathetic nervous system that creates alertness, and the parasympathetic nervous system that creates relaxation.
2 *Emotional balance.* It oversees the generation of emotional energy – making sure there is enough to feel alive and vibrant, but not so much that we become manic and overwhelmed.
3 *Fear modulation.* It has the ability to dampen down the immediate feelings of panic which often characterise our initial response to a potential threat.
4 *Response flexibility.* It allows us to pause and reflect on different options before acting.
5 *Intuition.* It is the seat of the intuitive knowing which emerges when we are open to what is happening in our bodies.
6 *Insight.* It creates the mental maps through which we become conscious of what is happening in our own mind.
7 *Attuning to others.* It is responsible for altering our internal state to resonate with that of another.
8 *Empathy.* It creates mental maps of another's internal world.
9 *Moral awareness.* It is capable of taking the larger picture into consideration, and acting in ways that are best for the whole.

At birth the middle prefrontal cortex is not yet on-line; in fact it does not reach maturity until we are in our mid twenties and its development is particularly responsive to the environment in which we grow up.

Daniela: What are emotions, and what role do they play in mental well-being?

Dan: Emotions are primarily non-conscious processes which evaluate a situation, and prepare us to deal with it. Emotions are created when attention, perceptions, memories and behaviour are integrated to create a particular feeling state, such as fear or joy. Well-being requires that our emotions are flexible and that they are appropriate to the environment in which we find ourselves.

Emotions divide into two basic types: (1) those that motivate us to approach what we perceive to be good for us, and (2) those that motivate us to withdraw from anything that we perceive to be a threat.

Approach drives us towards a thought, a feeling, a situation or a person. When our emotional state is set for approach, we are receptive. In social situations our facial muscles and vocal cords relax, our hearing is more sensitive and we attune to others more easily.

In contrast, when we detect a possible threat, a part of the brain called the amygdala is activated and we are catapulted into a defensive state. Unconscious processes assess whether fight or flight will help us escape the danger and then trigger the emotional state that will facilitate fight or flight. If, however, our unconscious assessment tells us that we are helpless, we collapse and feign death. Feigning death has its evolutionary roots in the fact that predators tend to eat only animals that they have killed, leaving animals that are already dead in case their flesh is rotting. Playing dead is a last ditch attempt to avoid being attacked.

The amygdala operates beneath awareness and can save our lives. Once, hiking with my son in the High Sierra, I felt a sudden jolt of fear and yelled, *'Stop!'* Only after I yelled did I become conscious of seeing a rattle snake lying on our path.

The system built around the amygdala is crude – it is the first port of call in assessing a situation and 'better safe than sorry' is its motto. That makes it prone to over-reaction so we have to be able to modulate the amygdala's response. Modulation occurs through the middle prefrontal cortex. Once the amygdala has sent out an alert, the prefrontal cortex reassess the situation and if it is not as dangerous as our initial reaction suggests, it releases a neurohormone into the limbic system that reduces its activity so we become calmer.

But this system is not fool-proof. The prefrontal cortex's ability to modulate the activity of the amygdala depends on the intensity of our fear. When our arousal is really great, the prefrontal cortex goes off-line – we literally 'flip our lid' – and our limbic reactions have free-rein. In this state our perceptions are biased and make the world seem even more threatening; we react impulsively, irrespective of whether our reactions are appropriate; we cannot take in new information or listen to others; and we cannot see the world from another's perspective. The prefrontal cortex is especially prone to shutting down when chronic childhood trauma has left us hyper-sensitised to danger.

Daniela: What role does our body play in the emotional system?

Dan: Our body is crucial! Emotions are initiated by the brain's reading of the environment. This then changes the state of both mind and body, but this happens beneath our awareness. To become aware of our feelings, information about what is happening in the body (for example, rate of breathing, muscle tension, butterflies in our stomach) has to be conveyed back to the prefrontal cortex of the right hemisphere. Phrases such as 'a heart-felt sense', or 'a gut feeling' are more than metaphors. This bodily awareness is called 'interoception', which literally means 'perceiving within'. It is the root of insight and best thought of as our sixth sense.

I see interoception as being a process of 'vertical integration' because information has to travel up from our body to the brain. When we suffer from chronic emotional wounding we may cut off this circuit. The emotions coursing through our bodies still influence our thinking, but we are protected from consciously feeling them. Cutting off from our emotional pain when we have no way to escape is adaptive because it allows us to function. However, when we shut down interoception to avoid pain and terror, we cut ourselves off from other emotions such as enjoyment and vitality. We become the walking dead.

Let me give you an example. One of my clients, who I call Ann, was three when her mother died. Her father remarried when Ann was five and had two more children with his new wife. Ann felt ignored by her father and described her step-mother as a harsh, hyper-critical disciplinarian. Aged 11, after a particularly painful dressing down, Ann went for a walk and promised herself that she would never feel anything again. Recounting this, Ann drew her index finger across her throat; a gesture that most of us would interpret to mean 'off with his head'. She was not aware that she had made this gesture, but she did tell me that her promise had worked. Her step-mother never made her feel bad again.

The pain of social rejection is mediated in the same part of the prefrontal cortex that registers physical pain from bodily injuries. Ann's mind would have been unable to tolerate the chronic pain of constant criticism; she would have been driven to stop it in the same way as she would have been driven to stop physical pain. However, because Ann was a child and could not get away from the cause of her pain, her only option was to prevent the pain from reaching her consciousness by shutting down her connection to her body. But that meant that she prevented all feelings from entering her consciousness, and by the time she came to see me her life felt empty and dead.

Ann's way of surviving her own childhood had repercussions for her relationship with her 11-year-old twin daughters. When describing them, Ann said that they were very independent, and 'did not bother with their parents', but something in the way she spoke did not feel real. Gradually Ann realised that having cut-off from her own body, she was unable to experience the feelings which would have enabled her to forge an emotional connection to her daughters. As a result, her daughters had no option but to become 'very independent' – even though, deep down, they still needed their mother's love and support.

Daniela: You mentioned that emotional information from the body goes to the right hemisphere – can you say something about brain lateralisation?

Dan: The brain of humans (and of other vertebrates) has evolved so that the two hemispheres specialise in different functions, and then are linked to form an integrated whole. Understanding the differences between the hemispheres gives us a clearer picture of how we attain emotional well-being, and highlights some of the problems that might get in the way.

The left hemisphere is specialised in the following ways:

- Approach Oriented. It mediates our propensity to seek out new experiences. Adventurous children have more activation in their left frontal areas compared to their right frontal areas, when they are resting.
- Modulates 'positive' emotions such as joy and contentment.
- Responsible for most verbal language.
- Poor at reading non-verbal emotional cues.
- Not directly connected to the body and does not have access to the raw emotions flowing through us. Instead, it modulates our non-verbal communication according to social rules. By the age of two we have learnt how to create socially appropriate facial expressions that are different from our internal emotional states. This is not necessarily a false self, but it may become one if we have to cut-off from our internal feelings.

- Sort the world into established categories and sees the world in a black-and-white way. Either this is true, or that is true. For the left hemisphere, only one view can accurately reflect reality.
- Concerned with anticipation and planning. It is goal directed. It analyses details and looks for solutions.
- Logical, literal and linear. It is concerned with linking cause to effect. We know the left hemisphere is coming on-line when two- to three-year-old children start to ask *'Why?'*.

In contrast, the right hemisphere is specialised as follows:
- Mediates withdrawal and turns us away from novelty. Shy children have more activity in their right frontal cortex than in their left, when at rest.
- Modulates 'negative' emotions such as pain and fear. It plays the primary role in coping with stress.
- Originator of our raw, intense, spontaneous and often private emotions.
- Some linguistic skill, such as poetry and metaphor, but it is less verbally adept than the left hemisphere.
- Responsible for non-verbal communication, both interpreting the signals of others and initiating the signals that we send into the world.
- Directly connected to the body, and capable of sensing our 'gut' reactions. It is responsible for interoception.
- Facilitates empathy. It creates images of our own minds, and the minds of others.
- Holistic. It looks at the overall pattern – at the gist of the experience. It has less need for linear causal explanations. It is at home with paradox and ambiguity. It sees a world of interconnecting possibilities: *'this AND that can be true. And together, wow, they could make something new!'*
- Less likely to interpret events in terms of pre-existing categories, and so it is more tuned-in to novelty, although it may also mediate withdrawal from such novelty.

Just as we need our left and right legs to be of equal length and strength to walk without limping, mental well-being requires that right and left hemispheres communicate with each other to create what I call 'horizontal integration'. When the left dominates we suffer from rigidity; when the right dominates we are lost in chaos.

Daniela: Can you talk more about what happens when integration between the hemispheres is impaired?

Dan: We can block intolerable emotions either by blocking vertical integration, as Ann did, or by living an existence that is dominated by our left hemisphere. We might also end up living in a left-dominated world if our caregivers were emotionally distant because then the right hemisphere would not have got enough stimulation to fuel its development. Either way, our life will be dominated by logical thinking and emotional flatness.

Alternatively, there are situations which lead to the right hemisphere being dominant. Then we are flooded by emotions and reactions that we do not understand. Julie came to see me because whenever her two-year-old son, Pythagoras, got upset she *'flipped'*. She said that Pythagoras pushed her buttons and made her *'unravel at the seams'*. She was terrified that she would snap, scream or even hit him. We started to explore Julie's childhood to see if we could discover what was driving her reactions.

Julie's father had been an alcoholic and she gradually began to express how helpless and scared she had been whenever he had got into a drunken rage. She recounted one night when he had chased her around the kitchen with a butcher's knife. When she locked herself in the bathroom, he broke the door down.

The brain helps us to anticipate what is about to happen by recalling memories of past experiences that seem similar to our present predicament. This happens without our awareness. Julie's sense of her own helplessness in the face of her son's distress seemed to evoke the feelings of the helplessness that she had experienced as a child when her father was in a drunken rage. The unconscious memories that were causing Julie to flip would have been held in her right hemisphere, and because, in these moments, there was no balancing left-hemisphere to provide the distance that could calm her, she unravelled.

Daniela: Can you talk more about memory?

Dan: Memory is created when our experiences are encoded in neural networks. We have many forms of memory. Short-term, or working memory, describes what is currently in our mind. If it has no use beyond the moment – for example, the phone number of a shop we have just called – then the neural network that encodes the telephone number dissipates and the information is quickly forgotten. But if working memory is concerned with something that could be important in the future it is passed onto another area of the brain where it becomes encoded as long-term memory. There are several forms of long-term memory; the two that are most relevant here are (1) explicit memory, and (2) implicit memory.

Explicit memory is what we generally think of as memory. When we retrieve an explicit memory we know that we are recalling something that happened in our past. This is because when the experience was encoded a part of the brain called the hippocampus tagged a time and place to the memory, recording when and where it occurred.

Implicit memory is different. When an implicit memory is retrieved we are not aware that something is being recalled from the past, instead we feel it as our present reality. For example, if we have learnt to ride a bicycle, as soon as we get on, implicit memory kicks in and based on what we have memorised we are able to pedal and balance and brake without having to consciously think back to when we first learnt to ride a bicycle.

Implicit memory is active in all areas of life; it can manifest as a physical skill such as riding a bicycle, an emotional reaction (as with Julie's helplessness), a perceptual bias or a behavioural pattern. Because of the nature of implicit memories, we do not realise when they have been activated even though they influence our attitudes and beliefs about ourselves and other people.

Elaine, a 26-year-old graduate, came to see me because she was scared that she would 'fall flat on her face' if she accepted the offer of a job that she really wanted. We were struggling to understand her fear, so we decided to see if focusing on her body would reveal anything. She did a body scan – a mindfulness-based guided meditation in which she systematically focused her attention on different parts of her body, taking in the sensations from each area. When her focus came to her arm, she gripped it and cried, *'Ouch!'* The pain then moved to her jaw. She started to cry. She remembered falling off her new tricycle when she was three years old. She had broken her arm and fractured two baby teeth. Elaine's arm healed and her adult teeth were fine, but her mind had created an implicit memory that coupled novelty and enthusiasm with intense pain. Her unconscious belief was that *'trying new things could result in disaster'*. She literally feared she would *'fall flat on her face'* if she took the job she had worked so hard to obtain. She was the prisoner of unintegrated, implicit memories.

We cannot access all of our implicit memories, and even when we do the factual details may not be accurate; however, the more we are able to recall the gist of what happened and integrate it into our explicit memory, the easier it is for us to distinguish present reality from what comes from the past to distort our present.

Daniela: Why do we remember some things explicitly, but not others?

Dan: First, it depends on age. Essentially, all of our earliest memories are implicit for the simple reason that the hippocampus does not come on-line until we are somewhere between 18 and 24 months old. Then it takes time to become fully functional, which is why we have few conscious (i.e. explicit) memories before we were five.

Once both memory systems are working, whether, and how an event is remembered is related to its emotional intensity. Experiences that are not intense are not remembered. Those that have middling levels of intensity, and are deemed meaningful, are stored as explicit memory. Those that are overwhelmingly painful and frightening are remembered implicitly, rather than explicitly. That is because the cortisol that is released when we are frightened shuts down the hippocampus, whereas the adrenalin which is released sears the experience into our implicit circuits. This is generally adaptive; it allows us to learn from dangerous experiences, and to act quickly next time we encounter a similar situation. However, the downside is that when something in our present reminds us of something painful from our past, it only takes a fraction of a second for an old, unconscious memory to emerge and shape our behaviour. In an instant we are on automatic pilot – the perceptions, emotions and bodily experience that were laid down in the past become present reality and we are driven by old defences that are often inappropriate.

Daniela: In your recent work you describe how top-down mental models colour our world view. What are top-down models?

Dan: Once we have experienced something several times, we create a generalised model of that experience. These are what I call top-down models, in that new information is processed within the light of these models. Top-down influences operate in all aspects of our life and have had huge value in our evolutionary history. Generation after generation, the more rapidly we could make top-down judgements about whether our situation was benevolent or threatening, the more likely we were to survive.

Neurobiologically, top-down influence is manifest via the cortex. The cortex is six cells deep. Cells are stacked on top of each other, creating columns. Information flows through these columns in both directions. Incoming sensory data enters the cortex at the bottom layer of neurons and moves up. When a toddler sees a rose for the first time he may first be attracted by its colour, then sniff its fragrance, touch its petals and maybe try to eat one. This is as close to a pure bottom-up experience as we can get. But if we have seen a rose before (or indeed any flower), a rich store of memories are activated and this top-down process then shapes our perception of what is in front of us.

By the time we are adults, perception is virtually always a blend of what we are sensing now and what we have already learnt. If you are on the streets of New York and you see me raise my hand, you will probably assume I am hailing a cab. If we are in a lecture, then without consciously thinking about it, you are likely to assume I want to ask a question. If, however, you had been hit as a child, we are having a heated discussion, and I raise my hand to emphasise a point, you might fear that I am about to hit you. In this instance, your trauma-created top-down model would dominate and you would misperceive my intention.

Daniela: Early relational experiences become top-down models through the attachment process – can you talk about this?

Dan: John Bowlby was the first psychoanalyst to develop the idea that all infants are born with an innate desire to be close to their parents. He and Mary Ainsworth worked together to explore what they called 'the attachment system'. At the most basic evolutionary level it helps the infant to survive, because parents protect infants from starvation, temperature change, predators, attacks from other humans and being separated from the group. But the attachment relationship does more than protect the infant: it is the medium through which the infant creates top-down models about how people will behave towards him. In time, these internal models colour our perceptions of everybody we meet. Eventually, they become character traits, and there is a real risk of attributing these ways of being to our innate make-up, rather than understanding them as implicitly learned memories.

Daniela: Can you talk about the different types of implicit models formed through the attachment process?

Dan: Mary Ainsworth collaborated with Bowlby to distinguish four attachment patterns, one of which is secure, whereas the other three describe different forms of insecurity, namely avoidant, ambivalent and disorganised.

Secure attachment develops when children have caregivers who are responsive to their needs and mental states. These children learn that their parents are trustworthy, and they generalise this learning and see other people as friendly and the world as safe. As they grow older they venture into the world, embrace new experiences and develop new relationships, knowing that they can return to their parents for support when it becomes too much.

Having perceptive and responsive parents also means that securely attached infants learn that their own needs are important, and their goals achievable. They come to think of themselves as worthy of being listened to and as lovable. Also, because their feelings are validated, they can learn about their feelings and how to regulate them. This opens the door to them being able to read the feelings of other people accurately, and to develop empathy.

A study that followed children from birth to 25 found that securely attached children fulfilled their intellectual potential, had good relationships and could regulate their emotions.

Insecure avoidant attachment is typical of infants whose parents are emotionally unavailable, rejecting and unresponsive. Such children develop an internal working model of parents who are unable to comfort them and as a result they learn to become self-sufficient, often acting like 'little adults' – as exemplified by Ann's children. Unconsciously, they tend to believe that they are unworthy of being listened to, helped or loved.

Because the parent is not there to validate the child's mental experiences, these children have few opportunities to learn about their own feelings, and to reflect on their own minds, and on the minds of others. Consequently, they are somewhat disconnected from themselves and from others, and find empathy difficult. However, never having known anything else, they are not necessarily aware of this.

As adults they are said to have a 'dismissing' stance. They tend towards dry, logical thinking. They value independence above all else; autonomy is at the core of their identity. Peers typically describe them as aloof, controlling and unlikable.

When asked about their childhoods they recall facts (e.g. schools, sporting events, etc.), but not relationships. When pushed to describe their emotional relationships with their parents, their descriptions are brief, idealistic and do not convey the lived experience. They typically claim that their family life had no effect on their development. One of my avoidantly attached clients, when asked about his childhood, replied: *'My mother was normal. She ran the home. My father worked. My brothers and I were fine. My family life didn't affect my development.'*

Insecure ambivalent attachment develops when parents are inconsistently available, and periodically invade their infant's mind. By that I mean that when a child triggers a parent's unconscious memories of trauma, the parent will act through the distorting filter of that trauma, rather than responding to the child's actual needs. For example, a mother who felt unloved as a child might grab her happily playing toddler and shower him with hugs – not because he needs hugging right then, but because the loneliness that the mother suffered as a young child has been triggered and she needs to soothe her own distress. Such children can never be confident that their own emotional needs will be met, and they live in fear of unpredictable intrusions. Consequently, they become hyper-tuned-in to their attachment figures.

Being seen through the filter of their parent's unresolved trauma also means that such children are unable to come to see themselves clearly, and so they end up with a confused sense of self, rather than the dismissing self typical of avoidant attachment. Instead of seeing themselves as separate to their parents, emotional entanglement means that anything that a parent does is interpreted as saying something about the child.

Parental intrusions that push the child into an over-aroused state mean that these children are unable to learn how to regulate their emotions, and so they become adults who are prone to being overwhelmed by their own chaotic outbursts.

In adults this pattern of relating is called 'preoccupied' attachment. Preoccupied adults are highly anxious and tend to see the behaviour of others only in terms of what it says about them. For example, a husband whose wife has to work late might believe that he is no longer a priority in her life, and she does not love him anymore. Preoccupied adults have both a powerful wish for closeness and a disabling fear of losing it. As a result they tend to over-react and to create their own worst nightmare, alienating friends, partners and even their own children. When asked about their early family history, they tend to confuse past and present. They may begin their answer by recounting something from their childhood, but switch into describing some dynamic that they are currently struggling with. In other words, they struggle with differentiation.

Disorganised attachment is the most extreme form of insecure attachment. Eighty per cent of children who are overtly abused show this pattern. It also develops if parents are frightened by their children, if parents are terrifying, either because they are abusing alcohol or drugs, or because they have rageful outbursts, if parents massively withdraw from their children, and possibly if parents repeatedly and intensely humiliate their children. Under any of these conditions, children face an irresolvable biological dilemma. Their survival circuits scream *'Get away from the source of terror, you are in danger!'*, whereas their attachment circuits cry *'Go toward your attachment figure for safety and soothing!'*. This is fear without solution.

Disorganised attachment can also come about as a result of early loss that is not processed. The loss will propel the child to seek comfort from the attachment figure, but that person is no longer there. This can have a profoundly damaging impact on a growing mind – especially if there is no other attachment figure around who can provide the child with a safe emotional environment in which to grieve the loss.

Parents, who behave in ways that constellate disorganised attachment in their children, typically suffer from unresolved emotional trauma themselves. Thus, when something in the interaction between parent and child triggers the parent's implicit memory, they lose control, just as Julie did. Generally, parents will not understand why they have just behaved in this way, and, feeling deeply ashamed will try to deny what has happened. Consequently, they will not soothe the child and repair the damage, whereupon the cycle will be perpetuated.

Children with disorganised attachment are unable to maintain a coherent sense of themselves. We all have multiple 'selves' to carry out the diverse activities of our lives; one self goes to the office, another looks after our children and another socialises with friends. Healthy development is not about creating a single self; it is about treating each self-state with respect, and moving fluidly between selves as appropriate. When we do this we experience a sense of self that is coherent. Children with disorganised attachment, who switch abruptly from state to state as they try to deal with an impossible situation, cannot create a coherent sense of themselves.

As adults they struggle to relate to others and to regulate their impulses and emotions. They have an increased risk of developing post-traumatic stress disorder, as well as dissociative disorders.[1]

For adults, there is a fifth pattern of attachment, *'earned security'*. These are people whose childhoods would normally have produced insecure attachment; however, as adults they are rated as secure, generally because a significant relationship with a close friend, romantic partner or therapist has allowed them to develop out of their insecure status. The key to creating 'earned security' is to make sense of our childhood; to acknowledge what was positive and what was negative; to understand how our childhood has affected our mind; and then to modify the internal models so they are more adaptive.

Encouragingly, although attachment patterns tend to be transmitted across generations, the best predictor of a child's attachment status is not what happened to his parents when they were children, but how his parents made sense of their childhood experiences. With enough deep work, the cycle of insecure attachment can be broken; the attachment patterns of children whose parents have achieved 'earned security' are indistinguishable from the children of secure parents.

Daniela: How do different attachment patterns affect the development of complexity and the kinds of relationships that people have?

Dan: Securely attached children, and adults who have achieved earned security, generally operate as an open, integrated complex system. They are not trapped in rigid ways of being; they do not get repeatedly lost in chaos. Rather than being defensive and closed down, they are open to the new experiences that provide the impetus for the system to grow and become even more complex.

Similarly, they are able to connect to other people without losing themselves. Having a sense of our self, yet being part of a *'we'*, is what I call interpersonal integration. It allows two people to create a complex super-system, and to become companions on a mutually created journey through time. These types of relationships are open only to securely attached individuals.

In contrast, avoidant children act as rigid systems. They are closed to the new experiences that could move them towards greater complexity, and their focus on independence prevents them from being able to form meaningful connections with others.

Ambivalently attached individuals also avoid the new experiences that would foster complexity, but the reason for their avoidance is that they do not want to risk falling into chaos. Also, because they struggle to differentiate themselves

---

1 Sieff: see Ellert Nijenhuis (Chapter 5) in this volume.

from others, they cannot form relationships that are based on a connection between two *separate* individuals.

Disorganised attachment is, by definition, an incoherent, unstable system that swings between rigidity and chaos. It is the antithesis of the integrated harmony and resilience that emerge with complexity. People who have developed disorganised attachment have no coherent self to form relationships.

Daniela: You explain that if we are securely attached, then we develop the capacity to understand what is happening in (1) our own minds, (2) the minds of others and (3) our relationships. You coined the term 'mindsight' to describe this. Why is mindsight important?

Dan: We constantly try to make sense of experience by understanding cause-and-effect relationships. We have evolved to do this because it helps us to anticipate the future; it is easier to avoid becoming a lion's dinner if you have figured out that a growl (cause) indicates the presence of a lion who might eat you (effect). Making sense of the social world is more complicated, but humans are a profoundly social species and being able to read another's mind is crucial. What does that scowl mean? Who do I trust? Is she or he attracted to me? I call the ability to read another's mind 'mindsight'.

Mindsight can be considered our seventh sense. Our first five senses (sight, hearing, touch, smell and taste) allow us to perceive the outside world. Interoception, our sixth sense, allows us to perceive internal bodily states – the quickly beating heart that signals fear or excitement, the butterflies in our stomach that tell us we are nervous. Mindsight, the ability to perceive intentions, emotions, beliefs, attitudes and thoughts, is our seventh sense. It is every bit as essential to our well-being as the other six.

Unless we are born with a condition like autism, mindsight is our birthright. However, it does not appear automatically any more than being born with muscles makes us athletes. We need the experiences embedded in secure attachment to develop this essential human capacity. If our caregiver is attuned, and reflects our reality back to us in a straightforward way, we come to sense our own mind with clarity, and building on this we learn to see the minds of others. However, if our caregiver is unresponsive, distant or confusing, and unable to accurately validate our internal experience, then our internal 'me-maps', and 'you-maps' become distorted.

Daniela: Would you call shame – the sense of being fundamentally inadequate – a distorted 'me-map'?

Dan: Absolutely! Shame occurs when we need attunement from our caregiver, do not get it, and when the caregiver does not recognise what has happened and does not put it right. Shame feels like a bottomless black hole and if constellated time and again, it becomes associated with a distorted and destructive me-map that states *'I am defective and unlovable'*.

From the point of view of survival, *'I am defective'* is safer than *'My parents are unreliable and may abandon me'*, however, it is practically impossible to live with the conscious belief that we are defective, and so this distorted me-map is relegated to the unconscious. From here, it runs our life. A patient, who I call Matthew, was successful at work, but his relationships with women caused him (and them) enormous pain. He would be attracted to a woman who seemed beyond his reach, but he would pursue her with such determination and charm that often she would fall for him. However, as soon as this happened, Matthew would begin to feel repulsed by the woman, and eventually the relationship would break down.

During our work Matthew stated that he felt that winning over 'high-profile women' would establish his worth. However, it was an unconscious strategy doomed to failure. Matthew's 'me-map' was built on the shame-defined premise that he was unlovable, so as soon as the woman had fallen for him, he began to believe that she *must* be flawed to love somebody as inadequate as him. An automatic response of repulsion would then set in. He would also back away when the relationship became intense because he was unconsciously frightened that his girlfriend would start to see 'just how inadequate and unlovable' he was.

To become a *'we'* – to be part of a truly intimate relationship – is an incredibly vulnerable experience at the best of times; when our 'me-map' is distorted by shame, it is practically intolerable.

Daniela: What is the relationship between mindsight and empathy?

Dan: Mindsight is a pre-requisite for empathy, allowing us to see and feel – that is, to empathise with – what is going on in another's mind. Without mindsight, people, whether they be our friends, our spouse or our children, become objects, and we struggle to see them as having minds of their own which are worthy of respect.

Daniela: You have coined the term 'resonance circuits' to describe the neurobiology that underlies empathy. What are these circuits?

Dan: Folk wisdom tells us that couples in a happy marriage look evermore alike. We now know that is because they have mirrored each other's expressions so often that the hundreds of tiny facial muscles have reshaped their faces to reflect each other's emotions. This mirroring is achieved through our 'resonance circuits', and the key component of these circuits is mirror neurons. On detecting that there is some purposeful meaning in what another person is doing or feeling, our mirror neurons cause our brains to create the same state in us. Then, so long as we are open to receiving information pertaining to our bodily state (interoception), we can become conscious of the other's feelings through what we are feeling in ourselves.

Daniela: In that case, when feelings are flowing through our body, how do we know whether those feelings derive from our mirroring of another person's emotional state, or whether they reflect our own emotions?

Dan: We do not yet have the answer, but we do know that when we confuse me with you (as with ambivalent attachment), we are in trouble. We are swamped by what is coming at us from others, and to protect ourselves we may shut down our resonance circuit, whereupon we lose our capacity for empathy.

Daniela: Recent research shows that when observing people in pain, doctors suppress the brain circuits associated with empathy and increase activity in areas linked to self-control. In the case of doctors it is probably adaptive; not only do they sometimes have to inflict pain on their patients as part of the healing process, but if they are overwhelmed by their patients' suffering they will burn out.

Dan: That is interesting, and there are indeed times when we need to suppress empathy and shut down mindsight. However, the danger is that this becomes a way of being. While studying medicine at Harvard I was told to stop asking questions about patients' feelings and stick to physical facts. The facts are crucial – being wheeled into an operating room we want a surgeon who knows the facts – but if we live only through the facts then our lives have no texture or vibrancy. If our lives are to be full and meaningful we have to tune into our own subjective, internal world, and we need to tune into the inner worlds of others. I went along with what was required of me at Harvard, but I felt disconnected from my inner world, and cut-off from the living part of myself. Eventually, my body went numb. I recall taking a shower and feeling nothing.

Daniela: If we do not develop mindsight growing up, how can we develop it later?

Dan: If we think of mindsight as the lens through which we see the internal world of both ourselves and of others, we can see that it has to be held steady for us to be able to focus. For this it needs a tripod, whose legs consist of (1) openness, (2) observation and (3) objectivity. To develop mindsight later in life we have to work on building this tripod.

Openness means that we are open to our emotional reactions; that we accept them without criticising ourselves. When we start thinking that we should be able to do X, or that we should not be feeling Y, we are likely to beat ourselves up. But when we attack ourselves, we automatically activate our defence system in an attempt to protect ourselves from the attack. And in a defensive state we shut down and so change moves ever further beyond our reach. If we are going to move towards well-being, we need to approach our internal world and embrace it with compassionate self-reflection.

Openness also means that we are willing to see things in a new way, and that means we have to be prepared to bypass some of the top-down models stored in our implicit memory. Looking through top-down models we cannot see clearly because our present is filtered through the past. Openness means embracing the uncertainty that allows new, bottom-up realities into our lives.

Observation means that we can watch ourselves, even while we are in the middle of an experience. It depends on an inner witness and enables us to become aware of our patterns, whereupon we can work, with self-compassion, towards changing them.

Objectivity means that we can have a thought or a feeling without being swept away by it. Getting lost in the flow of a piece of music can be wonderful. However, when we get lost in the flow of our tempers, or our panic, we are in trouble. Then we need to be able to step back and reflect. When we are in meltdown it is hard to reflect, but once we have recovered, objective reflection helps us to realise that our thoughts, feelings, memories, beliefs, behaviours and intentions are temporary; that they are not the totality of who we are. And that then allows us to take responsibility for our actions and feelings, and move towards change.

Daniela: What are some of the things that we can do to build the legs of the tripod?

Dan: Working with an empathetic and attuned therapist is an effective way to develop openness, observation and objectivity. Journaling develops our capacity to observe ourselves objectively, and it opens us to the working of our minds. Poetry inhibits hierarchical, top-down, left brain processes; through using words in unfamiliar ways it encourages us to see through fresh eyes.

I did a week's silent retreat which was powerful. The part of my mind that usually connects with other people turned its focus to the only person available: me! In our busy lives our minds are full and reactive; silence creates a rare opportunity to become intimate with our internal world. Interestingly, after the retreat I felt better able to tune into the non-verbals of others. Having focused on my own internal world for a week, I became more sensitised to others.

Mindfulness practices are particularly powerful methods for building the tripod. Kabat-Zinn, one of the leading mindfulness teachers in the West, defines mindfulness as: *'The awareness that emerges through paying attention, on purpose, in the present moment, and nonjudgementally, to the unfolding of experience moment by moment.'*[2]

Purposefully paying attention means actively noticing our sensations, thoughts and feelings as they unfold, and staying with them, whether they are joyful, neutral or painful. It shakes us out of our automated ways of perceiving, feeling and behaving, opening us to novelty.

Being non-judgemental does not mean that we get rid of judgements – the human mind is continually assessing what is going on and categorising it as good or bad. Rather, being non-judgemental means that we become aware that we are making judgements but then we actively choose to let them go, rather than become caught in them.

Mindfulness can be cultivated through many means. An attuned relationship can help us to become mindful, and so can more formal meditation practices. Most mindfulness meditation begins with a focus on the breath. This is powerful because breath marks the meeting of the external and internal world. It also helps to connect us to our bodies. For some people, practices like Tai Chi or yoga open the door to becoming aware of the present moment. Alternatively, guided meditations such as the one I did with Elaine, where we slowly move our attention from one part of the body to the next, can help us discover where we are blocked.

---

2 Kabat-Zinn, J. (2003) *Coming to our Senses: Healing Ourselves and the World through Mindfulness.* New York: Hyperion Press. pp. 145-146.

However, we do not need to do a formal practice to cultivate mindfulness; when we go for a jog, we can either focus our awareness on what we are doing in each moment, or we can daydream about our plans for that night. There is nothing wrong with daydreaming, but it is not mindful jogging. One of my practices is mindful washing up – instead of zoning out, I take the opportunity to focus my attention on what I am doing in the moment.

Regardless of the specific practice, mindfulness trains the mind to observe itself. It is a way to become aware of what is real for us in this moment. And it helps us to describe the internal seascape of the mind with words, and so bring it to consciousness.

Daniela: What is the difference between mindfulness and mindsight?

Dan: Mindsight is a term I created while in medical school to remind me of how we can see the inner subjective lives of others, and ourselves. Since then, I have expanded my understanding of mindsight to include the way we see the energy and information flow of the mind clearly, and so be able to move towards integration.

Mindfulness, in contrast, is a term that has been used in a range of ways. 'Contemplative mindfulness' reflects practices, some of which are 2,500 years old. It has no fully accepted definition, but generally includes being aware of things as they are happening without being swept up by judgements. 'Creative mindfulness' is about leaving one's mind open and not prematurely closing down on possible interpretations of an experience. 'Being mindful' is also a general term in common use, meaning to be intentional and aware, to be awake to possibilities, as in 'be mindful when you duck beneath a low doorway'.

You can see how some people would overlap mindfulness and mindsight, but they are actually not the same concept. When we have mindsight – when we see the mind of ourselves and others clearly and move towards integration – we likely have all three forms of 'being mindful': we are intentional and awake; we are open-minded and do not prematurely close our vision; and we are aware of things as they are happening. And so mindsight would include mindfulness within its functions.

Daniela: What are the therapeutic benefits of mindsight?

Dan: Mindsight enables us to look clearly and compassionately at difficulties in our internal world, and to use them as opportunities for growth. It fosters integration by encouraging us to ask: *'Where is there chaos and/or rigidity in my life? What is causing it? What needs to be differentiated? What is preventing linkage?'*

More concretely, mindsight enables us to recognise that many of our ways of perceiving, feeling, thinking and behaving are learnt patterns, etched into our implicit memory as a result of our early environments. It helps us to become aware of how these patterns limit us, and create (self) destructive knee-jerk reactions that hurt both ourselves and others. It can also help us to disengage from these patterns – something as simple as learning to breathe with our abdomen combats stress, which is synonymous with breathing in the chest to prepare for flight or fight.

Mindsight also helps us get beneath the veil of well-worn stories that hide our deeper pain. It connects us to the difficult feelings, beliefs and emotions that are buried within, and however painful that is, it is crucial to emotional healing.

Daniela: What about the therapeutic benefits of mindfulness practices?

Dan: The therapeutic benefits of mindfulness overlap with those of mindsight and what is exciting is that there is mounting scientific data on the benefits of mindfulness practices to both physical and mental well-being. Those who completed Jon Kabat-Zinn's eight-week 'mindfulness-based stress reduction' programme showed a shift in brain activity so that left prefrontal areas became more dominant. This did not mean that they were not using their right brain, or that analytical left brain thinking took over; rather, the activation of the left prefrontal area allowed them to approach their internal world with acceptance and curiosity, rather than with dread, fear, hate or anger. As a consequence they were able to reflect on painful events rather than withdrawing or spacing out. We have to be able to do this to heal our wounds.

Studies at UCLA have shown that simply naming a feeling diminishes activity in the amygdala and soothes us. That said, the details of how we name a feeling are crucial: there is a profound difference between saying, *'I am sad'* and *'I feel sad'*. *'I am sad'* conflates who we are with what we feel. *'I feel sad'* acknowledges our feelings, but implicitly acknowledges that we are more than our feelings and that our feelings will pass. Knowing this allows us to create an internal sanctuary from which we can experience what arises in each moment, rather than rushing to escape.

Daniela: The internal sanctuary sounds a little like dissociation. People who are terrified, or in great pain, often feel themselves to be observers, watching from a safe distance. How can we ensure that mindfulness practices do not foster dissociation?

Dan: That is a danger. A phrase that is often used in the mindfulness world is 'blissed out', but that is not a state that brings healing. Rather, being 'blissed out' describes a state of numbness in which we are cut-off from our inner reality.

Similarly, an exclusive focus on the present moment can be an escape from a painful past. I had a patient who had practised, and indeed taught, mindfulness meditation for decades. He initially refused to explore his childhood memories with me, explaining that if he did so he would not be 'living in the present'. I explained that we can be present with images of the past. After some resistance he agreed to try. You can imagine what was buried there: a world of pain and abuse. His meditation practice had been a 'spiritual bypass' through which he sought to escape from painful memories by sticking rigidly to the here-and-now. In reality, however, being present to the moment means being open to how the moment is influenced by the past.

Daniela: You propose that mindfulness enables us to become our own best friend, and can help to develop an adult attachment status of 'earned security'. Can you talk about this?

Dan: Through helping us to become aware of our feelings, thoughts and beliefs, mindfulness enables us to create a healthy relationship with ourselves. Parents who raise secure children bring *C*uriosity, *O*penness, *A*cceptance and *L*ove to their children (the acronym COAL helps me remember this). When we practise mindfulness we bring curiosity, openness, acceptance and love to our own minds. In doing so, we become our own best friend. Then we can develop a secure attachment to ourselves, and heal some of the wounds we carry from having had parents who could not attune to us.

I came to this realisation while preparing for a conference where I was sharing a platform with Jon Kabat-Zinn. Reading his books I was struck by the fact that practitioners of mindfulness meditation develop the same mental and emotional characteristics as securely attached individuals. I also realised that these characteristics are identical with the functions of the middle prefrontal cortex. I began to think that attunement – internal attunement in the case of mindfulness, and interpersonal attunement in the case of attachment – might lead to the healthy growth of middle prefrontal fibres, the integrative and regulatory circuits of the brain that we talked about earlier. Research is beginning to support this. One recent study showed that the middle prefrontal region of long-term meditators is thicker than in non-meditators. Another study shows that child abuse and neglect impairs the growth of integrative fibres of the brain.

Daniela: We have talked about mindfulness in healing – what is the role of a therapist?

Dan: Although mindfulness helps us to change our relationship with ourselves, the human brain evolved to be shaped by interpersonal experiences, so therapists play a crucial role in the journey towards emotional well-being. In fact, research suggests that the most important factor in healing is the relationship between therapist and patient, rather than which therapeutic technique is used.

Daniela: What are the qualities that are important in a therapeutic relationship?

Dan: A therapist will have several roles within the relationship. She/he may become an attachment figure for the patient. She/he may be required to act as a guide or teacher. At times she/he may even need to be an expert on the mind, well-being and the brain. But what is most important is that the therapist is genuinely open to the unknown, to what emerges as the patient begins to explore his or her inner world, and that the therapist is fully committed to being present and attuned and resonant with the patient during that process of exploration.

Past experiences in particular unresolved trauma, prevent us from being present to those who are in front of us, because it biases our perceptions. To be a mindful and effective therapist it is vital that we know how our own biases and wounds restrict our ability to be fully present to our patients. When we, as therapists, impose old (unconsciously held) stories on our clients' reality, they feel it and are likely to be retraumatised rather than healed.

Daniela: What is the relationship between presence and attunement?

Dan: Presence is opening to unfolding possibilities. Attunement is purposefully focusing our attention on whatever is happening in the moment, so as to take it in. We can attune to nature, focusing on the ways the breeze brushes through the branches of a tree. We can attune to other people, focusing on their unfolding reality and discoveries. In therapy, attunement means that the therapist focuses on what is emerging for his or her patient. It can feel very risky. After all, it requires that the therapist is okay with not knowing what is going to happen. Similarly, the therapist has to let go of any desire to be in control of the outcome. But unless a therapist is willing to risk attunement, the patient cannot find healing.

Daniela: How do you differentiate attunement from resonance?

Dan: With attunement we focus on another person so as to become aware of their internal state. Resonance is a step beyond; we allow ourselves to be *influenced* by the internal state of that other person. Resonance links two autonomous individuals into a functional whole that is bigger, more complex and more vital than the sum of its parts. Resonance creates the heightened moments of connection that are crucial to growth and healing.

Physically, resonance means an alignment of the autonomic nervous system, leading to the mirroring of bodily states such as breathing patterns and heart rates. Subjectively, we experience resonance when we see that the other person is changed because of our internal world. Talking about a childhood experience a patient might notice a tear forming at the edge of the therapist's eyes, or feel the therapist's outrage that a young child could be treated that way. It is crucial that therapists do not pretend: it is only if therapists are genuinely affected by their patient that the patient 'feels felt' and begins to experience the 'we' that was missing during childhood.

The sense of 'we' at the heart of resonance is the simplest way of describing love. It is also at the heart of healing. People do not often speak about a professional form of love because they are frightened that they will be misunderstood and be accused of bringing romance or sexuality into the clinical setting. However, caring for patients with curiosity, openness, acceptance and love is crucial. The therapeutic relationship is intimate in the most profoundly meaningful and existential way.

Daniela: You have said that resonance creates the trust that is vital in therapy. Can you talk about this?

Dan: When we trust another person, we feel safe enough to be vulnerable with them, and then we move into the open, approach-oriented receptive state that fosters change. We grow up being able to trust if we have experienced a resonant 'we' during our early years; however, if we have not had that, then we develop a defensive stance. We may deny our own feelings, cut ourselves off from bodily sensations, rationalise why what is happening does not matter, or withdraw from others and convince ourselves we do not need anybody. With repeated violations of our trust, our defensive adaptations are woven into our personalities. So one of the first requirements of therapy is to create the emotional environment in which the patient can begin to develop trust. To create such an environment a therapist must bring his or her full self to the relationship with their patient.

Daniela: You write that out of a foundation of trust, truth emerges. What do you mean by truth?

Dan: Humans are story-telling animals. We make sense of our lives by creating narratives that connect past, present and future. Some of our stories are conscious; many are not. Some help us to understand our experiences in a valid way; others are the best that we could come up with at the time, but are deeply misleading. Our personal identities are wrapped up in these stories. They create hidden top-down models, within whose confines we live our lives, irrespective of whether they are valid or not. If, for example, our parents were not there for us and we made sense of that by deducing that we are unlovable, this shame-filled story becomes a belief about our fundamental nature, and like Matthew, we act accordingly.

Truth refers to seeing things as they really are. To do that we have to be free of the distortions we created to survive. Truth emerges when we link many layers of facts and experiences into an integrated whole. Truth may be painful, but it allows us to rest in what actually happened, rather than expand huge amounts of energy trying to avoid our reality. Truth acts as an infusion of energy that destabilises obsolete and rigid ways of being, bringing new life. Paradoxically, the truth, however painful, brings freedom and vitality.

Daniela: It is not only emotional truth that is healing; scientific truth can also be healing. When I learnt about attachment dynamics and about implicit memory, my understanding of myself changed. Instead of believing that I was inadequate because of how I sometimes behaved, I realised that I had implicitly learnt that behaviour as a way of adapting to my childhood. That healed some of my shame. It also gave me hope: if my behaviour was learnt, maybe I could learn to behave differently.

Dan: That is important. Understanding the brain fosters discernment. As you say, instead of thinking that we are inadequate for how we behave, we can begin to understand the biological meaning behind our behaviour and develop self-compassion. Also, at an interpersonal level, when something we read illuminates our inner world, we feel understood and less alone. There is a joining between author and reader which can be healing.

Daniela: Feeling felt, experiencing trust and discovering truth leads to the change that brings healing – are there other factors that we need to be aware of?

Dan: Lasting change requires growth and change in the neural structure of our brain. There are six main requirements for this; some we have already talked about.

1   *Novelty* provides the new experiences that are essential if we are to build new neural connections.
2   *Relationships*, either with others or with ourselves, re-shape the brain when they are meaningful.

3   *Aerobic exercise* may help the brain grow for many reasons, possibly including the enhanced release of 'brain derived neurotrophic factor', which facilitates the creation of new neural connections.
4   *Paying attention* leads to the release of both acetylcholine, and brain-derived neurotrophic factor, both of which facilitate the creation of new neural connections.
5   *Diet*, in particular Omega 3, is necessary to build new neural connections.
6   *Sleep* is when lasting synaptic change occurs, so it is important we get enough sleep.

Daniela: Can you talk more about how paying attention facilitates the creation of new neural structures, because this speaks to the importance of mindfulness?

Dan: When we focus our attention on something, the nerve cells in that area of the brain are activated. And the more activated a region is, the more it develops. Animals who are rewarded for noticing sound have expanded auditory centres. Violinists show dramatic growth in the regions of the cortex that represents the left hand, which must finger the strings precisely, often at high speed. Similarly, mindfulness practices focus our attention in ways that build up the integrative centres of the brain.

Daniela: Where do genes and temperament come into development?

Dan: Our personality emerges as our inborn, genetically influenced temperament interacts with parents, peers and teachers. Random events – in the womb, in our early years and later – also contribute in unpredictable ways to how we develop.

Temperament is highly heritable: around 50 per cent of our personality can be understood in terms of the genes that we inherit, including whether we are constitutionally shy, socially anxious and sensitive or whether we are more comfortable with novelty and extraverted. That said, our genetic inheritance is greatly influenced by the environment, and parents can either exacerbate a child's inherent tendencies or ameliorate them. For example, some parents (unconsciously) try to help their shy children by minimising their distress, and protecting them from novelty. In doing so, they reinforce the child's predisposition to see the world as a dangerous place that needs to be approached with extreme caution. In contrast, parents who support and encourage their shy children to explore new situations enable them to develop more outgoing and confident behaviour. As adults, such individuals will still have a greater physiological stress response to novelty and social situations, but their lives will not be constrained by their anxiety. Similarly, good therapy is about developing emotional security so that we can take pleasure in our makeup, not about changing our personalities.

Daniela: What happens as we start to take pleasure in our makeup, become increasingly mindful and integrated?

Dan: Instead of criticising ourselves, we look upon ourselves with compassion and openness and acceptance and love. We become our own best friend and develop an attachment status of earned security.

We are open to sensing what is happening in our body and to listening to its wisdom. We allow ourselves to feel all of our emotions, but we are not swept away by our emotions.

We free ourselves from the prison created by the implicit memories that were laid down during our childhoods. We start to live more fully in the present, responding to what is in front of us, rather than seeing it through a distorting, unconscious filter.

We are able to engage in meaningful relationships: we retain our individuality, allow the other person their individuality, but we can be open to the other's internal world, and allow ourselves to be moved by it.

We become aware of inhabiting a bigger world. Our identity as an individual does not disappear; rather, it expands and we see ourselves as part of an interconnected whole. We understand that we are a part of the human species, and a part of nature. We realise that we are connected to those who have lived before us and to those who will be born after us. Our circle of compassion widens. Many people believe that psychotherapy promotes self-indulgent naval-gazing, but in my experience the very opposite is true. As we become more secure and more integrated, we find ourselves wanting to give back to others.

We move from a closed rigid and/or chaotic system into an open and integrated system. That said, 'integration' should be seen as a verb, not a noun. We never get to the point where we can say that we are now integrated, and rest on our laurels. Rather, integration is an ever-unfolding process – a life-time project. Each new phase of our life, each new relationship and each new experience will offer us new opportunities for integration. If we shy away from those opportunities our lives will stagnate, but if we take those opportunities, then our internal world will become increasingly integrated and we will become wiser. I find that a really exciting prospect!

Part III
Evolutionary perspectives

8 Live fast, die young

An evolved response to hostile environments?

James S. Chisholm and Daniela F. Sieff

Summary

Early attachment relationships have long-lasting effects on developing minds and bodies. They influence our fear system and sexual development. They shape our attitudes to romantic relationships, our parenting style and how we see both ourselves and others. Typically, the trajectory that develops from being sensitively nurtured and securely attached is seen as normal and healthy, whereas the trajectory that follows from being inadequately nurtured and insecurely attached is seen as abnormal and unhealthy.

Modern evolutionary theory has a different perspective. No single trajectory is best for all individuals of a species; what is optimal in one environment is rarely optimal in a different one. In particular, it is now thought that the pathways described by secure attachment offered advantages to ancestral humans who were living in benign environments, whereas the pathways described by insecure attachment offered our ancestors more chance of surviving and reproducing in harsh physical environments or when social support was lacking.

For ancestral infants to develop along the pathway that would be most adaptive for them as individuals, they needed information about the environment into which they were born. The quality of parental nurturance provided that information in an implicit and embodied form. Parents are more attuned to their infants when living in benign environments and when they have plentiful social support, than when they are struggling. Thus, the quality of parental nurturance became the crucial, albeit unwitting, cue which influenced development.

The adaptive value of insecure attachment does not mean that it has no costs. It does. It creates profound suffering at both emotional and physical levels. However, for those of our ancestors who were born into harsh physical or social environments, that suffering was the price of surviving and bearing descendents.

Daniela Sieff: Your research has brought a modern evolutionary approach to child development – why is this important?

Jim Chisholm: Our species, being part of the natural world, has been shaped by natural selection. We are all the descendents of a long line of ancestors, each of whom managed to adapt to the challenges of their environment well enough to leave descendents. Our ancestors survived infancy and childhood. They learned how to find food and how to avoid being eaten by predators. They forged relationships with others of their own species. They attracted mates. And they raised at least some offspring who survived to have offspring of their own.

The adaptations that enabled our ancestors to leave descendents emerge as we move through infancy, childhood, adolescence and into adulthood. The emergence of these adaptations is the result of natural selection operating on the actual process of development itself. Evolution does not only shape traits like brain size or bipedalism; it also shapes developmental processes. Knowing how developmental processes have been influenced by considerations of survival and reproduction makes a valuable contribution to our understanding of how we become who we are.

Evolutionary knowledge also offers us a broad context in which to understand why some developmental trajectories lead to a life of well-being, whereas others lead to suffering. Moreover, an evolutionary perspective helps us to see what needs to be done to help people move away from the developmental trajectory that leads to suffering and onto the one that creates well-being.

Daniela: How has evolution shaped the actual process of development?

Jim: The basic instructions for building a creature like ourselves are created at conception. They come from ancestors in the form of genes. However, the genes that we inherit cannot know about the specifics of the environment into which we have been born, so mechanisms evolved that enabled young individuals to garner information about the local environment. This information is then used to direct development along the trajectory that will offer us the best chance of surviving and leaving descendents in a particular environment – or rather along the trajectory that offered our ancestors the best chance of surviving and leaving descendents in similar environments. In short, evolution has shaped development to be directed by the interplay between information that comes from the past (via our genes) and information that comes from the present (via our environment).

Among humans, one mechanism for acquiring information about the present is learning: the skills needed to survive in the Arctic are very different from those needed to survive in the African savannah, and it is through learning that these skills are acquired. However, evolution has resulted in equally important, albeit less familiar, mechanisms, through which information about the present can shape development. They operate at molecular levels to shape developing hormonal and nervous systems through what is now known as 'epigenetics'. They are particularly potent before birth and just afterwards. In fact, any interaction with the environment has an immediate effect on our nervous and hormonal systems, and it is through these effects that we are informed about the kind of environment we are living in.

What is more, we are changed by that information, and directed towards the developmental trajectory which offered our ancestors the best chance of surviving and reproducing in apparently similar conditions.

These (and other) evolved mechanisms, which acquire information about the present environment, create opportunities for developmental plasticity – the ability of an organism to take on different forms depending on the environment it encounters. Developmental plasticity does not mean that anything goes. Rather, the range of alternatives that exist in a particular species are the ones that have been selected by evolution because they gave ancestral individuals a better chance of surviving and reproducing in the specific environments which they commonly faced.

Daniela: How do today's evolutionary researchers think about the variety of alternative forms that result from developmental plasticity?

Jim: Early zoologists who studied animal behaviour were influenced by the philosophy of essentialism. 'Essentialism' – a cornerstone of Plato's world view – sees things as having an 'ideal type' and a fixed essence. For zoologists that meant identifying species-typical behaviours, which were seen as 'normal', whereas less common behaviours were seen as abnormal. In the essentialist paradigm there was little space for exploring the consequences of developmental plasticity. However, in the 1960s zoologists moved beyond the search for species-typical behaviours and began to study individual differences. As they did, they developed the concept of 'optimality'. Optimality does not mean the 'best imaginable', but rather the most adaptive form that can be lived by a particular individual in a specific environment. There is no a priori definition of 'optimal'; what is optimal and adaptive in one environment is likely to be suboptimal and maladaptive in another. Optimality thinking compelled researchers to go beyond what is 'average' and 'normal' for a species and look at the range of variation. It demanded the examination of potential adaptive function of individual differences, and of the developmental plasticity which lay behind such differences.

As an aside, 'adaptive', as used in modern biology, does not mean that the characteristic adaptations always alleviate suffering and promote well-being; it means that adaptations offer the individual the best chance of surviving and reproducing in that particular environment.

Let me give you an example of how optimality thinking helps us understand one aspect of development. The young of some species engage in play. Play has few immediate benefits and quite high costs in that it uses precious calories that are often hard to come by. However, play can have considerable future benefits: it increases neural interconnectivity and animals that play as juveniles tend to be more adaptable and flexible as adults. They are more motivated to explore their environments, better able to switch between different behaviour patterns and have a greater capacity to reverse previous learning and engage in new learning. Animals that are in good condition play more. That makes evolutionary sense because youngsters who have plentiful resources are likely to have a relatively long life, and therefore they have a great capacity to benefit *in the future* from the delayed effects of play. In contrast, animals in poor condition play less. This, too, is evolutionarily prudent. When resources are scarce, it makes little sense to use precious calories to fuel play, when that might leave an animal malnourished and without the energy needed to fight disease or to grow. Additionally, animals that are in a poor condition are less likely to survive long enough to reap the long-term benefits of play. In short, from a modern evolutionary perspective, there is no one ideal pattern of play – what is optimal depends on the environment in which the individual is living, and the trade-offs necessary to survive and reproduce in that environment.

The dynamics surrounding play are observed in a myriad of species, including humans. Emotionally secure human children engage in more play and exploration (especially social play and exploration) than children who are not secure in their relationships to their caregivers. Moreover, emotionally secure children are the ones whose caregivers are attuned to them, and so in ancestral environments would have had the best chance of surviving. However, the issue is not the narrow one of whether there is abundance or a shortage of early resources that affects play. Rather, the important issue is the wider one of how certain early experiences move the developing organism along a developmental route that is *optimal* for the conditions it can expect to encounter in later life.

Daniela: You were one of the first people to argue that human developmental trajectories have evolved to be particularly sensitive to the level of danger in the environment. Why is danger so important?

Jim: A crucial adaptive problem for any species, but especially for our slow-developing, long-lived, highly intelligent and intensely social species, is that of environmental uncertainty, risk and danger. Every single one of our direct ancestors managed to negotiate the uncertainty and danger that was embedded in both their physical and social environments. Every one of them managed to survive long enough to grow up and to bear at least some children who then managed to survive and bear surviving children of their own.

There was considerable variation in the level and types of danger faced by our ancestors. Some were born in times and places where there were few predators, little disease and plentiful food. Others were born where predators were common, disease was prevalent or food was scarce.

Some of our ancestors were born to healthy mothers who found it relatively easy to secure the resources needed to nurture their children; others were born to mothers who were challenged by poor health or inadequate social support.

Humans are unique among primates in that they do not become self-sufficient once weaned; instead they continue to depend on adults for food for many years after weaning. Among our early human ancestors, mothers provided the bulk of that food but other adults – including fathers, grandmothers, aunts and cousins – made vital contributions. Consequently, those of our ancestors who were born to mothers with a large and supportive social network grew up in a more benign environment than those born to mothers with only a small social network.

Finally, some of our ancestors were born with qualities that meant that their mothers were particularly committed to them. Others were born small and sickly, or of an unwanted sex, or too soon after an existing child, and as a result their mothers would have been less committed to them.

Irrespective of the specific risks, being able to sense how benign or dangerous the environment was, and being able to follow a trajectory that could respond to that danger, would have been evolutionarily adaptive in that it would have increased the chance of surviving and of leaving descendants (who would then inherit the faculty to travel down a similar pathway in similar conditions).

Daniela: One system whose development is especially sensitive to cues of danger is the fear system: if our early environment indicates that the environment is dangerous then our fear system becomes more reactive than if we appear to have been born into a relatively benign environment. How can an evolutionary approach help us to understand this?

Jim: An evolutionary approach encourages us to explore whether these differences in reactivity might be adaptive. Some of the most informative research comes from Michael Meaney's group. These scientists compared the development of two different groups of rat pups: one group was the offspring of attentive and nurturing mothers; the other was the offspring of mothers who spent comparatively little time nurturing their young. In the wild, rat mothers who are stressed are less caring and they become stressed when a high number of predators bring danger into their environment.

When these two groups of pups became adults those raised by less nurturing mothers were more fearful and less likely to explore open spaces than those raised by more nurturing mothers. The system that mediates the fear response, including the fight–flight reaction, is called the hypothalamic-pituitary-adrenal (HPA) system, and includes parts of the nervous system as well as certain hormonal processes. Meaney's team showed that pups nurtured by less attentive mothers had an HPA system that was sensitised to make them more reactive to fear, and they identified the molecular pathways involved in sensitisation. The scientists then concluded that having a highly reactive HPA system rather than being maladaptive, actually gave these rats a better chance of surviving in a dangerous environment where predators are common.

A very similar dynamic occurs in humans. In both traditional and modern societies, a mother who is stressed (often because she is struggling to secure resources or because she has little social support) is less attentive to her infant than a mother who is not stressed. As a result of her lack of attentiveness, her infant's HPA system will be repeatedly activated. Repeated activation of an infant's HPA system then 'in-forms' the infant that the environment is dangerous, and sets the infant on the developmental pathway that results in a fear system that is calibrated for a dangerous environment. As a result the individual will have a heightened awareness of danger, as well as a quicker reaction when danger is present.

That said, although a sensitised fear system would have been evolutionarily adaptive for ancestors who were living in particularly uncertain and dangerous environments, having an HPA system that is adapted to danger can bring severe costs in terms of subjective well-being and long-term health. A highly reactive

HPA system compromises the immune system, meaning that adults are more susceptible to a range of diseases from cancer to the common cold. A highly reactive HPA system also increases the risk of having problems with cognitive function and can lead to the loss of neurons in an area of the brain called the hippocampus (which is crucial to memory). Additionally, it increases the likelihood of suffering from anxiety disorders and depression.

Another cost of being sensitised to danger is being continually on the lookout for possible threats. That compromises mental and physical well-being in and of itself. It also means there is limited 'spare capacity' to invest in activities that will contribute to a sense of well-being, such as play, creativity and healthy relationships. Moreover, when on the look-out for danger it is all too easy to see threats when they do not exist, and to create self-fulfilling prophecies.

However, most of these costs kick in later in life, so in a dangerous environment, when what matters is surviving long enough to have children, the costs are evolutionarily worth paying, irrespective of the suffering they cause. In safe and predictable environments the benefits of being sensitised to threats are not worth the future costs and it would be more adaptive if our developmental trajectory is one that entails less reactivity to danger.

Daniela: Patterns of reproduction are also shaped by the levels of danger in an individual's early environment – how can evolution help us understand this dynamic?

Jim: There is considerable variation between species in how early they become sexually mature, how young they are when they start reproducing, how choosy they are about their mates, how big their babies are, how long they breast feed, how long the interval is between offspring and how many offspring they have in total. Individuals within any particular species also vary along all of these dimensions, albeit remaining within the range that is possible for their species. The branch of modern evolution that explores the possible adaptive value of these variations is called 'Life History Theory'.

The fundamental premise of Life History Theory is that the life cycle, and the developmental processes that underlie it, has been subject to natural selection. Thus we can explore the variation in the life cycle by asking evolutionarily informed questions. One of the most important questions is: will an individual be likely to leave more descendants if she/he waits longer before having children and then has few children to whom she/he commits a considerable amount of care, or is an individual likely to leave more descendants if she/he starts reproducing as early as possible and has many children to whom she/he can offer only limited care? In essence this question is about how to best allocate limited resources in order to leave descendants. Years of research, across many different species, has shown that the life history pattern that will result in most descendants varies depending on how dangerous the environment is.

All other things being equal, in a comparatively safe environment, where relatively few children die before adulthood, an individual will leave more descendants (children, grandchildren, great-grandchildren, etc.) if she follows a reproductive trajectory that is oriented to the long term, which means having a few offspring who are healthy, strong and adaptable. The reason why this pattern results in more descendants in a relatively safe environment is that when mortality is low the population expands until it reaches the maximum that can be supported in that environment. At that point, there will be fierce competition for resources, and thus individuals will leave more descendants if they produce highly competitive offspring who can secure those resources.

To produce healthy, strong and competitive offspring a mother needs to take her time before she starts to bear children. During most of our evolutionary history energy, in the form of calories, was limited and so the bodies of teenagers could either use any available calories to fuel their own continued growth, or they could use those calories to produce children. Delaying reproduction so as to continue growing for longer has a long-term pay-off in a world that is relatively benign: larger women produce large, healthy infants who not only have a better chance of surviving, but they also tend to grow into healthy children and adults. Starting reproduction relatively late also allows a woman more time to develop greater knowledge of the local environment and better food-collecting skills. It also gives her (or sometimes her parents) more opportunities to select a high-quality mate who will be able to help with provisioning the youngsters and it gives her more time in which to establish a supportive social network. A woman can also raise stronger, healthier and more competitive children if she has a few children who are widely spaced, because that enables her to commit more resources and care to each child. Because of the relatively late onset of reproduction, and the greater spacing between births, this pattern is sometimes called a 'slow life history', and it is oriented towards the long term.

In contrast, in a relatively dangerous or unpredictable environment where mortality is high, a mother will leave more descendants if she follows a 'fast life history' that is oriented to the short term. That means truncating her own growth and starting to bear children as early as is physically possible, and then having the maximum number of children that she can bear, even if there are not enough resources to make each child successful (or indeed contented). The reason why this is evolutionarily adaptive in a dangerous environment is because the longer an individual waits before starting to reproduce, the greater the chance of dying before bearing children, and from the perspective of evolution, dying without issue is a dead end. Also, when the environment is dangerous and there is little that parents can do about the dangers, then investing a lot of time and energy into only a few children is risky because they may all die. Under these circumstances, parents are more likely to leave at least some descendants if they have as many children as possible, because that gives them more tickets in what is essentially a lottery.

We see both the 'fast' and 'slow' variations in a myriad of non-human species, among humans who are living traditional lives, and also in modern environments. For example, there is great inequality between neighbourhoods in many American cities, and one study of 77 neighbourhoods in Chicago found that in neighbourhoods where life-expectancy was short, a much higher proportion of women had given birth as teenagers. This finding has been replicated in other populations in the USA and in the UK. The problem of teenage pregnancy is one that many Western governments try to address, but without an evolutionary perspective there is no context in which to understand the motivating forces.

Daniela: How are the different reproductive trajectories mediated?

Jim: The age at which girls start menstruating (which is called menarche) is a significant biological event because it marks the moment when resources that were being used for growth and development are now re-allocated to reproduction. The age of menarche is partially determined by the genes that a girl inherits; however, more than a score of studies have reported that in addition to genetic effects there is a correlation between early stress and early menarche. In environments that are perceived to be threatening, all other things being equal, girls are physiologically shifted towards the fast trajectory. The age at which boys start to become reproductive is harder to measure because it requires invasive techniques to collect hormones, but evidence is beginning to mount that boys also become sexually mature earlier if they suffered stress early in their lives.

The work of Meaney's group on rats points to the mechanisms that underlie this. Rat pups who are cared for by less nurturing mothers are like humans in that they become reproductive at younger ages, and interestingly, the HPA system plays a crucial role in calibrating the system that is responsible for the timing of sexual maturity. A relatively low level of HPA activation means that the system responsible for the timing of puberty kicks in relatively late, whereas a high level of HPA activation accelerates the hormonal changes that initiate puberty.

The link between these two systems makes sense: it would have been adaptive for those of our ancestors who were living in a benign environment to have had a relatively resilient fear system and to be on the slow reproductive trajectory, whereas in a dangerous or stressful environment it would be adaptive for them to have had both a highly reactive fear system and to be on the fast reproductive trajectory.

Daniela: In today's world, these two trajectories are sometimes separated. Some groups of people who have experienced their environment as dangerous go for the slow reproductive trajectory and try to produce ultra-competitive children who will be safe because they are high-achieving and respected, yet they have fear systems that are highly sensitised and live with a constant feeling of danger. I am thinking of Holocaust survivors – many of whom brought up their children to live in a dangerous environment, but who invested heavily in a few children and placed huge value on education and achievement. There are probably other groups as well.

Jim: Absolutely. In the modern world there are more routes to apparent safety than there were in the past. In addition, we all have a deep need to belong to a group, and so there may be a tension between what is evolutionarily optimal in terms of reproductive strategies, and what is evolutionarily optimal in terms of remaining within the group and within its values. Evolution is always about trade-offs! That said, for our ancestors there would have been fewer opportunities to uncouple these two systems (if only because there was no contraception) and so for them, and for nearly every other species we know about, the reproductive trajectory would generally have been linked to the fear system.

Daniela: Do the fast and slow reproductive life history patterns differ in terms of their effect on our health and subjective experience of well-being?

Jim: Unfortunately, yes. From the perspective of evolution, neither the fast nor slow reproductive pattern is better than the other, neither is 'biologically normal' or 'evolutionarily adaptive'; rather what is 'normal' and adaptive depends on the environment. However, in terms of an individual's health and well-being, there can be severe costs to the fast life history for both mothers and their children.

Copious data collected in Western societies show that women who go through early menarche have an increased risk of reproductive cancers, depression, addiction and delinquency. These women also tend to be shorter (in part because they have stopped growing early in order to divert resources into reproduction), but they are relatively heavy and prone to obesity. Also, when women begin childbearing at a young age their education and career opportunities are typically cut short.

Data also show that, on average, young mothers give birth to smaller babies, and small babies have a greater chance of dying during infancy. Even if they survive, small babies grow into adults who suffer an increased risk of heart disease, hypertension and diabetes later in life. Additionally, the children of women who follow a fast pattern tend to get less emotional and material support, in part because the mother has not yet had time to accrue resources, and also because any available resources are shared between a greater number of closely spaced children. As a result, in the West, these children are less likely to graduate from high school, more likely to be dependent on public financial support, and will tend to accelerate the birth of their own first child compared to children of mothers who are older.

The deep tragedy built into this system is that once it is in place, it sets the stage for a potentially vicious, self-perpetuating intergenerational cycle of risk and uncertainty – with the danger no longer necessarily coming from the outside environment, but now coming from the (young) parents themselves.

In sum, when our evolved bodies perceive that the probability of producing descendants is low, the optimal reproductive pattern is to follow the fast reproductive pathway; to become pregnant early, and to bear many children. It is a pathway that typically brings real suffering and which instigates a vicious spiral that spans generations, but from the perspective of evolution that is simply the cost of continuing. Evolution is about producing descendants, not well-being. Extinction, as they say, is forever.

Daniela: What other aspects of human behaviour are sensitive to the environment into which an individual has been born?

Jim: Physical growth and psychological development are both sensitive to the relative safety of an infant's early environment. Infants who are 'in-formed' by sensitive mothering that the environment is safe generally do better in the realms of physical growth, cognitive-perceptual development and social-emotional development. An evolutionary perspective can help us to understand why: being relatively sure of the future, these children will have an evolutionary advantage if they allocate resources to maximising the quality of their development, rather than channelling resources into reproduction as soon as possible.

Self-control is another domain that is sensitive to early experiences. Self-control depends on the ability to delay gratification – to bypass an immediate reward in order to secure a greater benefit in the future. It can be thought of as an investment in the future. As we have already seen, investing in the future pays off when the environment is safe and we can be relatively sure that we will still be around in the future. However, if the future is risky, then it is unwise to make long-term investments and it is better to try to grab things as soon as they become available. In the industrial world, those who live in poverty are chronically oriented to the present. The propensity to take risks is not restricted to those who live in poverty: it may apply to anyone who perceives that their life is relatively risky, whether that risk is real or imagined. Middle-class US college students who expect to have short life spans relative to their peers report taking greater risks sexually, financially and with their social relationships. In one experiment with children, those who were the most emotionally secure could wait longest for a reward, whereas those who were the least secure had most difficulty waiting.

Empathy is also a characteristic whose development is influenced by the early environment. Those who grow up in a tough environment are often less empathetic. There are several factors that contribute to this, including, possibly, the ability to delay gratification. Empathy requires that we put aside our own feelings and take the time to feel what another is feeling, if only for an instant. That has long-term benefits in that we can better deduce what is going on for the other person, and we are better able to build the kind of social bonds that will bring us benefits in the long term. However, putting aside our own feelings, and allowing somebody else's feelings into our inner world, is risky in a dangerous environment. We risk feeling their pain, we risk feeling their dislike of us, and most dangerous of all, we delay our ability to react. In most environments the small delay would not matter, but in an uncertain and dangerous environment, delay can be a matter of life or death.

Daniela: Recent research shows that when environmental conditions are tough or parental care is lacking, children are more likely to use aggression and bullying to obtain resources for themselves. The researchers argue that in the environment in which we evolved, children who struggled to secure resources (for whatever reason) might have increased their chances of survival through the use of bullying.

Jim: That makes sense to me. It also concurs with the patterns of aggression that we see in adults. From an evolutionary perspective, the function of aggression is to create fear in others in the implicit hope that they will then give us the resources that might ultimately contribute to our ability to leave descendants. Those resources might be material, for example cattle or money, or they might be social, for example reputation and status.

Using aggression is risky because we might just get hurt and lose the very resources that we are seeking. However, when the environment is already dangerous and the future is uncertain, it may be evolutionarily prudent to take risks in order to have at least some chance of leaving descendants.

This is one reason why violence is concentrated among young men from the poorest parts of society. In terms of leaving descendants, being young and male is risky in and of itself. The number of children that a woman can bear is limited by the need to carry a nine-month pregnancy to term and, throughout our evolutionary past, to breast-feed for an average of two and a half years. However, all else being equal, the number of children that a man can father is limited by the number of women that he can inseminate. That means some men might father many children with several different women, whereas other men might father none. When men are young, they do not know if they are going to be one of the males who fathers children or one who does not. That is particularly true for those who come from relatively impoverished sections of the population and who have limited opportunities to secure the resources that will make them attractive as husbands or fathers. As a result, it makes – or made – evolutionary sense for young males to take risks to gain the resources that could increase their chances of fathering children.

For example, Canadian researchers Margo Wilson and Margin Daly studied 500 homicide cases. Those who killed were overwhelmingly young, unmarried men who were unemployed, poor and undereducated. Most homicides involved ostensibly trivial altercations that escalated into murder when one or both felt that their honour had been challenged – that they had been disrespected – so felt they had 'nothing left to lose'. Wilson and Daly proposed that the contingencies of being male, young and poor created an embodied sense that the future was uncertain and they suggested that could be the developmental trigger that increased a young male's motivation to engage in aggressive and risky activities.

In another study, researchers enrolled over 200 male teenagers living in an inner-city housing project to complete an anonymous questionnaire in which they were asked the degree to which they expected to be alive at 25, and also about their use of violence. Those who were most confident of being alive at 25 had never used violence.

At an implicit level we know this pattern – it is encapsulated in the phrase 'Live fast, die young' – although an evolutionary perspective suggests this phrase is back-to-front! When our ancestors had a high risk of dying young, the most evolutionary prudent thing for them to do was to live fast.

Daniela: How do young animals, including humans, 'know' whether they have been born into a benign or a dangerous environment?

Jim: Young animals acquire information about the kind of environment that they have been born into from those individuals who form their immediate environment. That is first and foremost their mother, but can also include other caregivers including their father.

Individuals start to acquire this information in the womb. If a mother is stressed or anxious while pregnant, she will have elevated levels of the stress hormone cortisol, some of which will cross the placenta and enter the foetus' bloodstream. High levels of cortisol act as information about the world into which the foetus will be born, and in response to this cortisol the foetal HPA system starts to become more sensitive and reactive. By the time these infants are born, they are already physiologically prepared for life in a dangerous environment.

This process continues after birth, only now the quality of the relationship between mother and infant is the conduit for this information. John Bowlby was the first person to realise that infants of all mammal species, including humans, are born with a drive to become emotionally attached to their caregivers. As we have already seen, mothers living in benign environments are better able to respond in a sensitive and attuned manner to their infants' attachment needs than mothers living in hostile environments. Of course, the infant, whether it be a rat infant or a human infant, does not consciously think *'My mum is attuned and therefore the environment must be relatively benign'* or *'My mum is not very attuned – that must mean that she is struggling and that the environment is hostile and I better prepare myself for it!'* Rather, if caregivers are responsive, then the infant's stress system will not be repeatedly activated and the infant will head down the developmental trajectory that is described by a relatively resilient fear response, a slow life history and a subjective sense of inner security. However, when caregivers fail to be responsive, the infant's stress system will be repeatedly activated, and as a result the infant will move towards the developmental pathway that embodies a more reactive fear system, a fast life history trajectory and a subjective sense of insecurity – all of which leave the individual better adapted to a dangerous environment.

Once infants become toddlers, they begin to garner information about risk and uncertainty through direct engagement with their environment. Whether the perceived danger takes the form of food shortages, illness, a preponderance of predators or aggression from other humans, there will be a secondary impact on the stress system, on the cascade of systems that unfold from that, and on the subjective inner experience of security or insecurity.

Children have also evolved to perceive danger when there are few people they can turn to for help. A path-breaking study in the Dominican Republic found significantly higher cortisol levels in the children of single mothers without adequate kin support than in the children of single mothers who did have social support.

High local death rates suggest the environment is hostile and we now have data showing that all other things being equal, children who experience the death of someone who lives in close physical proximity are more likely to head down the developmental trajectory (including earlier menarche) that is best suited to a dangerous environment, compared to similar children who do not have a direct experience of death.

There is also considerable evidence that the absence of a father hastens menarche in girls and pushes boys towards a developmental trajectory that is characterised by a reactive fear system, an exploitative attitude towards women and a propensity to aggression and violence. In other words, the absence of a father leads to children growing up to follow the fast life history and all that goes with it. These patterns have been recorded in Western cultures (particularly among the poorest strata) and in traditional herding and horticultural societies which are prone to raiding livestock.

The pattern observed in boys is so obvious that long before evolutionary theory addressed this phenomenon, social anthropologists and sociologists named it 'The Absent Father Syndrome'. In the West the behaviour associated with 'The Absent Father Syndrome' is seen as problematic, whereas in these small-scale raiding societies it is seen as desirable. The fact that the behavioural consequences of father absence are the same for boys in these very different social and ecological contexts suggests that it represents the outcome of a naturally selected capacity to develop in different ways according to the presence or absence of a father or father-like person. It is as if the absence of a father 'tells' young boys that they have been born into a tough environment where resources are hard to come by, and violence is rife. But, of course, there is a built-in circularity in this phenomenon: growing up without a father means that there is no male to protect and help provision the child and so the child's environment is intrinsically more dangerous.

The Shel Silverstein lyrics of the Johnny Cash ballad 'A Boy Named Sue' capture this dynamic. A father, just before walking out on his wife and toddler, names his son 'Sue'. As a result, the boy is teased horribly, grows up fast and becomes a mean fighter. On reaching adulthood Sue goes looking for his father; he wants to kill him in revenge for the trouble that being named Sue has caused him. Sue eventually finds his father, and attacks him. His father fights back. When they get to the stage of pulling guns on each other, Sue's father pauses and smiles; he then says that it is a rough world, that men have to be tough to make it, and that because he was not going to be there to help his son he named him Sue, knowing that would force his son to grow up tough.

Daniela: Early attachment dynamics affect not only physiology, but also how we come to see our caregivers and then are subsequently generalised to other people. Why have our minds evolved to develop in this way?

Jim: Through the tens of thousands of cycles of interaction between caregiver and infant over the first few years, the infant creates an unconscious expectation about how his caregiver will respond to him. Bowlby called such expectations 'internal working models' and argued that over time they are generalised to include not only caregivers, but adult romantic relations and relations with one's own children, and even social relations in general. The working models include implicit beliefs about whether the infant is lovable, worthy of support and able to affect others enough to get help or comfort when needed. These unconscious expectations about relationships are believed to be represented in the infant's emotional brain in the form of developing neural pathways connecting the amygdala, hippocampus and related structures with the prefrontal cortex.

The evolutionary significance of internal working models is that they help the infant to predict how mother, or mother-like people, are likely to behave. Our survival, growth and eventual reproduction depend on material resources such as food and protection, but for mammalian infants access to these resources is always by way of mother. Human infants are born into a particularly vulnerable position: alone among the primates, human mothers give birth to subsequent offspring while the preceding child still needs mother (and others) to provide food. This means that only human mothers have to decide which child is the better beneficiary of their limited resources. Additionally, as Sarah Hrdy has shown us,[1] there are good evolutionary reasons why human mothers may sometimes commit infanticide or abandon their offspring. In other words, throughout our evolutionary history infants were never assured of receiving the care needed to survive. Selection is therefore expected to have favoured the neurobiological mechanisms that enabled our infant ancestors to create internal working models of self–mother relations. After all, the better an infant was at predicting mother's behaviour, and adjusting their own behaviour accordingly, the more likely they were to survive.

Daniela: Why might the internal working models formed during infancy be generalised to adult romantic relationships, and to parenting children?

Jim: There is a suite of elements that contribute to living either a fast or a slow life history trajectory. Our romantic relationships, as well as how we parent our children, form part of that suite.

Those who are classified as 'secure' children generally go on to be classified as 'secure' adults. Compared to those adults who are classified as insecurely attached, they are older when they enter romantic relationships and more choosy about their partners. Once in a relationship they are less likely to be promiscuous, and their relationships are more likely to be long-lasting. They are more apt to describe their romantic relationships as happy, friendly and trusting. They are also more attentive to their own offspring.

This pattern of romantic relationships and parenting is congruent with the 'slow' reproductive trajectory which is adaptive in safe environments. Being older when entering romantic relationships is, as we have seen, intrinsic to the slow reproductive trajectory. Being picky about one's partner can be seen as an attempt to choose the best mate to father/mother one's children – where 'best' means the mate that will help children to be as competitive – successful in love and work – as possible. For the most part the choice of mates is unconscious and reflects two different concerns. First, an individual is expected to 'want' a mate who has 'good genes' – meaning outward signs of health, strength, intelligence, sociability and so forth. Second, an individual is expected to want a mate who will be able to secure adequate resources, generously share them with children and also remain faithful. In short, the pattern of romantic relationships typically followed by those who are classified as secure are conducive to providing maximum nurturance to a few children who will grow up to be highly competitive, in the best sense of that word.

In contrast, adults who are classified as insecure tend to be younger when they first enter romantic relationships and less picky when choosing partners. They tend to have more sexual partners and their relationships generally do not last as long. They are apt to describe their romantic relationships in terms that suggest extreme sexual attraction but limited emotional intimacy and lack of trust.

---

1 Sieff: see Sarah Blaffer Hrdy (Chapter 9) in this volume.

These traits are congruent with the 'fast' reproductive pattern, adaptive in harsh or unpredictable environments. Engaging in romantic relationships earlier and being less picky are symptomatic of 'living fast' and being focused on the short term. And the bias against monogamy under impoverished environmental conditions is rooted in the fact that it is simply not in men's or women's interests. When the environment is dangerous and life-expectancy is short, relying on a single man makes little sense because he may die before his children reach independence. Even if he stays alive, a single man may be unable to secure enough resources to provision his family, and women may secure more resources by maintaining relationships with more than one man. In the Dominican Republic study I mentioned earlier, some children lived in monogamous two-parent families and others in female-headed households where women had relationships with more than one man at a time. When these two types of families were compared, women in female-headed households had healthier children, fewer pre- and post-natal medical complications, more surviving children to age five, more protein per capita in their children's diets and better psychological health. That said, these kinds of family structures frequently occur in a context of three or more generations of women in extended families, where grandmothers and other female relatives are available to help with child-care.

Daniela: How does a modern evolutionary perspective see Bowlby's conceptualisation of attachment?

Jim: Bowlby's insights are seen as profoundly important. Bowlby broke new ground not only in articulating attachment dynamics, but also with his insistence that we need to understand the environment in which it evolved. Bowlby coined the term 'environment of evolutionary adaptiveness' (EEA) to denote that environment, and his clarity regarding the importance of evolution effectively made him the first evolutionary psychologist. However, there are some elements of attachment theory that can be updated. In particular, modern evolutionary theory has a very different way of thinking about the long-term trajectories embodied in insecure attachment.

Bowlby believed that sensitive, responsive mothers and their securely attached infants were nature's prototypes, and that insecure attachment was essentially abnormal, maladaptive and a disorder. His belief accorded with the essentialism that infused zoology at the time. It was also rooted in an implicit assumption that the environment in which we evolved was, apart from predators, relatively benign (in which case secure attachment would indeed have been most adaptive). However, when essentialism gave way to the optimality paradigm in the mid 1960s, researchers realised that they needed to look beyond some species-specific, apparently normal standard and so they began to study individual differences in the development of attachment. They also began to explore how attachment dynamics unfolded in different social-cultural, ecological and historical contexts.

In addition, in the last 20 years we have discovered that the environment in which our species evolved was anything but stable and benign. In fact, crucial periods of human evolution occurred during periods of rapid climatic fluctuations, with some decades being relatively benevolent while others were extremely harsh. At one point, environmental instability made life for our ancestors so difficult that our numbers dropped to below 10,000 individuals in total, and our species almost became extinct. Even when the environment was more stable, it is estimated that between 40 and 50 per cent of children died before becoming adults. Also, it now seems certain that the main threat facing ancestral infants was not predators, but rather the infant's parents – who at times, because of their circumstances, were unable or unwilling to care for particular children.

As a result of these discoveries, today's evolutionary researchers reject the idea that insecure attachment is a disorder or even abnormal, even though it does bring suffering. According to the modern perspective, there is no 'normal' pattern of attachment. Instead, parents unwittingly create the emotional environment which will predispose their children to develop along the pathway that, during our evolutionary history at least, would have given them the best chance of adapting to the environment into which they had been born. Secure attachment develops as an adaptation to consistently sensitive and responsive parenting because in the environment in which we evolved, sensitive and responsible parenting was reliable evidence that parents possessed both the resources and motivation to nurture offspring for extended periods. Insecure attachment develops as an adaptation to what we call insensitive, intrusive, unresponsive or rejecting parenting because for our ancestors this style of parental behaviour was reliable evidence that parents were unable or unwilling (not necessarily consciously) to nurture offspring and/or that the environment was dangerous.

In other words, a modern evolutionary approach sees informing the infant of the kind of environment that he or she has been born into as one of the functions of attachment. This does not negate Bowlby's ideas; rather, it is an expansion of Bowlby's view that parental care is fundamentally about protecting children from environmental risk and uncertainty by providing them with resources. Bowlby saw those resources as consisting of energy, nutrients, temperature regulation and protection – particularly from predators; today's evolutionary thinking views information about the intentions of caregivers as well as information about the levels of danger in the wider social and physical environment as an equally crucial resource.

Daniela: Mary Ainsworth and John Bowlby identified two sub-types of insecure attachment: avoidant attachment and ambivalent attachment. Avoidant attachment generally results from being looked after by uninvolved, distant caregivers and these children tend to become avoidant of their caregivers, overly self-sufficient and unlikely to form intimate relationships. In contrast, ambivalent attachment generally results from being looked after by inconsistent caregivers who are sometimes attuned, sometimes distant and sometimes intrusive. These children tend to become hyper-focused on caregivers and somewhat 'clingy'. You have suggested that an evolutionary framework can help us to understand why these two patterns exist.

Jim: It is possible that they are adaptations that have evolved for solving different problems. In the environment in which we evolved there were two persistent (and not mutually exclusive) threats to youngsters: (1) parents' *inability* to commit to a child, and (2) parents' (not necessarily conscious) *unwillingness* to commit. The two different insecure attachment patterns may be tailored to these two different threats.

For insecure-avoidant children, the immediate reason to avoid caregivers is to avoid the pain felt when rejected. However, for our ancestral infants frequent rejection may have been a reliable indicator of a caregiver's relative unwillingness to care, because she/he preferred to care for already existing children, or to bear more children. In that case there would have been little point in hanging round the caregivers and a great deal of benefit in becoming as self-sufficient as possible.

In contrast, for insecure-ambivalent children the immediate reason to be overly focused on their caregiver is that she/he is inconsistent and the child cannot be sure of what she/he will do next. However, from an evolutionary perspective, such inconsistency may have been a reliable indicator of a mother's relative inability to nurture her child because of a lack of resources, and a child's preoccupation may have been an adaptation for staying close so as to nab any resources that did become available.

When I developed this hypothesis there were no data to support it, but Tanya Behne and her colleagues showed that infants as young as nine months could distinguish between the unwillingness of a caregiver to hand them a toy, and the inability of a caregiver to do so. Obviously, this does not prove my hypothesis, but it suggests that it is a viable idea which could benefit from more research.

Daniela: Does a modern evolutionary perspective affect how we define pathology in the context of development?

Jim: It does, and in a very unpalatable way. The grim fact of nature is that under harsh and dangerous conditions, what we define as pathological may in fact be, or at least once was, normal and adaptive, in that it allowed insecure ancestral infants to survive and reproduce. Evolution is a natural process that keeps itself going through reproduction. It is driven by the fact that individuals have different numbers of surviving offspring. Any characteristic – physical or behavioural – that enabled our ancestors to have more surviving offspring than their fellows will have spread, irrespective of whether it brought well-being or suffering.

Nobody likes suffering, but suffering may just have been the cost of reproduction in risky or uncertain environments. When the future was risky, the most evolutionarily adaptive pattern was to be hyper-vigilant, to grab hold of whatever resources were available and to convert them into children as quickly as possible – to live life as if there is no tomorrow. The costs in terms of physical health and emotional well-being are often so desperate that we call these pathways 'pathological', but from an evolutionary perspective, had our ancestors not paid these costs, we would not exist.

Daniela: Can an evolutionary perspective suggest how we might combat the suffering caused by our adaptations to a dangerous environment?

Jim: Absolutely! We now know that we – and animals in general, incidentally – have evolved to be reliably affected by the relative levels of danger, risk and uncertainty in the environment in which we develop. If we experience our environment as being relatively low in risk and uncertainty (and if we develop an implicit confidence that we can secure the resources that we need for life) then, for very good evolutionary reasons, we are likely to end up on a developmental pathway that will allow us to develop a healthy fear system – rather than a hyper-sensitised one, and a concordant subjective experience of inner security. We are also likely to be oriented towards the long term and to follow a slow life history trajectory, with all the advantages in physical and psychological well-being which that brings. Children will play more, they will develop greater empathy and they will be less likely to grow into sexually impulsive adults. Conversely, if we experience our environment as high in uncertainty and danger, and if we have little opportunity or ability to reduce that risk, then there are good evolutionary reasons to devalue the future and orient ourselves to the short term, even though the result is both physical and emotional suffering. Thus, evolution tells us in no uncertain terms that reducing environmental risk and uncertainty would make a very real difference.

It is not just changing the absolute level of danger and uncertainly that will make a difference – we need to tackle inequality, too. Those at the bottom of any hierarchy invariably experience their environment as relatively more risky than those at the top, simply because they have less power to affect their own lives.

The idea that we need to create environments in which people can move from the fast to the slow life trajectory is in line with the thinking of Marta Nussbaum, a philosopher. She sees three broad ways that a human life can be lived:

1   A life so impoverished that it is not a human life at all, for instance, the state of some people at the end of their lives where they lose consciousness.
2   A human life, in which we possess the minimum that we need to think of our life as human – that is, we are just managing to subsist.
3   A good human life, in which we have good health, adequate nourishment and shelter; opportunities to imagine, think, reason, play, laugh and learn; relationships with people who we can love and who love us; empathy for other people and concern for the rest of nature.

Nussbaum exhorts the moral importance of enabling as many people as possible to cross the threshold from living a 'human life' to living a 'good human life'. I agree, and I would argue that this is the same as crossing the threshold from following the developmental trajectory that has evolved to enable us to survive and leave descendants in a dangerous and unpredictable environment, to following the trajectory that is evolutionarily optimal in a relatively safe and predictable environment.

Daniela: What are the therapeutic implications of this modern evolutionary perspective?

Jim: First, an evolutionary perspective compels us to question our assumptions about normality and pathology and to recognise that such questions have important therapeutic implications. An evolutionary perspective forces us to accept that it is impossible to define normality and pathology unless we specify the environment in which it occurs. Modern evolutionary theory emphasises that attachment does not take place in a vacuum. An infant's environment is that of his or her caregivers, but caregivers are inescapably embedded in a more extensive physical and social environment, and the relative danger or benevolence of that wider environment will have an influence on how they attend to their children. It is true that parents who have followed the fast life history create relatively insecure environments for their children, irrespective of what is happening in the wider world, but that is only one aspect of attachment dynamics and a modern evolutionary perspective shows us that to gain a fuller understanding of attachment (and of what may or may not be normal), then the wider environment must also be taken into account.

Second, an evolutionary perspective forces us to acknowledge that our nature was not shaped by the need to create well-being, but rather by the need to leave descendants. Had our ancestors not left descendants we would not exist. The developmental adaptations that enabled ancestral humans to leave descendants in conditions of chronic risk and uncertainty typically diminish well-being and entail suffering. If the goal of therapy is to increase well-being – but if evolution centres on producing descendants rather than well-being – then effective therapy is ultimately contingent on understanding how these forces may pull in different directions.

Finally, an evolutionary perspective tells us that anybody presenting for treatment should be viewed not only as a unique person with a unique developmental and medical history, nor only as a representative of a particular culture or social group with its own unique cultural and medical history, but also as a member of the human species, with its own embodied adaptations and evolutionary history.

9 The natural history of mothers and infants

An evolutionary and anthropological perspective

Sarah Blaffer Hrdy and Daniela F. Sieff

Summary

Humans are a product of evolution. To understand the relationship between mothers and infants we need to understand how evolution has shaped this relationship, and to identify the challenges that ancestral mothers and infants faced.

Modern society defines mothering as caring for children, but for ancestral women mothering encompassed everything that contributed to leaving descendants: choosing mates, procuring food, building shelters, striving for high rank and creating a supportive social network. The allocation of time between these tasks was also part of mothering, and a matter of life or death for both mothers and their children.

The allocation of limited resources between children was an equally crucial part of mothering for our ancestors. Today we see mothering as synonymous with unconditional love, but this is a relatively modern concept. During our evolutionary history, when resources were scarce, when mothers had insufficient social support, or when children were spaced too closely together, if women were to have any surviving descendents they needed to favour some children over others. During particularly difficult times, that meant nurturing some children while abandoning others to die. Most at risk of abandonment were infants. This ancient facet of mothering, which is at least a quarter of a million years old, was visible in European societies until relatively recently, and remains part of life for many of today's hunter-gatherers.

Knowing this helps us to understand why human infants are so exquisitely sensitive to signs of maternal abandonment and why they experience a mother's lack of commitment as genuinely life-threatening. It also deepens our understanding of some of the dilemmas that mothers face by rooting those dilemmas in the context of our inherited legacy.

Daniela Sieff: You have spent many years researching the emotional makeup of human mothers and infants in the light of evolution; what has motivated you?

Sarah Hrdy: I have always wanted to understand not just who I am, but how creatures like me came to be. What does it mean to be a mammal, with an emotional legacy that makes me capable of caring for others? What does it mean to breed with the ovaries of a primate, and to possess the mind of a human being? What does it mean to be a woman who has descended from ancestors who spent the Pleistocene (the time span between approximately 1.8 million and 10,000 years ago) trying to gather enough food to prevent starvation and to obtain enough help from others so that her offspring would survive and prosper? In short, what does it mean to be a human mother, and just as importantly, what does it mean to be an infant of such a mother?

We are not, as biblical accounts would have it, ready-made out of somebody's rib. We are one of the products of evolutionary processes that have been going on for billions of years. I have wanted to understand how that deep, deep history affects us.

Daniela: What does it mean to look at mothers and infants in the light of evolution?

Sarah: Evolution is driven, primarily, by natural selection, which is an impersonal force: some individuals are better suited to their environment than others and therefore leave more offspring who will, for the most part, inherit the traits that made their parents well suited to their environment. This is what survival of the fittest means – those individuals best suited to their current environment, not the survival of the best in any kind of absolute sense.

Darwinian natural selection is the most powerful and comprehensive theory available for understanding the basic natures of mothers and infants. In the middle of the last century, a tremendously humane and astute psychiatrist named John Bowlby recognised this, and set out to interpret the endocrinological, sensory, emotional and cognitive makeup of mothers and infants as composites of ancient dramas of survival encompassing innumerable past lives.

Daniela: How does our mammalian heritage affect mothering?

Sarah: Mammals, defined by the fact that they produce milk for their offspring, evolved more than 200 million years ago. Mammalian mothers are alchemists able to transform fodder – shellfish, grass, insects, other mammals, plants – into biological white-gold: a blend of highly digestible nutrients and antibiotics. In what is typically a very challenging world, a lactating mother provides a stable environment for her young.

The first social relationships were those forged between a mother and her offspring. With the evolution of mammals, mothers needed to become even better attuned to their young. New modes of hearing, sensitivity to touch and odours, as well as new capacities for distinguishing one's young from others evolved, alongside cognitive systems for sensing the needs of others.

At the same time, natural selection favoured babies who were attracted to maternal body warmth and smell, able to squirm close to her and latch onto her teats, capable of signalling their needs effectively as well as their whereabouts when separated.

The requirement for mothers to bond with babies, and babies with mothers necessitated the evolution of new brain structures. This led to the first glimmerings of empathy and for the first time natural selection favoured brains capable of caring relationships.

Daniela: What goes into being a mother?

Sarah: Our society's vision of the ideal mother is a woman who selflessly looks after her children round the clock. However, most women who have tried to turn their lives over to their children feel frustrated and conflicted at least some of the time. That was certainly my experience. I had read Bowlby and desperately wanted to give my daughter all that she needed to be emotionally secure, but I could not let go of my desire to succeed in my career. I fretted over whether my desire to continue with my work meant that I was a bad mother. Fortunately, I have never been content to agonise when I could analyse instead. I set out to use every perspective, and every source of information I could locate, to explore what it means to be a mother, what infants need from their mothers and why. Even if I did not find answers in time to help me rear my own children, I could pass what I discovered onto others.

And what I concluded was that from an evolutionary standpoint, mothering involves anything and everything a female does to ensure her genes make it into subsequent generations. For our ancestresses, that meant not only looking after young, but also getting enough to eat, finding water, striving for high rank, making deals, manipulating others, planning, being opportunistic, building a social network, helping others and enlisting critically important assistance.

Daniela: How did women juggle these different roles?

Sarah: With difficulty! There were always trade-offs. For example, an early human mother could either carry her baby with her while she foraged, or leave her baby in the custody of caregivers back at camp. If the caregivers failed to look after the baby, it would die. But if taking her baby foraging hampered the mother's ability to gather food, then both mother and infant would starve.

In modern times the struggle to balance subsistence needs against direct caregiving is exacerbated because mothers' workplaces are so incompatible with infant care. But whereas in the past the cost of getting it wrong resulted in infant death, in today's largely predator-free world, where we live in walled houses, vaccinate our children, have access to clean water and pasteurised milk deliverable in rubber-nippled bottles, child neglect is reflected instead by its psychological toll – insecurity among infants, stress in their mothers.

Daniela: You have said that women's ambition has its evolutionary roots in motherhood – could you talk about this?

Sarah: Competitiveness, status-striving and ambition are generally seen as the domain of men, incompatible with being a 'good mother', who in contrast is expected to be selfless and nurturing. What a fallacy! For many primates, including our ape ancestors, a mother's ambition, status and social strategising determined her 'local clout', which in turn determined her access to the material and social resources that were crucial to the survival of her offspring.

The chimpanzee, Flo, was followed for many years by Jane Goodall and her assistants. Flo was infinitely patient and nurturing with her offspring. But over time, it became clear that her success at keeping her young alive also depended on her high rank in the local female hierarchy, which allowed her to carve out a prime territory within the centre of her community's home range. Flo's central territory offered both a good food supply and protection from potentially infanticidal males in neighbouring groups. Just as important, her high rank enabled her to protect her infants from being harmed by rival females in her own group. Given the opportunity, a female chimpanzee will kill and eat babies born to subordinate females unable to defend them. This was not the image of female chimpanzees most people started out with.

In short, far from being opposing forces, a female's quest for status – her ambition, if you will – was inseparable from her ability to keep her offspring and grand-offspring alive and remains a very ancient, conserved feature of women's natures.

Daniela: In today's world high-status women generally have fewer children, so can we really say that evolution has a role?

Sarah: In the world of our ancestors, where females did not have access to consciously chosen birth control, and where no female was ever celibate, any female with sufficient access to resources – that is, fat enough to ovulate – was going to give birth, and the higher her status, the better her chances would be of keeping her infants alive. In terms of fertility, there was no downside to ambition. Today, however, status-striving has become decoupled from child survival. So will there come a time when selection operates against women whose ambition to succeed discourages them from reproducing? Probably – if our species survives long enough, and the workplace environment does not change.

Daniela: Is there a relationship between female sexuality and motherhood?

Sarah: Yes! At the most basic level, when a female chooses her mate, she is choosing the genetic father of her children, a hugely important maternal decision.

But female sexuality can also make a less obvious contribution to being a successful mother. In many mammals, females are only able to mate when they are fertile, around the time of ovulation, but in humans as in some other primates, sexual receptivity depends on circumstances as well, not just cycle state. Why would this be?

In a number of species, when a new male takes over a group, unweaned infants are at great risk. A lactating female is not fertile and the male needs the females to be fertile if he is to have any chance of fathering offspring before he is deposed by the next new male. Killing unweaned infants returns females to fertility, and explains why in chimpanzees, gorillas and many other species, infanticide by novel males is a major source of infant mortality. But if a mother's new mate has previously mated with her, and has some chance of being the father of her infant, then the infant is safe.

Years ago, during my research on wild langur monkeys, I discovered that when roving males approached a troop, females would solicit and mate with them, regardless of whether they were ovulating, at an infertile time in their cycle or already pregnant. If one of these former sexual consorts subsequently took over her group, he would be less likely to kill her infant. For langurs, then, such opportunistic 'promiscuity' is a maternal strategy, likely to enhance her infant's chances of survival.

Human infants confront similar risks when a widowed or abandoned human mother takes a new mate. The Aché are hunter-gatherers who live in Paraguay. The husband of one young pregnant woman was killed by a jaguar. Following his death she was courted by a bachelor whom she married. However, when she gave birth to the child of her deceased husband, she buried the newborn alive as she understood that her new husband would not want it. Her story is not unique. In environments such as the Aché's, where so much of the diet is meat provided by men, it makes little sense for a male to provision a non-related infant.

Additionally, sexual relations with men other than her mate can be a way for a mother to (unconsciously) enlist more men to help provide for her children. This is particularly adaptive for those who live in environments where fathers are important but cannot be relied upon, either because high adult mortality rates mean that many fathers die before their children reach independence, or because fathers abandon their children, or because men's success in hunting or fishing varies unpredictably from day to day. In large swaths of Amazonia, all the way from eastern Brazil to lowland Peru, north to Venezuela and southward down to Paraguay, hunter-horticulturalists subscribe to a folk belief known as 'partible paternity'. They assume that foetuses are built up by repeated application of semen, and that every man with whom the woman has sex contributes to creating the child. As such, they are expected to provide the child with food, and the benefits of this are measurable. Among the Bari of Venezuela, 64 per cent of children who had no secondary father survived to age 15, whereas 80 per cent of those with a secondary father survived. In some of these groups, as soon as a woman suspects she is pregnant, she attempts to seduce the tribe's best hunters and fishermen, like a groupie after a rock star. That said, if there are too many candidates for fatherhood this extreme uncertainty with regards to paternity may dissuade all possible fathers from helping. It is a delicate balance.

As a strategy to gain extra provisioning for children this does not work in agricultural and pastoral societies, where wealth can be passed on to offspring (hunter-gatherers have no land or livestock to pass on) and there is consequently an obsessive concern with paternity. Wives submit to being monogamous so that they, and their offspring, are protected from other males and also gain access to the resources under a man's control.

But the motivational underpinnings that led women to seek multiple mates as a maternal strategy remain; ready to be expressed under conditions when resources become unpredictable, adult male mortality rates go up or whenever it becomes imprudent for a mother to rely on protection or provisioning from a single man. We are seeing this in the breakdown of the nuclear family. The specific demographic and ecological conditions that motivate some inner-city women to line up multiple 'fathers' may be new, but the emotional calculus behind their decisions is very old.

Daniela: How important is a woman's social network in the context of mothering?

Sarah: It is crucial! Bowlby assumed that in the environment in which humans evolved, the mother was the infant's sole source of warmth, protection and nutrition, just as she is in the other great apes – chimpanzees, bonobos, gorillas and orang-utans. But not all primates have exclusive maternal care. In more than half of all 400 or so primate species, group members other than the mother help carry young infants, and in some of these, adults other than the mother also help with provisioning. Biologists use the term 'allomother' to describe any individual other than the mother who helps to rear an infant (from the Greek 'allo' for 'other than'). We call species in which allomothers not only care for young, but also provision them, 'cooperative breeders'. During the course of my research it became clear to me that unlike chimpanzees, bonobos, gorillas and orang-utans, the apes in the line leading to humans must have evolved as cooperative breeders.

In the months following birth, no chimpanzee, gorilla or orang-utan mother ever allows another individual to hold her infant for fear that they will try to kill it, or that they will be unable to protect it from a more dominant individual who might try to kill it. By contrast, a hunter-gatherer mother allows other group members to hold her baby from the outset. Among the Hadza, who live in Tanzania, infants not yet a day old are held by somebody other than their mother some 30 per cent of the time. Among the Efé, who live in the Democratic Republic of the Congo, babies average 14 different caregivers in their first days of life, and are held by somebody other than their mother for 60 per cent of the day. By great ape standards, these levels of trust are extraordinary. Hunter-gatherer babies are powerfully attached to their mother, and she still holds the baby more than any other single individual and babies spend their nights nestled next to their mothers, but from day one, human mothers lay the groundwork for creating the emotional bonds that will bind her baby to potential allomothers and vice versa.

Similarly, in almost all of the hunter-gatherer groups for which we have data, lactating women will on occasion feed other women's babies with their own breast milk. Group members other than the mother – allomothers – may also provide snacks to babies through mouth-to-mouth kisses laced with the juice of ripe berries, or sugary ground powder from baobab pods. Children as young as three months receive premasticated mouthfuls of food from allomothers, who push these delicacies into the babies' mouths with their tongue. And once children are weaned, men then start to take more of a role in helping to provision them. Among chimpanzees, gorillas and orang-utans nothing comparable to alloparental provisioning occurs.

Daniela: What is the role of human fathers in helping to raise children?

Sarah: Fathers are important. They can be the most important allomothers of all, but their role varies enormously from culture to culture and from individual to individual. Among the Aché, where meat provides over 80 per cent of the diet, an infant who loses his father before the age of two is four times more likely to die. In other environments a father's disappearance has little impact on child survival so long as there are other alloparents willing to compensate.

However, in many societies – even ones in which fathers are crucial – men do not necessarily have much direct contact with babies. That is partially because small initial differences in responsiveness to infants become magnified. Mothers and fathers are equally sensitive to urgent cries of 'help', but mothers are more sensitive to less intense signals – like a baby waking up from a nap. So mothers tend to respond first, conditioning the baby to be comforted and soothed by her. Fathers then follow the path of least resistance, with the result that the baby builds a stronger initial attachment to its mother.

That said there is an enormous potential for nurture in human males. Human males are physiologically altered simply by spending time in intimate association with pregnant mothers and new babies; as in other cooperatively breeding primates like marmosets, testosterone levels fall, and prolactin levels rise. This implies that men have been an integral part of human parenting for a long time, but whether paternal nurturance is manifest depends on the environment in which they live. Among the Hadza, hunting takes men away from camp – and away from pregnant women and infants – for long periods of time. When in camp, men hold their infants only 7 per cent of the time, and it is even less among the !Kung. In contrast, among the Aka, who live in the Central African Republic, men spend long periods of time at camp with infants held by their fathers 22 per cent of the time.

Daniela: When fathers do not play a major role in child-care, who have mothers turned to?

Sarah: In some societies a sister, sister-in-law or co-wife acts as an allomother, although these women typically have their hands full raising their own children. Thus, pre-productives (i.e. girls who are not yet married, who are on hand and who have no children of their own) have been a mother's mainstay. However, pre-productives have limitations. They are most eager to help with childcare when they are younger and inexperienced. As they mature their energy is redirected into looking for their own mates, their own feeding ground (which in the West means a job) and into building their own social network (which means hanging out with their friends). Modern Western teenagers who do not want to do household chores exemplify this!

More reliable, are post-reproductive women. They are experienced in child-care, adept at local subsistence tasks, repositories of useful knowledge and undistracted by babies of their own. In fact, the anthropologist Kristen Hawkes proposed that the unusually long post-menopausal lifespan enjoyed by human females evolved because of the positive impact that grandmothers had on grandchildren, an idea that makes a lot of sense to me.

Daniela: In what ways do grandmothers make an impact?

Sarah: From an evolutionary perspective, child survival is what matters, and support from grandmothers not only improves health, social maturation and mental development of children, but under some circumstances can be essential for child survival.

Hadza grannies, long past their prime, are the most dedicated food-gatherers, and work particularly hard digging up tubers. Tubers are buried beneath a deep layer of sun-baked earth and extracting them takes skill and hard work. Kristen Hawkes and her colleagues noticed that in times of food shortage, the nutritional status of Hadza children was improved if they had a grandmother or great-aunt helping to provision them with tubers.

Under some circumstances the presence of a grandmother or other dedicated allomother has been shown to make the difference between life and death. The Mandinka are horticulturalists who live in the Gambia, and back at the turn of the last century had staggeringly high mortality rates, with almost 40 per cent of those born dying by age five. However, with an older sibling (especially a sister) or a post-reproductive grandmother nearby, this mortality rate was cut in half, down to 20 per cent.

Similar patterns have been found in some eighteenth- and nineteenth-century peasant societies. Records for 500 Finnish women and 2,400 Canadian women show that these mothers also lost 40 per cent of their infants on average. However, when women had their own mothers still living in their community, they lost significantly fewer children.

Child mortality rates of 40 per cent were typical for African and Western populations before the introduction of modern medicine. They are in the range of other primates, and presumably of our hominid ancestors as well. If grandmothers reduced the mortality of their grandchildren by half, the evolutionary impact would have been enormous.

That said, in harsh worlds without modern medicine, grandmothers may no longer be alive when grandchildren are born. For a sample of Aka infants only one in two infants had a living grandparent. For Efé infants, it was only one in four. Archaeological records from Palaeolithic gravesites suggest that a 20-year-old mother had roughly a 50 per cent chance of her own mother being alive to help her raise her children. And so women have had to rely on fathers, possible fathers and older children to provide the bulk of alloparental care.

Daniela: What role do grandfathers have?

Sarah: They seem to have little *direct* effect on the survival of their grandchildren. Even in cultures with lots of hands-on male child-care, it is fathers, cousins and older brothers who babysit, rather than grandfathers. That said, in hunter-gatherer societies older men have an important role in promoting in-group harmony, and thus ensuring there are enough hunters, gatherers and alloparents around to help with child-rearing.

Daniela: How important are non-related individuals in rearing children?

Sarah: Because there is an element of luck in determining whether grandmother (or indeed father) is alive, and because the composition of hunter-gatherer groups is fluid, non-related individuals can be an important source of help, and humans have developed a special talent for enlisting them as alloparents. Strategies include naming a newborn after somebody that the parents would like the child to become affiliated with, encouraging more than one man to think that he might be the father or inviting people to become 'God-parents'. We use culture to expand our network of kin and to create 'as if' kin.

Women, in particular, are expert at foraging alliances on their children's behalf. Beginning in girlhood, women become increasingly adept at making friends. From adolescence onward, many girls are more concerned with popularity than with achievement per se. Social bonds themselves became a resource to be protected, and girls can be competitive and ruthless in excluding others from a group. This is likely to reflect ancestral environments in which social bonds would have been critical for successful childrearing.

Daniela: We believe that maternal love is unconditional – is that right?

Sarah: No! The idea of a self-sacrificing mother totally committed to loving and rearing every child she gives birth to is wishful thinking. In nearly every species mothers have to make 'decisions' (at some level) about how much of their time, commitment and energy to invest in each infant if they are to ensure that at least some survive. These decisions are typically unconscious, but sometimes it pays a mother to be fully committed, other times its better for her to cut back – even altogether.

One circumstance in which it can pay a mother to bail on her infants is when food is short. The American black bear exemplifies this. Females mate during the abundance of the summer, but the fertilised ovum does not implant; instead, it enters a state of suspended development. As winter approaches, the mother retreats to her cave to save body fuel by hibernating. If she has stored enough fat to sustain lactation, the fertilised eggs implant, and gestation and birth ensue. If she has not got enough fat, the earliest abortion nature offers takes place: implantation never occurs and the mother waits for a better year.

In other species, it is the lack of social support that leads to a mother bailing out on her young. The Californian mouse is monogamous and mothers whose mates stay alive long enough to help rear their offspring have four times as many surviving young as single mothers. Mothers who lose their mates may terminate investment by ceasing to lactate before their pups are ready to be weaned. The pups are likely to die, but it frees the mothers to start afresh with a new male, and that can make more evolutionary sense than attempting to rear pups alone. This is, in principle, not very different from the Aché woman whose husband died while she was pregnant, and who buried her newborn before going on to start a family with a new husband.

Daniela: How common is it for human mothers to abandon newborns?

Sarah: Through prehistory and history it has been, and continues to be, more common than we like to think. In circumstances where life is tough and 40 or more per cent of children die before the age of 15, a mother has to assess what resources are available to her when 'deciding' whether to commit to a particular child.

Imagine a !Kung woman living a traditional life in the Kalahari desert of Botswana. Sixty per cent of her calories come from plants that women gather. However, there are few weaning foods, and nothing that a child younger than four can chew and digest. If a woman who is still nursing a three-year-old gives birth, what does she do? She is not well enough nourished to provide breast milk for both, so does she wean the three-year-old, in whom she has already invested around three-quarters of a million calories, knowing that there is little for him to eat and so he is likely to die? Or does she leave her newborn in the bush?

When the !Kung lived as hunter-gatherers about 1 in 100 babies was abandoned at birth and left to die in the bushes. Infanticide was almost always undertaken with regret, but it was culturally sanctioned. Indeed, in many different hunter-gatherer societies, infanticide was expected if a newborn was deformed, or perhaps the 'wrong' sex, or one of a twin, or born too soon after its still-nursing sibling, or if the mother did not have enough social support.

But abandoning a poorly timed infant does not mean that a woman will not be a good mother to those that she chooses to rear. Rather, as a black bear will prevent implantation of an egg if she has not stored enough fat, but tenderly care for later litters, a teenage mother who eliminates a baby will lovingly care for later children if the circumstances are right.

Daniela: How has the contingency of maternal commitment been expressed in Western cultures?

Sarah: We have denied the contingent nature of maternal love, primarily by decreeing that mothers who kill their own children must be deranged. Between 1902 and 1927, 48 per cent of women committed to Broadmoor, Britain's state asylum for the clinically insane, had committed infanticide. Today, being a devoted mother is still equated with mental health. But teenagers who kill or abandon their infants are not crazy; rather they are unconsciously responding to the fact that they have given birth under poor conditions, with insufficient support and typically at a young age (meaning they can look forward to reproducing in the future when conditions might be better).

Daniela: How extensive has infanticide been in Western culture?

Sarah: That is hard to answer because with the coming of Christianity, the abandonment of infants was deemed sinful and from the thirteenth century onward it became a crime that had to be kept hidden. For example, the euphemistic catch-all term 'overlaying' described the 'accidental' smothering of infants by their caregivers. Between 1855 and 1860, in London, 3,900 infant deaths were reported as being due to 'overlaying'. Subsequent inquests showed that over 1,100 of these were murder and the real rate was probably higher, given how hard it is to accidentally smother a baby while sleeping. Today some fairly obvious cases of infanticide are swept under the rug of Sudden Infant Death Syndrome. Sure – some babies spontaneously stop breathing, and there are also accidental suffocations, but not all SIDS cases are due to this.

During Roman times women abandoned, rather than killed, unwanted infants. The majority of women living in the first three centuries of the Christian era who had reared more than one child had also abandoned at least one. Between 20 and 40 per cent of children born were abandoned. Some abandoned children were brought up either as adopted members of another household or as labourers; others ended up as slaves and prostitutes. Many died.

Centuries later, to prevent abandoned children from dying, foundling homes were established. The 'Hospital of the Innocents' in Florence was completed in 1445, and 90 foundlings were left during the first year. By 1539, 960 babies were left. Eventually 5,000 infants a year poured in. It was still going three centuries later, but of the 15,000 babies left between 1755 and 1773, two-thirds died before their first birthday. Elsewhere in Europe it was the same. Of the 72,000 infants abandoned to foundling homes in Sicily between 1783 and 1809 fewer than 20 per cent survived.

Daniela: Why were death rates so high?

Sarah: There were not enough wet-nurses to go round and without nutritionally fortified baby formulas and sterile water to mix them with, malnutrition and illness were rampant. The scale of mortality was so openly acknowledged that residents of Brescia in Northern Italy proposed that a motto be carved over the gate of the foundling home: 'Here children are killed at public expense.'

I still remember the autumn day when, at a conference on abandoned children, the full extent of this phenomenon sunk in. As child abandonment was described, epoch by epoch, for England, Sweden, Italy and even Portugal's colony in the Azores, it dawned on me that this affected not tens of thousands or even hundreds of thousands of infants, as I had long assumed, but millions of babies. I grew increasingly numb. I had difficulty breathing. As I distanced myself emotionally from these findings by seeking to analyse what they meant, I may have experienced (in a remote way) what mothers long ago must have done in an attempt not to see or feel what they were doing.

The women who abandoned these babies were seen as unfortunate. Their infants died from malnutrition or dysentery, not infanticide. But this is a sleight of mind – contrived to hide the fact that in the West the abandonment of infants has been responsible for more deaths than several plagues combined.

Daniela: Although a mother's decision to commit to her child is most cut-and-dried just after birth, she will (unconsciously) need to reassess her commitment whenever conditions change. For example, during food shortages if a mother shares food evenly between her children, none may get enough to survive. But if she favours a couple of children – giving them extra calories at the expense of their sibs – she will improve the odds that at least one makes it through to better times.

Sarah: Those kinds of (unconscious) decisions were an intrinsic part of being a mother for the women who were our ancestors; they are part of mothering for women who live in subsistence economies today. We may find that shocking, but we have to remember that current Western populations live in an unprecedented state of freedom from famine. For the first time in human history, the survival of children rarely depends on choices mothers make about how much food to allocate to one child versus another.

That said, we see echoes of these ancient choices in the way that parents in our culture allocate their resources. For example, Western parents are twice as likely to treat a growth-impairing hormone inadequacy in a son as in a daughter. The decision is most likely based on an unconscious calculation about which sex will benefit most from the intervention. Even in modern society, height is a more important predictor of success (including salaries and marriage options) for sons than for daughters.

Daniela: Do the characteristics of a child affect a mother's commitment?

Sarah: I am afraid so. Mothers are more likely to commit to a newborn whom they perceive to be healthy and strong. An incident recorded by anthropologists working with the Eipo subsistence horticulturalists of Papua New Guinea illustrates this. The Eipo have limited land and food and the average completed family size is two-and-a-half children. They have no birth control and low child mortality. They keep family size small through infanticide; 41 per cent of infants born are eliminated. One woman, during late pregnancy, said that she would not accept a baby girl because she already had a daughter and did not yet have a son. However, on giving birth to a particularly healthy-looking female infant, she became ambivalent. Without cutting the umbilical cord, she wrapped her newborn daughter in fern leaves, and sat by the bundle. The infant screamed lustily, and her pudgy hands and feet burst through the leaves. After a while the mother left, apparently abandoning her infant after all. However, two hours later she returned, cut the umbilical cord, and picked up the baby, explaining: *'This daughter was too strong.'*

Two thousand years earlier, in a completely different culture, Soranus, a Greek physician, wrote an influential text called *Gynaecology.*[1] In it he advised,

> Now the midwife, having received the newborn … [and having] examined beforehand whether the infant is male or female … should also consider whether it is worth rearing or not.

To determine whether it was worth rearing Soranus wanted to know: was the mother healthy during pregnancy? Was the infant well formed? Was it plump? Was it full term? Did it respond well to sensory stimulation? Did it cry normally? Was it neurobiologically normal?

Some cultures developed viability tests for newborns. From Ancient Greece through to the medieval period, infants were subjected to ice-cold baths to toughen them up and *'in order to let die, as not worth rearing, one that cannot bear the chilling'*. Scholars think the submersion of infants during Christian baptism derives

---

1 Soranus (1956) *Gynaecology*, Oswei Temkin, trans. Baltimore, MD: Johns Hopkins University Press.

from this practice. The practice of subjecting infants to ice-cold baths arose independently in highland South America and some more tropical climes, too.

In the West, making abandonment a crime did not prevent parents from being reluctant to rear infants that seemed weak. Out of this conundrum came a set of folk beliefs about changelings. Sickly babies were believed to be the babies of fairies, elves or goblins who had been exchanged for human ones. Parents could then leave the 'changeling' in the forest overnight. If the baby died, it was assumed that the fairies had refused to take it back, but since it was not human the parents had committed no crime. If the baby disappeared overnight it was believed that the fairies had taken it back, though more likely it had been eaten by a wild animal. If, however, the baby survived, it was believed that the original healthy human child had been returned by the fairies – although what this actually proved was that the baby was pretty healthy and tough after all, and thus worth rearing.

A mother's preference for a strong child can take more subtle forms. In the 1980s, the psychologist Janet Mann undertook a study of 14 pre-term twins born at extremely low birth weights. Eight months after the twins were brought home, all seven mothers in this small sample were directing more attention to the healthier twin, even though they were not conscious of doing so. Mann cautiously proposed that mothers might have an innate template for assessing infant quality, and biasing their care accordingly.

Daniela: Could this explain why we find plump babies cute?

Sarah: As it happens, birth weight is the most visible indicator of whether a baby is full-term and a good predictor of survival. It is also a moderately good predictor of future development (including cognitive development) and adult health. Thus it is not surprising that selection has shaped us to find plump babies more attractive, more worth caring for. The contemporary practice of sending out birth announcements that inform relatives and friends not only of a baby's sex and date of birth, but also its weight, is a vestige of this deeply engrained mode of assessing newborns.

Daniela: Given the contingency of maternal care, is there a role for 'maternal instincts'?

Sarah: That depends on what you mean by instincts! In 1952 the psychoanalyst Alice Balint wrote: *'It remains self-evident that the interests of mother and child are identical and it is a generally acknowledged measure of the goodness or badness of the mother how far she feels this identity of interests.'* [2] Many still believe this and regard any mother who does not instinctively love all her children unconditionally as 'unnatural'. But although pregnancy, labour and delivery alter a woman's brain to make her more sensitive to her newborn, a mother's commitment to her infant – which in humans is what we mean by 'mother love' – is, as with other mammals, biologically designed to be contingent on circumstances.

---

2 Balint, A. (1985) 'Love for the Mother and Mother Love'. In *Primary Love and Psycho-analytic Technique* by Michael Balint. London: Maresfield (originally published 1952).

Daniela: What are the mechanisms, by which the environment sets a mother's level of commitment?

Sarah: We do not know yet, but a reasonable guess is that they involve endocrinological and neurobiological mechanisms that alter a mother's threshold for responding to infant cues, rendering her more or less likely to become emotionally engaged.

Daniela: Given the contingent nature of maternal commitment, how does the process of bonding between mother and infant occur?

Sarah: Bonding between a mother and her newborn happens differently in different species. In herd-living animals with precocial (well developed at birth) infants such as sheep, mothers only accept babies who smell just like theirs do immediately after birth. This has evolved because young are up and running around soon after birth, and there is a real risk that an alien infant could pirate the milk of a female who is not his mother. But humans are different. Babies are born so helpless that there is no way a baby could *accidentally* end up on the wrong mother. Thus a mother has no need to imprint on her own baby right after birth and maternal commitment can unfold more gradually.

There are evolutionary advantages to this more flexible strategy. A mother can choose whether to nurture a particular newborn or whether to abandon it and try again at a better time. Equally important, individuals other than the mother can come to care deeply about a child, making alloparental care, as well as fostering and adoption, possible.

Daniela: What about a baby's drive to bond with its mother?

Sarah: A baby's drive to bond to its mother is different from the processes through which a mother bonds to her infant. From the moment of birth, babies invariably 'strive' for contact and what Bowlby called 'attachment' (i.e. bonding to mother), irrespective of circumstances. That is because, the mother (or surrogate mother) is the baby's only viable environment, and any baby unable to secure a place in that environment would surely die. If a baby finds a rubber pacifier soothing it is because for at least 50 million years, primate infants engaged in sucking could feel secure because their mother was invariably close at hand.

For human infants the stakes are particularly high, given the contingent nature of maternal care, and it is hardly surprising that babies evolved to be hyper-sensitive to any indication that their mothers are reluctant to commit to them, and to do everything in their power to counteract such reluctance.

Daniela: You have written about attachment being the dynamic through which a human infant sets its developmental trajectory. What do you mean?

Sarah: Researchers have identified four main attachment patterns which develop in children in response to different types of parental behaviour:

1   *Secure attachment:* caregivers are attuned and committed to the infant. Infants grow up believing themselves to be lovable; they learn that others

are trustworthy, that it is okay to ask for help; and they develop empathy for others.

2   *Insecure-avoidant:* caregivers are distant, inattentive or absent. Infants grow up not to trust others, to dismiss the importance of relationships, are extremely self-reliant and have little empathy.

3   *Insecure-ambivalent:* caregivers are sometimes distant, sometimes over-bearing – their behaviour is unpredictable. Infants grow up unsure as to whether their needs will ever be met. They become hyper-tuned into how others respond to them, and hyper-sensitive to criticism or rejection.

4   *Insecure-disorganised:* caregivers are either frightened of their children, or they frighten their children. Either way, the very person who is supposed to provide safety is the source of danger.[3] These infants typically grow up with a fragmented sense of self, are at risk of developing dissociative disorders,[4] and often struggle with aggression, self-harm and addiction.

Bowlby, and many of the psychologists who followed him, viewed secure attachment as adaptive and normal, and all forms of insecure attachment as aberrations. However, for the last three decades, evolutionary researchers have understood that we cannot automatically designate certain behaviours as adaptive, others as maladaptive. Rather, their adaptiveness depends on the environment in which that individual is living.

What is more, given that different environments call for different behaviours (and in some species different body shapes), some traits have evolved to take the environment into account as development unfolds. One striking example of this occurs in caterpillars belonging to a species of moths (*Nemoria arizonaria*) that breed in oak woodlands in the American Southwest. Mothers have two broods a year. Spring broods feed on the pollen of oak's flowers, called catkins. The second brood hatches long after these flowers have dropped and feed on tough, mature oak leaves, laden with tannins. Pollen-eating grubs metamorphose into knobbly, wrinkled caterpillars that resemble catkins and are thus camouflaged from insect-eating predators. But later-born grubs develop to look twig-like, adopting a different camouflage. The hatchling's developmental trajectory is triggered by what the caterpillars eat in their first three days. High levels of tannins trigger the development of the twig-like body.

Different attachment strategies can be viewed the same way – that is as different adaptive paths taken by immatures depending on the social world that they have been born into and are likely to inhabit. Just as the moth's diet during the first three days of its life tells it whether it has been born into a world where pollen-laden catkins or tannin-laden leaves will provide its sustenance, whether his human mother (or foster mother) is single-mindedly attentive, a bit distracted or absent

3 Sieff: see Allan Schore (Chapter 6) and Daniel Siegel (Chapter 7) in this volume.
4 Sieff: see Ellert Nijenhuis (Chapter 5) in this volume.

altogether gives the developing infant critical information about the social world he or she has been born into.

If mother is attentive to her infant, then it is likely that she has lots of social support, and her infant can set his or her developmental trajectory accordingly. This means following the path of secure attachment. To recap, securely attached infants grow up believing that they are lovable; they learn to trust others, are comfortable asking for help and, in turn, they develop greater empathy towards others. Such behaviour is likely to be adaptive given that her mother's social network will probably be there to support the child throughout childhood, adolescence and often into adulthood as well. In traditional societies, the social network that a child is born into is likely to follow that child through life.

In contrast, if a mother is absent and unresponsive, the infant would do better to respond as if born to a mother with few relations and limited social support. Being kinless would have been a dismal situation for any early human; for a kinless child, the survival prospects would have been particularly dim. But should such a child happen to survive, the path of insecure-avoidant attachment, i.e. believing that you are unlovable, believing that others are untrustworthy, being extremely self-reliant and having little empathy, would be more adaptive. Take what you can, because no one is going to give it.

The developmental trajectory of avoidant attachment would not only be adaptive for children born to mothers with a limited social network; for abandoned or orphaned children it might be the only way to survive. Some such children might be lucky enough to be fostered by kin, but others (if they survived at all) would have been exploitatively reared for their labour, or with girls, for their reproductive potential.

In Greek mythology, Telephos was born from the coupling of Hercules with a priestess to Athena. He was abandoned as an infant, suckled by a doe, reared by non-relatives. For such a child, brought up without a supportive kin group, it might well be adaptive to develop into an aggressive loner. Tellingly, when Telephos was wounded and informed that King Agamemnon alone could heal him, he took the king's son hostage to exhort Agamemnon's help. For a kinless human, little is likely to be proffered and what is needed must be snatched, secretly stolen, won by guile or daring exploits. The ancient Greeks intuited that early emotional deprivation sets humans on this path.

Daniela: Might one reason for the high levels of insecure attachment in our society be that at some unconscious level mothers are preparing their children to live in a world without kin, because people are so mobile and many move away from their families?

Sarah: That is an interesting idea and it would make sense. I know of no research that specifically addresses your question, but yes of course, some parents make a policy of maintaining emotional distance because they want their children to grow up to be self-sufficient and independent. But we have to be cautious since the conscious reasons people cite may not be why they do something.

Daniela: If avoidant-attachment is adaptive under certain social conditions, why is it so painful to live that way?

Sarah: Special centres in the brain were designed to reward us for tactile contact and for social connection with trusted others, as well as for behaving generously towards others. Deprived of the opportunity to engage in such activities, we feel lonely, left out and unloved, even if that developmental path was formerly adaptive.

Daniela: What might the evolutionary advantage of insecure-ambivalent attachment be?

Sarah: The more that our ancient ancestors worried about such questions as: *'Shall I ask my mother to hold this baby while I crack the nuts?'* or *'Should I carry my baby with me on a long trek to gather food, or leave him with auntie?'* or *'Should I get rid of this child altogether?'*, the more that natural selection would have favoured youngsters temperamentally inclined to keep watch on their mother's facial expressions, or monitor her body tones for any signs that would indicate a lapse in commitment, and so respond accordingly. An inconsistent mother is one who may well be thinking of abandoning her infant. Hence it would be adaptive for infants to become connoisseurs of their mother's emotions and intentions.

Daniela: Might one reason for a woman to become an inconsistent mother be that she has some social support, but not enough to feel secure about raising her child successfully? And if so, then her child would not have many people who he could go to for help, and it would pay him to grow up to be hyper-sensitive to how people respond to him, because he could not afford to lose anybody from his network. Could this be part of what is happening with ambivalent attachment?

Sarah: Daniela, that certainly makes sense to me, but I cannot really point to evidence which supports that. Bowlby's ideas have inspired a remarkable and increasingly robust body of experimental work, but until quite recently rigorous research has mostly focused on the mother's behaviour and her infant's responses and we still do not know much about how babies respond to multiple caregivers. Similarly, we do not yet have a fine-grained enough understanding of how the availability of social support affects maternal responses. There is a lot of suggestive evidence, but also a long way to go in our understanding.

Daniela: Can evolution tell us anything about disorganised attachment – the most extreme form of insecure attachment?

Sarah: This is one dimension of attachment where evolution cannot add that much. Today, in the West, nearly 99 per cent of all infants born survive childhood. For the first time in human history child survival has been decoupled from the responsiveness of caregivers. Prior to 1,500 years ago, I have trouble believing that children could have survived the kind of parenting that leads to disorganised attachment. Perverse as it sounds, disorganised attachment looks like a modern pathology resulting from the fact that children have begun to survive so well.

Daniela: You have suggested that attachment patterns affect not only how we view other people, but also how we experience our physical environment – can you talk about this?

Sarah: Hunter-gatherers tend to see their environment as a giving place. The Mbuti people of Zaire say that the forest gives *'food, shelter and clothing, just like parents'*. The Nayaka of Southern India simply say *'the forest is a parent'*. But in groups such as the Mbuti and the Nayaka, 50 per cent of children typically die before the age of 15, so at first glance it seems strange that they would view their environment this way. However, with child mortality so high, any child that survived would, by necessity, have been surrounded by many caring alloparents, and so as ethnographer Nurit Bird-David has pointed out, perhaps it is not surprising that they would internalise working models of their world as a giving place.

By contrast, children growing up amidst the emotionally much colder parenting of Northern Europe would come to view the natural world as dangerous and threatening. In the version of Hansel and Gretel that most of us know, it is their step-mother who plans to leave Hansel and Gretel in the wood when famine comes, so that she and her husband will have fewer mouths to feed, and will not starve. However, in the original folk tale the 'step-mother' was actually the children's real mother. The substitution occurred when one of the Grimm brothers decided it would be too much for his readers to present mothers this way. Either way, it is easy to envision how children raised in an emotionally precarious, often quite punitive environment, might come to see their physical world as a dangerous and hostile place.

Daniela: Are there specific traits that have evolved in human infants because of the importance of allomothers to their survival?

Sarah: Yes! Human infants are extraordinarily curious about other people's reactions and are experts at evaluating nuances of commitment and character. In the first months of life, before a child's brain is anything like fully developed, a human infant is intensely sensitive to how responsive caregivers are likely to be. A human baby gravitates towards enlivened eyes and a voice whose cadence and rhythms echo his own – all of which indicate that this adult is interested in the infant and likely to help to rear him or her.

Similarly, long before infants have words to describe helpfulness, they readily discriminate between someone likely to be nice and someone potentially nasty, and they act on this knowledge. After six-month-old infants watched a cartoon in which shapes either helped or hindered a third party who was trying to climb a steep hill, they were presented with toys that were replicas of either the helpful or the hindering shape. They showed a robust preference for the helpful shape by reaching out for it.

In addition, human babies appear to be attuned to the expectations and emotional reactions of caregivers. Children of less than a year appear to be acutely aware that they might have failed to meet somebody's expectation, and they exhibit embarrassment and what looks like shame when that happens. By four, the age at which a child in a hunter-gatherer society would be weaned, modern children begin to use their intersubjective gifts not only to intuit what others want, but also to flatter others and to ingratiate themselves with the sort of people upon whom children's survival once depended.

In short, beginning in infancy, humans have a unique gift for attributing mental and emotional states to others. Some call this theory of mind, others intersubjectivity – which is the term I prefer because it encompasses the emotional component of caring what others think. But, whatever term is used, this quest for intersubjective engagement is not nearly so well developed in other apes.

So why did eagerness to enter into the mental and emotional states of others develop in one line of apes, namely ours, but not the others? The most plausible explanation rests on the vast stretch of time (perhaps two million years) during which human infants with multiple caregivers would have been challenged in ways that no ape before ever was. The needy youngster would have had to decipher not only its mother's level of commitment but also the moods and intentions of others who might be seduced into helping. How best to attract care? Through crying? With smiles, funny faces, gurgling, or babbling? The youngsters who were best at mind-reading would have been best cared for and best fed, and with infant mortality running at 40 per cent and probably often higher, anything that increased the chance of survival would have been strongly selected for.

Daniela: Is there any research about the effects of having multiple caregivers on the development of empathy?

Sarah: As I have mentioned, most research on attachment has focused solely on mothers. Mothers are tremendously important, so this is a good beginning, but such evidence as we have indicates that infants nurtured by multiple trusted caregivers grow up not only feeling secure, but with a better-developed capacity to see the world from multiple perspectives. Fathers, older kinswomen and especially juvenile allomothers are not only carers, but also potential competitors for food and other resources. When children spend time in a mixed-age play-group they learn about status-seeking, posturing and deceit, and further develop their ability to ascertain emotional commitment and predict generosity versus stinginess. In fact, the more opportunities a child has to interact with older, more experienced caregivers, the better they can read and empathise with other people's mental states, including being able to read between the lines. What is more, children with lots of caregivers exhibit these capacities at an earlier age.

Daniela: You have linked the unique empathic abilities of humans to the evolution of cooperation in humans – can you talk more about this?

Sarah: It has been suggested that the key difference between human and non-human primates is that only humans are biologically adapted to participate in collaborative activities with shared goals and intentions. Humans are the only mammals where we find large-scale cooperative endeavours involving people who are not necessarily close kin, engaged in such collaborative activities as tracking and hunting prey, processing food, playing competitive games, building shelters or designing space craft that reach the moon.

Similarly, humans are extraordinarily generous and altruistic compared to other apes. From a tender age, and without special training, modern humans identify with the plights of others and, without being asked, volunteer to help and find pleasure in helping. In fact, the dopamine-related reward centres of the brain are activated by helping in humans. In contrast, sharing is uncommon in non-human apes, and almost never spontaneous or reciprocal. Donors have to be begged, and when one animal allows another food, it is better described as scrounging than the spontaneous, often carefully considered, gift giving that is documented for every human society ever studied. No researcher has ever seen a wild chimpanzee spontaneously offer food to its child or to its mate, let alone to another group member. Yet this is something that humans do all over the world.

Our ability to cooperate rests on the combination of our aptitude for theorising about mental states and intentions of other people with this spontaneous eagerness to give or help. It is my contention that the enhanced empathy – a key precursor in this realm – was initially favoured by natural selection because of the advantage it provided to youngsters in securing the help they needed to survive. Once these abilities had evolved in youngsters, they would then be retained into adulthood, where they became part and parcel of caregiving. Paradoxically, it may have been the contingent nature of maternal care, and the critical need to ensure help from alloparents, that paved the way for humans to evolve into the most cooperative and altruistic of primates.

Daniela: How would you sum up what it is to be a human mother, as well as an infant of such a creature?

Sarah: In 1956 the philosopher and psychoanalyst Erich Fromm wrote *'Mother's love is unconditional, it is all-protective, all enveloping'.*[5] This is a fantasy based in wishful thinking rather than biological reality. Every human mother's response to her infant is influenced by a composite of biological responses of mammalian, primate and human origin, and the last 50 years of evolutionary research tells us that there is no one species-typical level of maternal commitment. With social support and otherwise propitious circumstances a woman may have the luxury of being fully committed to, and loving each child born. But over evolutionary time, only a few mothers were afforded that luxury; most had to factor into their decisions the resources available to them (including the availability of allomaternal assistance), the probable effects of a newborn on the well-being of older children, the likely responses of fathers or stepfathers, as well as the infant's own robustness and probability of surviving.

As a consequence, human infancy and childhood has not always been the warm, safe-in-the-arms-of-love tableau many imagine. Once upon a time, maintaining

5 Fromm, E. (1956) *The Art of Loving.* New York: Harper and Row.

202 Sarah Blaffer Hrdy and Daniela F. Sieff

maternal commitment and enticing others to care for you were just as important for an infant's survival as oxygen. That is why human infants, so helpless at birth and so dependent on others for years afterwards, have evolved to be exceptionally sensitive to signs of emotional distancing, and to do whatever is needed to avoid abandonment. Yet as part of the very same suite of Darwinian adaptations, humans have evolved to become the most sophisticated and empathetic of mind-readers and the most cooperative of primates.

10 Emotional evolution

A Darwinian understanding of suffering and well-being

Randolph M. Nesse and Daniela F. Sieff

Summary

To understand emotional suffering, it is vital to understand what the underlying emotions evolved to do. Emotional suffering is caused by 'negative' emotions, which we generally see as undesirable and try to eliminate as quickly as possible. However, negative emotions evolved over millions of years to warn us of danger and to motivate us to withdraw from threatening situations. Thus it is not always wise to eliminate these emotions; rather, it is prudent to first explore whether our suffering relates to our circumstances, and if so, act accordingly.

Sometimes, however, we are assailed by negative emotions which seem inappropriate to our circumstances. Then we are diagnosed as having a disorder such as depression, anxiety or panic attacks. Evolutionary thinking helps to explain why we are susceptible to these 'disorders', and enables us to contextualise the particular dynamics involved in terms of what we have inherited from our distant ancestors.

Evolutionary thinking also elucidates why happiness is elusive, why we turn to self-blame when misfortune befalls us and why we will sacrifice so much to remain within groups. It can even shed light on why psychological change is difficult. Most importantly, evolutionary perspectives help us realise that our emotional states result from our deep heritage rather than because we are abnormal, and that realisation makes it easier to develop self-acceptance and self-compassion.

Today we have a much greater understanding of the evolutionary forces that have shaped our emotional world than ever before. Incorporating this understanding into our lives, and our clinical practices, enhances our ability to alleviate emotional suffering and foster well-being.

Daniela Sieff: What can a Darwinian perspective contribute to our understanding of emotional suffering?

Randy Nesse: To understand emotional suffering, it is important to understand why we have emotions in the first place, and what their purpose is. Neurobiology tells us how emotions operate and how they develop during an individual's life, but it does not tell us why we have emotions or why our emotions came to be the way that they are. Only evolution can tell us that. Evolutionary explanations do not compete with neurobiological explanations, or indeed with psychological ones. They are complimentary. Working psychotherapeutically with emotions without knowing about their evolution is like doing art without knowing perspective, or doing engineering without knowing physics. You can do it, but understanding the Darwinian forces that underlie our emotional suffering can increase effectiveness.

Daniela: How did you come to realise that it was important to incorporate an evolutionary perspective into your understanding of emotions?

Randy: In my second year of college I became interested in why evolution has left us vulnerable to ageing. After finishing my psychiatric training, I found the answer, and started using evolution to understand other problems concerning physical health, including pain and inflammation. However, like most practising psychiatrists, I had not thought about how evolution related to emotional well-being, and I had only a dim notion of the role that natural selection played in shaping our emotional world. Then a new patient came to see me: handing me a nearly empty bottle of antidepressants, she said *'All I really need is a refill.'* For the previous year she had been taking Prozac for weight loss; she was one of the lucky ones who got that side-effect. *'I only lost a few pounds',* she said, *'but I want to keep taking it because it makes me feel better.'* She denied feeling unusually depressed before, but insisted that the drug made her more confident and energetic. I could discover no history of clinical depression; as far as I could determine, she was a normal person whose normal distress was blocked by the drug.

I wrestled with whether to renew her prescription. If the drug made her feel better, and she had no noticeable side-effects, then why not? There again, might side-effects later be discovered? Then a totally separate thought caused me to pause: Are bad feelings useful? If they are, is blocking them wise?

In that moment I saw that my work on evolution and disease could guide my study of emotions. Why do we have emotions? Are they useful? Why are there so many painful emotions? Why has evolution left us vulnerable to the emotional suffering caused by depression or anxiety? I set out to learn what I could.

Daniela: What have emotions evolved to do? Why do we have them?

Randy: Emotions evolved over millions of generations. They help individuals to take advantage of opportunities and to cope with threatening situations. Each emotion changes many aspects of our biology and psychology in a coordinated manner; attention, motivation, physiology, memory, cognition, behaviour, communication and subjective experience. The result is that we behave in ways that, in similar situations, helped our ancestors to survive and to leave more children. If a lover looks deeply into our eyes, sexual feelings are adaptive; those who responded with sexual arousal would have left more offspring. Those who responded to longing gazes with panic had few children, unless the gaze was from a lion, in which case panic would be as useful as an emotion can be!

The fact that emotions evolved as adaptations to situations that were common during our evolutionary history does not imply that they are crude, fixed responses to simple cues. Instead, emotions evolved to flexibly adjust behaviour to circumstances. A married woman who wants children and discovers that she is pregnant is likely to feel happy, whereas a single Catholic girl may feel anxiety, guilt and fear of being rejected by her community – fear that is justified because in our evolutionary past such rejection would likely have meant death.

Daniela: What is the evolutionary history of emotions?

Randy: The precursors of emotions appeared in single-celled bacteria that lived hundreds of millions of years ago. We were not there to watch, but some of today's bacteria are probably similar. These bacteria have a memory of half a second, and their behavioural repertoire is limited to two actions: move forward or tumble in a random direction. The algorithm that decides between these options is simple. If food concentration is higher than it was half a second ago, move forwards. If food concentration is lower, or if there is danger such as heat or acid, then swim in some other direction. It is safe to assume that a mechanism similar to this was the precursor of our emotions. At the most fundamental level, our emotions, and the underlying neural mechanisms that mediate them, still divide cues into good or bad. They motivate us to move towards what we experience as positive and to withdraw from what we experience as negative.

Over millions of years, this simple algorithm became increasingly nuanced, providing specialised responses to different kinds of threats and opportunities. The attack of a predator will arouse physiological and behavioural changes characteristic of panicked flight, while the threat of falling arouses freezing. The prospect of rejection elicits social anxiety, while the danger of losing one's mate elicits jealousy.

That said, the differentiation of emotions from each other is partial; the boundaries are blurred. A good analogy is the different musical modes pre-programmed into an electronic keyboard such as jazz, classical music, folk, rock, etc. Each mode adjusts the presence or absence of various instruments, the volume of each frequency band, the amount of distortion, the background rhythm, the reverberation and a host of other parameters. Each mode is separate, each has a different feel, but each is built from the same basic mechanisms, and any two modes will have many overlapping characteristics. This evolutionary approach explains why no agreement has been reached on which emotions are basic.

Daniela: How does an evolutionary perspective help us to understand emotional disorders?

Randy: Natural selection did not shape emotional disorders; traits that leave an individual badly adapted to the environment will be eliminated. However, an evolutionary approach can offer us an unparalleled understanding as to why we humans are vulnerable to certain disorders such as depression, anxiety and panic attacks. It can help us to understand why we are sensitive to social rejection. It can also help us understand why it is so easy to become caught in cycles of self-blame when misfortune strikes.

Just as important, natural selection can help us to distinguish what is a disorder and what is not. At the moment psychiatric diagnosis is muddled because it fails to distinguish three very different phenomena that get classified as a 'disorder'.

1. *Defects in our physiology and neurobiology.* There can be problems with a person's underlying neurobiology or hormonal systems that prevent them from functioning properly. Schizophrenia, autism and obsessive compulsive disorder are examples.
2. *Healthy defences that are mistaken for disease.* Emotional defence systems have evolved to be aversive and unpleasant in order to stop us from doing what we are doing and to avoid similar situations in the future. However, because they are aversive, it is easy to think that the normal emotion is the actual problem, rather than look for the underlying cause. I call this 'the Clinician's Illusion'. Thinking about physical pain helps to clarify this. Physical pain evolved to stop us doing things that might cause injury or death; to be effective pain must be so distressing that eliminating the source of pain becomes our highest priority. However, the pain itself is not the problem – the problem is what is causing the pain. Doctors used to get caught out by the Clinician's Illusion, but most now carefully separate diseases from our body's defensive responses. For instance, pneumonia results in fluid accumulation in the lungs. This is a harmful consequence of infection. In contrast, the coughing that typically accompanies pneumonia is a defence. Those who cannot cough, or whose cough is overly suppressed by medication, are likely to die. Defensive responses can be problematic (excessive coughing can cause cerebral haemorrhage), but the capacity to cough is part of the body's evolved defence system, rather than the problem. Similarly, many emotional states that we label as disorders, such as low mood and anxiety, are normal defences that have been shaped by natural selection because they are advantageous in certain circumstances.
3. *Dysregulation of healthy defences.* The regulation of our healthy defences can go astray. Allergies result when the body is overly sensitised to substances like pollen. In the emotional realm, a feeling of suspicion alerts us to the possibility that we are about to be betrayed, information that can allow us to protect ourselves. However, if suspicion is activated too easily, it can impose huge costs and we call it paranoia. Most mental disorders arise from dysregulation of healthy emotions.

Daniela: Are there any reasons, in addition to the 'Clinician's Illusion', that result in us mistaking defences for disease?

Randy: There are! Another reason why we struggle to differentiate emotional defences from emotional disorders is that diagnosis is currently based on symptoms (which are relatively easy to identify), rather than on the underlying causes (which can be very difficult to discover). But to say that somebody is suffering from depression simply because they show a particular set of symptoms is akin to saying that somebody who has a cough and a temperature is suffering from the disorder 'cough fever'. If we went to a doctor suffering from a cough and a fever, we would not be happy with a diagnosis of 'cough fever', followed by a prescription for medicine that simply suppressed both the cough and fever! Rather, we would want the doctor to look for the underlying problem before deciding upon the appropriate treatment.

The fact that specific psychological syndromes are now being defined by whether they respond to a particular pharmacological drug exacerbates the problem. For instance, if an anti-anxiety drug releases the symptom, that person is then diagnosed as having an anxiety disorder. But a single drug can affect many diverse conditions and just as the pain-relieving effects of aspirin are not a sound basis for discovering the cause of our physical pain, our response to a psychiatric drug does not help us get to the roots of our emotional suffering.

In other words, to determine if an emotional response is a normal defence or a disorder, we need to know what situations that emotion has evolved to cope with, and the details of the current situation. At present, we differentiate disorders from normality based solely on the severity of the symptoms and how much they interfere with our normal functioning. This is not valid. What is missing is a consideration of what underlies the emotion and how much 'negative' emotion is optimal in these particular circumstances.

Daniela: Turning to specific emotions, what can evolution tell us about happiness and sadness?

Randy: We tend to believe that happiness is the goal of life, but at the core of evolution is a very disturbing principle: natural selection did not shape us for happiness, health or long life. Natural selection has no goals as such, it simply increases the prevalence of any trait that on average results in having more offspring.

So, why do we have a capacity for happiness? Happiness occurs in situations that have tended, over evolutionary time, to increase an individual's number of surviving offspring. It motivates us to continue doing whatever it is that we are doing. So we enjoy things like food, caresses and sexual intercourse, and we are happy when our children are healthy and successful. Happiness is also a reward for having good friends and for public recognition, both of which would have helped our ancestors to attain the support that was critical to the survival and success of themselves and their children.

In contrast, sadness occurs after the loss of resources that could have been used to increase reproduction. These include health, social position, and material possessions, but the big one is children themselves. Nothing causes more sadness than loss of a child, although loss of a mate comes close. It seems paradoxical that it can be useful to have an emotion after a loss, but sadness is about the present and the future. It tells us to stop whatever we are doing, try to recover what was lost, warn others, and to take care to avoid a similar loss in the future.

We could, in theory, have a brain wired so that food, sex, being the object of admiration and having successful children were emotionally painful, whereas failure, death of a loved one and facing mortal danger were enjoyable. Such a proposition seems preposterous, and it is. Anybody whose brain was wired that way would not have survived and reproduced – it would have been an evolutionary dead-end.

Daniela: You have worked on the emotions and moods that arise in pursuit of a goal – can you talk about these?

Randy: My work on emotions and moods (which are longer in duration than emotions) started making much more sense when I realised that it was important to have mechanisms that can mediate how we invest our energy when *pursuing* a goal. Energy is hard to come by, and individuals of all species have to adjust their goals depending on the energy required to achieve that goal. A bumble-bee's search for food offers a classic example. As evening falls and the air cools, flying takes more energy. At a certain point the calories burnt while searching for food outweighs the calories gained by finding food. Then it is best to give up foraging for the day. Bumble-bees may not experience emotions, but for the human species emotions and moods are the primary mechanisms that mediate how we invest our efforts in ongoing projects.

When an opportunity presents itself, we feel the excitement and desire that inspires us to set out. If our efforts to reach our goal are going well, engagement and satisfaction encourage us to continue. When we encounter an obstacle, frustration spurs us to trying to find a way through. When our efforts to reach a goal are failing, despondency and low mood dampens enthusiasm and encourage us to explore alternative strategies. If no alternative strategy works and we persist in pursuing the 'unreachable' goal, ordinary low mood can escalate into clinical depression. Not all depression results from pursuing unreachable goals, but much does. Low mood and its extreme of depression force us to withdraw from pursuing a goal; they prevent us from persisting with futile or dangerous actions. Unable to act, we have little choice but to stop and turn efforts elsewhere. Severe depression is resolved more often by giving up unreachable goals than by finding new ways to reach them. Therapists have long viewed life crises as an opportunity for change. An evolutionary perspective explains why.

Daniela: What kinds of goals do we strive for?

Randy: Whatever goals would have enabled us to survive and to have children in our evolutionary past. As infants and young children, what is most important is getting our parents to care for us. Without that, we will not survive. As adults, our goals include finding a mate, having sex, conceiving offspring, nurturing those offspring, and providing for them so that they can grow up to be healthy and successful. In service to that end, having a strong social network, friends, social status, reputation, wealth and power have become important goals for our species.

Many of the goals that humans strive for have parallels in the lives on non-human animals, but no other species has our ability to conceive of long-term futures and to make plans to achieve long-term goals. No other organism can sit and think about which of five different strategies will be most likely to get us to a goal in a week's time, a year's time or even ten years' time.

The goals that we pursue differ on many dimensions. Sometimes one person reaching a goal means that others will not. For instance, competitions to win a golf tournament or become the CEO of a company are zero-sum games. Fortunately, many goals are win–win, for instance, playing a game for fun, or cooperating in a hunt.

Some goals are tangible – such as buying a house or writing a book. Once we have achieved such goals we have something solid to show for it. Other goals are more elusive – maybe we are trying to get our mothers to finally love us, or striving to lose weight. A wish to be universally popular is a goal that is as elusive as it is common, and therefore a common cause of emotional suffering.

Another important issue highlighted by an evolutionary approach is that we pursue multiple goals simultaneously, and so we are constantly making compromises. We are told by the media and the self-help industry that we can have it all, but evolutionary success has depended on judiciously allocating effort among diverse and competing enterprises, including acquiring material resources, attracting and keeping a partner, taking care of children, making and maintaining friends and gaining social status. Even a person with substantial resources may face impossible dilemmas. A woman in her mid thirties and keen to devote herself to raising children may find herself in an impossible situation if her much loved fiancé is unlikely to ever get a job good enough to support her and children. An ambitious young executive may be torn between his desire to spend more time at home caring for his children, and the need to take on more out-of-town assignments to get promoted. This is no different, in principle, from the dilemma of a hunter-gatherer who has to choose whether to forage far afield where hunting is better, or to stay at home and protect his family. Needing to balance the trade-offs between competing goals can leave us feeling painfully conflicted, but such conflicts are neither a personal problem, nor pathologies of modern life; they are biological realities.

That said, the unconscious processes that mediate these trade-offs are partially influenced by motivational systems that are influenced by childhood experiences. Sometimes that results in more conflict and suffering than is necessary. Becoming aware of those motivational systems takes years of psychotherapeutic work and is a very difficult process – incorporating an evolutionary perspective can help with that process.

Daniela: Depression seems particularly prevalent in the modern world – why is that so?

Randy: That is a huge question! Modern life is seen as especially stressful and around 20 per cent of people experience low moods severe enough to be diagnosed as depression; however, our ancestors undoubtedly faced more stress than we do. Although family networks were stronger in the past, our ancient ancestors had no police, no food reserves, no medicine and no laws. Infections were rampant and 50 per cent of babies typically died before adulthood. Around 16 per cent of women died in childbirth. Most of us lead lives that exceed our ancestors' wildest fantasies. We have fabulous food and as much of it as we want. Central heating keeps us warm. Most miraculous, our children are unlikely to die. We have what we thought would make us happy, but depression is common. Why?

If depression is an extreme version of low mood, and if it evolved primarily to mediate our withdrawal from fruitless goals, then the amount of depression in a culture will be related to size of enterprises that people pursue. Just a few thousand years ago individuals allocated their effort among a limited variety of tasks: gathering food and water, taking care of family, participating in the group, etc. It is relatively easy to give up looking for nuts when several days of foraging has proved fruitless. However, in modern environments, the size and duration of goals has expanded from plans about what to do next week to plans for the next decade. Big rewards now go to those who allocate a huge proportion of their life's effort to one domain, and sometimes even just to one goal. Hunter-gatherers never experienced a situation of being five years into a doctoral training programme and realising that no jobs are available in the field. They never spent ten years training for an Olympic gymnastics competition only to not make the cut. They never worked 20 years at a specialised job in a particular industry, only to be let go when a new crop of younger employees turned out to be willing to do the job for less. After years of working towards such a goal, there may be no satisfactory alternatives. In short, our motivational systems were not designed to cope with efforts so long in duration towards goals so large, with all-or-nothing outcomes that offer few alternatives.

The problem is compounded because we evolved a desire to imitate the successful. Our ancestors would have benefited from imitating the best hunter, or gatherer, or tool-maker in the group. However, our ancestors would have been seeking to emulate the best in their local community, whereas the media now shows us the very best in the world; trying to emulate the world's best is very unlikely to be successful. Our mood-regulation systems did not evolve in a situation where people are exposed to so many ultra-successful role models.

Positive psychology can also be problematic because it can reinforce the idea that 'happiness' is a valid and attainable goal in and of itself. But pursuing happiness does not lead to happiness. Happiness emerges when we are making good progress towards other goals; the idea that we ought to be able to attain happiness per se paradoxically sets us up for failure and for low mood.

Daniela: Sometimes depression means we do not have the energy to make a new start. If its evolutionary function is to get us to pursue a different path, why does that happen?

Randy: There are times when it is more adaptive to persist with our current path, rather than start anew. When we have spent years building a marriage, a reputation, a career or raising children, walking away may be a bad idea, even if we are very unhappy. There are real costs to breaking commitments. There are no guarantees that we will find anything better. We may also lose our reputation, our security and our identity. Depression prevents us from walking away because it leaves us without the energy needed to embark on a new path. There are times when pessimism, low self-esteem and a lack of initiative can prevent calamity even as they perpetuate misery.

Daniela: How might seasonal affective disorder – the form of depression that hits us during the short days of winter – fit into this framework?

Randy: Seasonal affective disorder (SAD) might have evolved as a way to reduce our incentive to go out looking for food in winter, when it would have been more prudent to minimise activity levels and conserve energy. In winter not only is food scarce, meaning that the calories we burn up searching for food may well outweigh the calories we can procure, but in some environments being out brings dangers that we would be wise to avoid.

On the day of my grandmother's baptism in February 1881, on a tiny island off the coast of Norway, my great-grandfather sighted a swirl of mackerel just offshore. Off he went with some other fishermen. They were optimistic and in high spirits. The fishing was good. They filled not only their boat, but also a dingy connected by a chain. A wave swamped the overloaded dingy, the chain could not be cut. All drowned. A fellow villager, who was perhaps more prone to seasonal depression and less optimistic, may not have gone out that day. He would have forgone the opportunity to catch fish, but he would have lived to help look after his daughter as she grew up. As important, from an evolutionary perspective, he would have had the opportunity to father additional children, and they would have been likely to inherit his propensity to seasonal depression.

Seasonal affective disorder illustrates the paradox embedded in depression: it is most useful when things have a chance of improving. It is worth battening down the hatches in winter because spring will come and food will be more plentiful and less dangerous to obtain. It is worth withdrawing from a goal if there is the potential to later pursue a different path. If things are going to stay the same indefinitely, there is no point to depression no matter how hopeless things seem and something else kicks in. I call it the 'what the hell effect'; you simply get on with it.

Daniela: Post-natal depression is especially common in women who perceive that they have little social support. Given that during our evolutionary history women needed a strong social network if they were to successfully raise children,[1] could post-natal depression have evolved as a mechanism to get women to step back from an infant who they had little chance of rearing because they did not have that support?

Randy: Having a child in a situation where the child is unlikely to survive was unfortunately common in ancestral times, and my anthropologist friends tell me it

1 Sieff: See Sarah Hrdy (Chapter 9) in this volume.

is not so different today for some people. One told me about a family with a cow, one child and money enough for food for the cow or the baby. Feeding the baby would have meant they all starved, so the cow got fed and the baby died. It is nearly impossible for us to imagine the choices that people have had to make. Such dire situations have recurred often enough to shape emotional responses, but I do not see how depression would be useful. Some have suggested that it offers a woman a way of manipulating others to provide more help than they would otherwise. Perhaps sometimes, but there is plenty of evidence that depression gets you extra help for only a short time – after that, people avoid you.

Ideas about attachment do seem germane, however. In some cultures where infant mortality is high, women do not even name their babies until they are past the risky first year of life. This would help to minimise grief.

Daniela: How does an evolutionary perspective affect the treatment of depression?

Randy: Evolution warns us that psychiatrists need to explore what is happening in a person's world before prescribing antidepressants, just as medics need to look for the cause of pain before prescribing pain-killers. Not all depression is caused by the pursuit of unreachable goals, but we do need to ask whether there is an underlying reason that needs to be addressed. Otherwise, alleviating depression with medication may create more serious problems. If low mood is a result of pursuing an unrealistic goal, then antidepressants may lead to struggling on and wasting yet more time and energy on that goal. Alternatively, when depression sets in to prevent us from walking away from long-term commitments, antidepressants may offer enough energy to leave but that may create more problems than it solves.

However, I am against generalisations about using medications. Most of the time depression is about as useful as pain, which is to say, not very. It is a bit subtle but important to realise that low mood and sometimes depression can be useful and normal, but it can still be safe to use medications to block them. Much general medicine consists of relieving the suffering caused by normal defences. People routinely take aspirin for pain and fever, and pills to relieve nausea and diarrhoea, with no ill effects. We get away with it because natural selection has shaped bodies along the lines of better to be safe and to activate the defence, however unpleasant the defence is, than sorry and possibly dead. It is the same with emotional defences. Also, depression is sometimes due to the dysregulation of an otherwise normal capacity and there is no situation arousing it.

In terms of treatment, it can also be useful for patients to learn about the evolutionary origins and functions of low mood. Bolstered by modern media, we tend to believe that a normal life is happy, that anything other than happiness is abnormal and that there is something wrong with us when we feel depressed. The revelation that there is some evolutionary sense to our emotional suffering can help us to quit blaming ourselves and other people, and concentrate on what we need to feel better.

Also, when we realise that we are pursuing various goals because natural selection has shaped us to do so, it is easier to laugh about what we are doing and not be so identified with success.

Daniela: If our capacity for happiness and depression is the result of natural selection, then are our emotions determined by genes?

Randy: Absolutely not! Genes interact with environments to make brains and bodies which then express emotions in situations where they tend to have been useful. The nature–nurture debate has been dead for years among professional biologists. Just as it is senseless to ask if the area of a rectangle is caused more by its width or its length, it is senseless to ask whether a trait is determined by genes or by the environment. However, is makes perfect sense to ask if *variations* among a group of rectangles comes mostly from variations in the width or changes in the length. Similarly, it is important to ask if *variations* in vulnerability to a mental disorder result mostly from genetic differences or environmental differences. So, for instance, we know that most of the variation in who gets schizophrenia results from variations in genes.

The body also has systems that monitor the environment and change development accordingly. For instance, early exposure to heat increases the number of sweat glands formed in an infant's body by triggering increased activity in the genes that code for the creation of sweat glands. Similarly, prenatal exposure to cues that indicate that foetus is about to be born into a stressful world tend to sensitise the stress system. A similar developmental process may occur with the propensity to depression. If an individual is born into a propitious environment, it would be advantageous to set the threshold for depression quite high because such individuals would benefit from taking risks and investing energy in big goals. However, if an individual's early environment is impoverished, it makes sense to have a lower threshold for depression. Despite the suffering this would cause, it would prepare the individual for an environment where risk-taking is unlikely to pay off, and where it is not worth chasing after goals that are unlikely to be achieved.

Daniela: How does an evolutionary perspective contribute to the understanding of anxiety and fear?

Randy: Anxiety, or fear, has evolved to warn us of possible danger, and to help us escape and avoid that danger. Danger, from an evolutionary perspective, is anything that threatens our ability to secure the resources that we need if we are to raise children. Those resources include not only our own lives and the lives of our children, but also mates, social relationships, property, status, reputation and skill. An evolutionary perspective tells us that fear is likely to be aroused by anything that suggests we might suffer loss in one of these domains.

In addition, an evolutionary perspective helps us to see that we are predisposed to become frightened of specific dangers that were common during our evolutionary history, including: snakes, spiders, heights, storms, thunder, lightning, darkness, blood, strangers, social scrutiny, separation and leaving the home range. In contrast, we rarely develop fear of evolutionarily recent dangers such as fast cars, guns, cigarettes or alcohol, even though they kill far more of us than snakes, spiders and heights. Not having been part of our evolutionary history for long enough to alter our genetic endowment, modern perils are feared too little. That said, we have evolved to become frightened of anything that has actually hurt us.

If we are badly hurt by something, we may become extremely fearful of it and avidly avoid anything that is reminiscent of it. Often, this is seen as an over-reaction and labelled as an anxiety 'disorder', but it becomes understandable given the high evolutionary cost of being dead!

An evolutionary perspective also helps us to gain a deeper understanding of the four main sub-types of fear-responses available to us:

1   *Freezing, hyper-alert immobility.* Frozen immobility, coupled with remaining hyper-alert, helps an individual to avoid detection and to assess the danger. It is a response that evolved long before the origins of primates, and is the first line of defence against becoming a predator's dinner. When prey animals start to run, predators go into chase mode; standing still was a way to avoid triggering the hunting behaviour of predators. Today, our first reaction to most possible threats is still to freeze and to lock onto the source of the threat.
2   *Escape (flight).* When freezing is not enough to avert danger, animals will try to escape by running away. Many aspects of what we call a 'panic attack' would help us to escape from the life-threatening danger posed by predators.
3   *Aggressive defences (anger, clawing, biting and fighting).* There are times when an individual simply cannot get away from the danger. Then the fear-response is expressed as aggression which attempts to fight off the danger. Animals have long used aggression as a way to save their lives when a predator is upon them. Many also use aggression to protect other evolutionarily important resources such as mates, territory, possessions, status (dominance) or even, in humans, our reputation.
4   *Submission/appeasement.* This is particularly useful in the face of social threats from one's own group – perhaps from an individual who is working his or her way up the dominance hierarchy. Then there are situations involving challenging one higher in rank. If you lose, then 'involuntary yielding', that is, withdrawing from conflict, submitting and experiencing oneself as unable to compete, will prevent further attacks by the winner of the battle.

Daniela: How has evolution shaped the regulation of anxiety?

Randy: Anxiety is beneficial only when it is regulated. If we have too little fear, we open ourselves to danger. If we have too much fear, we are crippled. The optimum balance depends on just how dangerous our particular environment is. The process of finding that balance begins in utero: the sensitivity of a foetus' stress system is set by the mother's stress levels during pregnancy. For humans, as well as for many other species, if a mother is stressed while pregnant, the foetus' stress system develops so that it is triggered at a relatively low threshold, making the individual more prone to anxiety. High levels of maternal stress hormones induce responses in the developing foetus that are useful in a dangerous world, even if those responses cause diseases later in life.

Daniela: The challenge of matching anxiety levels to the environment does not only apply to individuals of a specific species; it can also shape the average fear levels of different species. In particularly safe environments, fear can be eliminated from the species' experience. This typically happens on islands that have long been free from predators. Mauritius was one such island. Free of threats, one of its bird species not only lost its ability to fly, but it also lost its fear. That bird was the dodo. It was extremely successful until humans settled on Mauritius in 1638. However, the dodo's flightlessness, coupled with its lack of fear, made it easy prey not only for human settlers, but also for the animals that the settlers brought with them. Within 50 years of the arrival of humans, the dodo was extinct, illustrating just how dangerous fearlessness can be.

Randy: That is a great example.

Daniela: How do you distinguish fear from panic?

Randy: Panic is a special kind of fear. Like vomiting, it is an all-or-nothing response. The output of the regulatory system for panic is a 'go/no go' decision, but there is rarely definitive information available for making that decision. When there is a rustle in the bush we cannot be sure whether it is a predator, but must instantaneously decide whether to flee or not. Once again, it makes evolutionary sense to be safe rather than sorry. Imagine a scenario where panicked flight costs 100 calories, and not fleeing and being injured by a predator costs 100,000 calories; it is worth 999 'false' flights for every one that is a response to an actual predator. In short, a relatively inexpensive all-or-nothing defence like panicked flight should be expressed if there is even a small chance of catastrophic harm.

I have dubbed this the 'smoke-detector principle'. We do not want a smoke detector that almost always detects a fire – we want one that goes off every single time there is any kind of blaze, and so we are willing to accept false alarms. The smoke-detector principle tells us that the supposed over-responsiveness of many all-or-nothing defences is an illusion.

The smoke-detector principle is visible in the apparently excessive caution we display. We tune into bad news, whereas good news does not grab our attention in the same way. We wear seat belts, even though they are not necessary 99 per cent of the time. In the USA we prohibit parking adjacent to fire hydrants although the chance that a fire truck will use that hydrant on a given day is less than 1 in 100,000. The latter may be one case where cumulative costs are not worth it – it might be safer if communities added parking meters adjacent to hydrants and gave the extra revenues to the fire department!

Daniela: Some of your work has focused on social selection and on its shadow side, social anxiety. What is involved in these dynamics from an evolutionary perspective?

Randy: Darwin identified two kinds of selection: natural selection, whereby individuals who are better adapted to their environment leave more descendents; and sexual selection, whereby a trait becomes prevalent because it helps to attract mates. The peacock's tail is the classic example of a sexually selected trait: it does not help the animal to adapt to its physical environment, but peacocks with grand tails are preferred by peahens, so they have more descendants who inherit their grand tail. Social selection is like sexual selection, only instead of being chosen as a mate, the individual is chosen as a social partner.

Social selection is particularly important in species that rely on others for help, and humans exemplify this. For our ancestors, procuring food was typically unpredictable and individuals needed social partners (friends) who would share food with them and their children on days when their efforts at hunting or gathering were unsuccessful. In fact, there were times during the course of human evolution when having a strong social network would have been a matter of life or death. However, the relationships that make up social networks require time and energy, both of which are limited, so earlier humans would have benefited by being discriminating when choosing who to include in their network. The challenge thus became: *'How do I get others to choose me to become part of their social network? How do I become popular?'* The answer was (and still is) to excel at something so that your skills are valued by your community, and to be altruistic because people prefer altruists when choosing friends or group members.

But there is a dark-side to social selection – it predisposes us to social anxiety. Because being chosen to be part of somebody's social network was literally a matter of life or death, we hanker after popularity, we constantly monitor how people respond to us, we are very sensitive to cues which tell us how secure we are in the group and we are terrified of being left out. When these concerns dominate our lives, they bring profound anxiety and suffering.

Daniela: What can an evolutionary perspective contribute to the treatment of anxiety disorders?

Randy: The smoke-detector principle has significant clinical implications, telling us that the threshold for a panic response is set at a level where false alarms are inevitable, and that much apparently excessive anxiety is actually normal and healthy. Understanding this can make a real difference. People suffering with agoraphobia often feel silly avoiding a place where they once had a panic attack. But, if asked what the best response would be if years ago they had been attacked by a lion at that spot, most quickly realise that 100 false alarms would be worth a single escape from an attack. Similarly, explaining to somebody who has social anxiety that being thrown out of a group would have been fatal for our ancestors enables them to understand their fear in a bigger context. This frees them from worrying that there is something wrong with them for their anxiety, whereupon their anxiety tends to decrease.

Daniela: You mentioned that an evolutionary perspective can help us to understand why we often turn to blaming ourselves, even when we are not to blame.

Randy: The smoke-detector principle is relevant once again. When something goes wrong we churn it over and over, unable to stop thinking about what we might have done to prevent it. Rumination often appears to be pathological in that we get stuck in self-blame and exacerbate our suffering, when in reality there was nothing we could have done. However, the emotional costs of self-blame are, from an evolutionary perspective, insignificant compared to putting ourselves in a potentially dangerous situation. Evolution does not care how we feel: if there is *anything* at all that we can do to prevent a similar danger in the future, then we need to know about it. Despite the anguish it brings, from the viewpoint of evolution it makes sense to set the default at *'It is my fault – what could I have done to have prevented it?'*.

Daniela: Can an evolutionary perspective shed any light on why psychological change is so difficult?

Randy: I suspect that during our evolutionary history there was little advantage to evolving psychological mechanisms that could facilitate major psychological changes. Modern humans are extraordinarily mobile. We can move to new cities, we can move into new jobs and we can move into new social worlds. With every move we have opportunities to build new relationships that are based on different foundations to the ones that we grew up with. The lives of our ancestors were different. Relationships were much more stable in the hunter-gatherer bands that characterised our evolutionary history. People might move to a new camp, but individuals essentially remained within the same relatively close-knit social group. Thus, the models and expectations built during childhood would have stood them in good stead for their entire lives, and there would have been no selection pressure to evolve mechanisms that would make psychological change possible.

Also, as we have seen, throughout most of our evolutionary history, being a valued member of a group was crucial to survival, and so we have evolved built-in mechanisms to make us absorb the values we see in our first five years of life and stick to them, no matter what. For instance, we rarely eat foods that were taboo when we were children. I suspect our evolved predisposition to absorb (cultural) values as young children is part of what makes change so difficult.

In addition, as we grow up we become increasingly adept at using certain strategies for conducting relationships and because strategies are sometimes mutually exclusive (we can influence others either by using threats or through affection) personality patterns are stabilised.

Daniela: Might it be fair to say that trying to change a personality pattern would be like an adult who had learnt to write with his right hand having to learn to write with his left? First he would lose his ability to write altogether. Then he would need to start anew. It would take considerable time and perseverance. In our ancestral environment, adults would not have had that time. Life expectancy was typically around 45 years, and people spent most of their waking hours searching for food, collecting water and firewood, and looking after children. It seems to me that the kind of change made possible by psychotherapy is one of the gifts of the modern world, and because we did not have that opportunity in the past, we have not evolved the mechanisms that would allow us to do it easily.

Randy: Yes, I certainly agree with that, Daniela.

Daniela: To conclude, what do you see as the main contributions of an evolutionary approach to our understanding of emotional suffering?

Randy: Our understanding of animal behaviour was revolutionised when biologists who were already studying the mechanisms and development of behaviour began to study behaviour from an evolutionary perspective as well. However, the task of building bridges between evolutionary thinking and psychiatry is just beginning. In fact, most therapists and psychiatrists view evolution as either irrelevant or as a threat. It is neither! Evolutionary explanations elucidate why emotions came to be part of human experience, and such explanations are complimentary to both neurobiological and psychological ones. Incorporating them is essential to a full understanding.

Before learning about evolution, I used to think that negative emotions were bad, or at least to be minimised whenever possible. However, an evolutionary view reveals that both positive and negative emotions are useful. Had any of our ancestors been able to dampen down negative emotions they would have been happier, but they would have been deprived of crucial adaptive tools and less likely to leave descendants. In contrast, those whose emotional experiences mapped accurately onto the situations in which they were useful had a selective advantage, irrespective of the suffering they had to endure.

The utter mindlessness of natural selection is terribly hard to grasp and even harder to accept. When I first came across it, I had many sleepless nights. However, the understanding that it offers makes a huge difference to how we see ourselves and to how we experience our emotional suffering and our so-called emotional disorders. When we stop thinking of ourselves as abnormal and inadequate for what we are feeling, healing becomes possible.

I believe that history is going to remember this millennium not only for the mapping of the genome, and for the explosion in neurobiological knowledge, but also for being the first time in history that humans actually grasped where they came from in terms of the evolutionary forces that shaped our emotional world, as well as many other dimensions of being human. Incorporating that understanding into the clinical realm can only enhance our ability to help those who are suffering.

Part IV
Concluding perspective

11 Connecting conversations

Expanding our understanding to
transform our trauma-worlds

Daniela F. Sieff

Summary

When we are emotionally traumatised, we live in an inner world that is fundamentally different to the world in which we would have lived, had we not experienced trauma. This world is organised around the implicitly embodied conviction that important aspects of our physical, emotional or mental survival are at risk. It is built upon the distorting foundations of fear, dissociation and shame. Living in a 'trauma-world' leaves us no choice but to experience ourselves and others in ways that create new layers of pain and suffering.

Understanding trauma from a variety of perspectives helps us to experience ourselves and others more authentically. It encourages us to develop an embodied awareness of our unconscious fears, and recognise how they shape our relationships. It emboldens us to reach deep inside our minds and bodies, and reconnect to the dissociated parts of ourselves. It frees us to dismantle the shame-full belief that we are fundamentally inadequate, and relate to ourselves with more clarity, compassion and responsibility. In short, a multi-faceted understanding offers us guidance, support and inspiration as we engage in the challenging inner work required to transform our trauma-worlds.

To illustrate this, insights from different conversations are brought together to address three questions: (1) Why are particular types of childhood experiences likely to leave us traumatised? (2) Why does emotional trauma leave us prone to reacting in ways that create new suffering? (3) Why is it hard to make the changes that take us out of our trauma-worlds? The answers that emerge speak not only to these specific questions; they also help us to understand what it means to heal emotional trauma and live a more vibrant and fulfilling life.

Trauma-worlds

When we are emotionally traumatised, we live in an inner world that is fundamentally different to the world in which we would have lived had we not experienced trauma. The inner world of emotional trauma is organised around the implicit conviction that important aspects of our physical, mental or emotional survival are at risk. This conviction is written into our unconscious minds and subjective experiences, as well as into our neurobiology, hormones and musculature.

The trauma-world that exists in each of us differs, depending on both our individual disposition and our unique personal experiences. However, as is clear from the conversations in this book, certain dynamics are common to all who suffer trauma: first, our fear system becomes extremely sensitive; second, we develop some form of dissociation; and third, our identity becomes interwoven with shame. As a result, we find we have no choice but to experience ourselves and others in distorted ways.

When our fear system becomes sensitised in response to trauma, our experiences are distorted by a mesh of hyper-vigilance and distrust. Thus we scan our external world for the dangers that we perceive to be surrounding us [Chisholm, Hrdy, Nesse[1]]; we scan our relational world for the abandonment or attacks that we perceive to be inevitable [Hrdy, Nesse, Nijenhuis, Schore, Siegel, Woodman]; and we scan our inner world for the essential wrongness that we perceive to be part of our makeup [Lloyd, Siegel]. In an attempt to pre-empt danger, we unconsciously strive to control ourselves, other people and our environments [Woodman]. Hyper-vigilance has many costs: our emotional and physical health suffers [Chisholm, Schore]; we have little spare energy to pursue more fulfilling avenues [Chisholm]; and we become predisposed to see danger where none exists, often reacting to that imagined danger in ways that bring about the very situations we most fear [Chisholm, Kalsched, Lloyd, Siegel, Stromsted, Woodman].

The dissociation that results from trauma distorts our experience of ourselves, others and the world because it cuts us off from aspects of our own reality, as well as from the reality of the situation [Kalsched, Lloyd, Nijenhuis, Schore]. There are several different forms of dissociation, all of which can leave us disconnected from reality in many debilitating and harmful ways.

We may dissociate the parts of our personality that are unacceptable to our caregivers, as well as any specific emotions that our caregivers are unable to accommodate [Kalsched, Lloyd, Nijenhuis, Stromsted, Woodman]. When this happens, our life is built around the person we have become in order to survive, rather than around our genuine potential and inclinations [Lloyd, Woodman]. As a result, we are not rooted in our own being, so our foundations are likely to be insecure, and our inner sense of danger heightened.

We may dissociate our emotions more generally. If our childhood pain and fear is overwhelming, and there is nobody to help us process these emotions, we have little choice but to prevent the pain and fear from reaching our awareness. To

---

1 References in square brackets refer to the conversations in this book.

achieve that, we must cut-off from our bodies, because it is in our bodies that our emotions arise [Nijenhuis, Schore, Siegel, Stromsted]. However, cut-off from our bodies, more-or-less all emotions are blocked from reaching consciousness [Kalsched, Lloyd, Schore, Siegel, Stromsted], whereupon life feels flat, dead and, at times, unreal [Lloyd, Nijenhuis, Schore, Siegel]. Additionally, our embodied emotions guide us in our relationships, and in other important aspects of our lives [Nesse, Schore, Stromsted], so when we are disconnected from feelings we have to rely more heavily on our thoughts for guidance. Often, these thoughts are distorted by our trauma, but even without such distortion, thinking can provide only half the picture and without access to the texture and nuanced meaning that comes from emotions, we find it harder to navigate our inner and outer environments. This intensifies our sense that our survival is at risk [Schore, Stromsted].

We may also dissociate our actual memories of traumatising experiences [Kalsched, Nijenhuis, Siegel, Stromsted]. Sometimes, the trauma is so extreme that our personality fragments into quasi-independent parts [Nijenhuis]. Some of these parts are concerned with navigating daily life and will need to be distanced from the memories of the trauma; other parts will hold the traumatic memories and be organised around those memories [Nijenhuis]. Traumatic memories that are kept out of consciousness, or that are held within parts of a fragmented personality, have ways of hijacking our behaviour when they are reactivated [Nijenhuis, Siegel, Stromsted, Woodman]. Thus we have little choice but to feel terrifyingly out of control during these times [Nijenhuis, Woodman].

Shame, the third dynamic that occurs in the wake of trauma, creates an equally malevolent and distorting way of experiencing ourselves and others [Kalsched, Lloyd, Siegel]. It leaves us with a visceral conviction that we are intrinsically flawed as a human being. Often that conviction is kept out of consciousness – it is simply too painful to live with on a daily basis [Lloyd, Siegel]. However, irrespective of whether we are aware of our deep sense of inadequacy or not, it contaminates our relationship with ourselves, and with others [Lloyd, Siegel]. Certain that we fail as a human being, we despise ourselves, feel victim to our supposed defectiveness, and strive to become more than we are [Lloyd, Siegel]. At the same time, terrified that if others get to know us they will see us as the flawed person we mistakenly believe ourselves to be, we unconsciously create all kinds of barriers in our relationships [Lloyd, Siegel, Woodman]. These ways of relating to both ourselves and others add to our existing shame, and can leave us increasingly isolated and lonely [Lloyd].

Connecting the conversations

One of the most pernicious features of our trauma-worlds is that they spawn self-perpetuating cycles of distortion and suffering. Trauma-worlds are constellated in response to painful and frightening experiences that originate in the external environment, but once established they create closed, rigid, internal systems. These internal systems compound the dangers we face; leave us feeling increasingly alienated from both ourselves and others; and exacerbate our implicit conviction that our survival is at risk [Chisholm, Kalsched, Lloyd, Nijenhuis, Siegel, Woodman]. They keep us locked into a small and limited life, and prevent us from expanding our potential.

If we are to break out of our trauma-worlds and into a bigger and more vibrant life, it is important that we understand their nature. Such an understanding helps us to reach into our unconscious minds and bodies and give form to the traumatic reality which has defined our lives. It is equally important that we understand the inner territory that must be traversed if we are to travel beyond out trauma-worlds. Such an understanding helps to contain, guide and inspire us as we engage with the healing journey.

To these ends, each contributor offers us profoundly important and innovative insights. When these insights are juxtaposed and integrated, new understandings emerge. In the following part of this chapter, I shall address three questions to illustrate what can emerge when we bring together insights from these different perspectives. I have chosen these particular questions because, first, they address different stages in the process of trauma and healing, and second, they allow me to draw out some key principles which are important in addressing emotional trauma more generally.

1   Why are particular types of childhood experiences likely to leave us traumatised?
2   Why does emotional trauma leave us prone to reacting in ways that create new suffering?
3   Why is it hard to make the changes that take us out of our trauma-worlds?

At this point, I wish to add a personal note. All the contributors have made a profoundly important contribution to my inner work with my own trauma; however, I was originally trained as an evolutionary anthropologist, thus I am especially drawn to the insights that emerge by integrating an evolutionary perspective into our understanding of trauma. Other people, who come to these questions from different personal and intellectual starting points, will uncover different connections between these perspectives. Trauma is a multi-faceted phenomenon and our ability to understand and work with it is enhanced when different people illuminate different aspects of the phenomenon.

Why are particular types of childhood experiences likely to leave us traumatised?

It has long been known that we are especially susceptible to emotional trauma during childhood. In the last decade there have been hugely important advances in understanding the neurobiological and physiological mechanisms which underpin this vulnerability [Schore, Siegel]. When our caregivers are not attuned to us, or when they actively neglect or abuse us, the parts of our brains, nervous and hormonal systems which mediate our emotional life become structured in ways that constitute 'trauma' [Chisholm, Nijenhuis, Schore, Siegel]. The effects of this can last not only for the duration of our own lives, but, unless brought to awareness and challenged, may be unconsciously passed on to our children and grandchildren as well [Chisholm, Lloyd, Schore, Siegel, Woodman].

Our deepening understanding of the mechanisms through which early relationships affect emotional well-being raises new questions. Why are the brains and bodies of children so sensitive to early relationships? Why do children find certain kinds of relational experiences so painful and frightening that they are traumatised by them? To answer these questions we need to bring in an evolutionary perspective.

It seems likely that most of the relational experiences that traumatise children are ones which, throughout our evolutionary history, would have literally threatened our lives.

Woodman offers a visceral description of how an 'archetypal Death Mother' can impact on our developing minds and bodies. For Woodman, the 'Death Mother' personifies the psychological energy we face when our mother wishes that we, or some part of us, were dead. An evolutionary perspective suggests why encountering the 'Death Mother' energy is so traumatising. During our species' evolutionary past, ancestral mothers cared for some of their children with the utmost dedication, but abandoned others at birth to die [Hrdy]. A mother's commitment to a particular child was influenced by her circumstances, as well as by the characteristics of the infant [Chisholm, Hrdy]. For earlier members of our species, and indeed in some traditional societies today, the Death Mother was not only a psychological force, but also a concrete reality. As a result, ancestral infants would have evolved an implicitly embodied knowledge of Death Mother [Hrdy], and that knowledge is still part of our makeup today. Thus, even though infanticide is rare in modern Western societies, when, as infants, we meet the 'Death Mother' energy, we respond with an anciently embodied conviction that our life is genuinely at risk.

Understanding the Death Mother as a real part of our species heritage can similarly enhance our understanding of why human infants have evolved to be so sensitive to the quality of attention they receive from their caregivers [Schore]. Ancestral infants had a better chance of surviving if they were able to ascertain how their mothers felt about them, because that gave their minds and bodies an opportunity to adjust their behaviour if they were at risk of being abandoned [Hrdy]. Infants could not gain that knowledge in a conscious or explicit way; however, they could acquire an implicit sense of their mothers' intentions through their embodied experience of how their mothers behaved with them [Hrdy]. If their mothers were attentive and nurturing, there was a good chance that their mothers were committed to raising them; if their mothers were not attentive, then they may have been at risk, in which case hyper-vigilance would have been adaptive.

Among ancestral humans it was not just newborns who were at risk of being abandoned; older children were too. Human mothers, unlike other great apes, need to provide food for several children simultaneously. During times of shortage, mothers would have struggled to secure enough food for all their children, so less-favoured siblings would have been likely to lose out [Chisholm]. Thus, had we sensed we were a less favoured child, it would have been important to discover whether that was because our parents did not like something about who we were, and if so, to dissociate that part of ourselves. The price of survival could have been a compromised self.

Many of the contributors emphasise that it is not pain and fear per se that constellate trauma; rather trauma is constellated when we experience pain and fear *and* there is nobody to accompany us and help us process our emotions [Kalsched, Lloyd, Schore, Siegel]. An evolutionary perspective suggests why this might be the case.

For our human ancestors, being part of a strong social network was crucial to survival. In the environment in which we evolved, children and adults who had no social support were likely to die [Chisholm, Hrdy, Nesse]. As a consequence, we have evolved to feel safe when accompanied, but at risk when alone. Being on our own, whether or not we are in a dangerous environment, is sufficient to trigger our fear system and propel us into a more vigilant state [Chisholm]. It is therefore possible that being emotionally wounded, and having nobody we can turn to for support, constellates a trauma-world not only because of the pain and fear, but also because our aloneness is experienced as life-threatening in and of itself.

So how might this understanding of why infants have evolved to find certain kinds of experiences so traumatising contribute to helping us break out of our trauma-worlds? The *Diagnostic and Statistical Manual of Mental Disorders* (DSM) defines the criteria by which mental disorders are officially diagnosed. In early editions, for an experience to qualify as 'trauma' people either had to be in mortal danger or they had to witness somebody else in mortal danger. Thus, emotional abuse was not recognised as 'traumatising'. However, even by the DSM's old standards, 'trauma' was exactly the right word to use because during our evolutionary past, infants and children whose mothers were less than fully committed to them, or who were unsupported during tough times, were in mortal danger.

This understanding can help us recognise and contextualise our lived experience. Often we do not have the knowledge to recognise what we have experienced, and how that has affected us. However, without such knowledge we mistakenly believe that our way of being is innate to who we are [Schore, Siegel], whereupon, at some implicit level, we feel a victim to ourselves. Then we develop a shame-based identity [Kalsched, Lloyd] which leaves us little choice but to relate to ourselves through a cacophony of self-abusive, self-traumatising, disempowering thoughts: *'There is something wrong with me for feeling like this, and for behaving this way. I am not normal. If others see this wrongness in me, they will abandon me, so I need to hide it. At the same time, I need to find something or somebody to rescue me from myself, and plug the hole of my loneliness. But maybe that won't work because my wrongness will probably get the better of me in the end. And so it's probably hopeless. There is nothing I can do.'* Living in an internal world populated with thoughts like these – regardless of whether they whisper to us from the shadows, or scream from centre stage – is exceedingly painful. It also makes healing impossible.

However, once we gain some knowledge about the psychological, neurobiological and evolutionary dynamics involved in early trauma, and can integrate that knowledge into our personally lived experience, we begin to recognise that whether or not we faced overt physical danger, the way our caregivers related to us triggered our anciently evolved fears of being abandoned to die by 'Death Mother'. That allows us to start to relate to ourselves within a context of compassion and curiosity.

If we also learn about the developmental pathways that human children typically follow when feeling that their lives are at risk [Schore, Siegel, Chisholm, Hrdy], we begin to challenge the implicit, shame-based belief that it is our own innate and immutable deficiencies which are to blame for our suffering. That gives us hope. It also encourages us to stop feeling that we are a victim of ourselves, and to start taking responsibility for doing the deep inner work that will bring about lasting change [Kalsched, Lloyd, Woodman].

That said, we will only take responsibility for our own healing process if we forgo the temptation to blame our childhood relationships for our suffering [Kalsched, Lloyd, Nijenhuis, Woodman]. Our trauma-worlds will indeed have been created in response to our childhood emotional environment – and we need to recognise that. However, if our energy becomes focused on blaming parents and caretakers, then all we have done is replace the feeling that we are a victim of ourselves with a feeling that we are a victim of others, and little actually changes. So long as we feel ourselves to be a victim of any kind, there can be no genuine healing. Irrespective of what caused our original wounds, it was in our own bodies and minds that the fear, dissociation and shame were formed. Thus, it is only through taking responsibility for ourselves and working with our own bodies and minds – albeit within the context of a healing relationship – that we can bring about change [Kalsched, Nijenhuis, Lloyd, Schore, Woodman].

Refusing to see ourselves as a victim should not prevent us from having compassion for ourselves and for what we have suffered. Relating to ourselves with compassion is fundamentally different to experiencing ourselves as a victim, and that difference is hinted at in the words themselves. To be a 'victim' is to suffer harm at the hands of another, so we are a 'victim *to*' or a 'victim *of*' something or somebody. Thus when we feel ourselves to be a victim, we experience our pain in relation to some malevolent external or internal 'other' and feel alone, helpless and abandoned in our pain. As a result, we contract further into our distorted and disempowering trauma-world. By contrast, 'compassion' means 'to suffer *with*'; so when we relate to ourselves through compassion we accompany ourselves in our suffering [Kalsched, Lloyd, Siegel, Woodman].

Being able to accompany ourselves in our suffering is an important part of healing because it reverses the deep feelings of isolation and loneliness that are intrinsic to living in a trauma-world. It also creates a safe and supportive internal environment, and that, in turn, enables us to start to reconnect to the parts of ourselves that were dissociated, and relax our hyper-vigilant, controlling defences.

Why does emotional trauma leave us prone to reacting in ways that create new suffering?

One consequence of living in a trauma-world is that when our unconscious mind and body perceives, or imagines, the slightest similarity between our current situation and the one in which we were traumatised, we react in extreme ways and become passengers on a rollercoaster to hell [Kalsched, Lloyd, Nijenhuis, Schore, Siegel, Stromsted, Woodman]. Woodman describes this as experiencing life as 'a minefield in which we are knocked down by explosions that are inaudible to others'. These 'trauma-reactions' leave a trail of destruction in their wake. Every time our trauma-reactions are activated we vow *'Never again!'*, but our vows are futile. We cannot help ourselves – these reactions continue to be triggered. As a result it is impossible to feel emotionally secure [Schore], and to trust ourselves. So what is happening on this rollercoaster? How can we understand our reactions?

Both our ability to regulate our emotions and our general level of emotional reactivity are influenced by our early childhood attachment relationships with our parents and other caregivers [Schore, Siegel]. When we are born, the most developed part of the emotional brain is the amygdala. The amygdala makes lightning-quick assessments of whether we are safe or in danger, and 'better safe than sorry' is its motto [Schore, Siegel]. Because the amygdala operates below consciousness, and its responses are crude and intense, we need our caregivers to help us regulate the powerful emotions [Schore]. If our caregivers do a 'good enough' job in helping us to regulate our emotions, then, in time, we will learn to do that for ourselves. This sets the stage for us to become comfortable with our emotions, resilient and to feel secure in ourselves [Schore]. However, if our caregivers are unable to help us regulate our emotions – and childhood wounding typically becomes 'trauma' when there is nobody to help us to regulate our fear and pain – we grow up at the mercy of the amygdala's crude, intense, emotional responses. Thus, we become prone to being emotionally over-reactive [Schore, Siegel], whereupon emotional security and resilience moves beyond our reach.

Focusing specifically on the fear response, its level of reactivity is also influenced by our earliest relationships. One of the biological systems that mediates the fear response is the hypothalamic-pituitary-adrenal system (HPA system), and this system can be structured so as to leave us more, or less, reactive to possible danger [Chisholm, Nesse, Schore]. If we experience high levels of stress either in the womb or during our early years, our HPA system develops in ways that make us relatively sensitive to danger. As a result we grow up to be more vigilant, more easily frightened and quicker to react to possible threats. This makes evolutionary sense [Chisholm]. If we experience a lot of stress in our early life, it suggests that we have been born into a dangerous environment; in which case we are more likely to survive if we are hyper-vigilant and react quickly [Chisholm, Nesse]. However, as with many adaptations to danger, there are costs. A sensitised fear system predisposes us to see danger when none exists, and to 'over-react' to anything that we feel, or imagine, might be dangerous [Chisholm]. Further, it increases our risk of developing heart disease, cancer and other illnesses as we get older [Chisholm].

Turning our attention to specific trauma-reactions, understanding the role of implicit memory is crucial [Siegel]. Generally we remember particularly painful and frightening experiences; however, such experiences tend to be recorded as 'implicit' rather than 'explicit' memory [Siegel]. This means that the original experience is encoded as the visceral feelings and embodied reactions that constituted the experience, rather than as a conscious memory of something that happened in our past. Siegel suggests this is adaptive because it allows us to react extremely quickly when we reencounter what originally traumatised us, and this can make the difference between life and death. But again, there are costs. When we sense, or imagine, even the vaguest parallel between current circumstances and those in which we were traumatised, we are catapulted back *into* the original traumatising experience. As a result, we are taken-over by the feelings of pain and fear which were originally present. Worse still, unaware that our traumatic past has come back to life, we believe that our experience genuinely represents present reality [Nijenhuis, Siegel], and so we behave in ways that can create a situation that did not previously exist.

An equally illuminating way to envision our trauma-reactions is in terms of the 'archetypal self-care system' described by Kalsched. In response to trauma, we unconsciously dissociate the essential, vulnerable, relational part of our psyche [Kalsched, Lloyd, Stromsted, Woodman]. Simultaneously, other parts of us move forward to become the protectors of this dissociated essence [Kalsched]. The protective energies reside in our unconscious mind and body, and are so determined to prevent us from going into situations where we might possibly be retraumatised that they can become viciously self-critical, destroy our relationships, sabotage our attempts to heal and even create physical illnesses [Kalsched, Stromsted, Woodman].

When the traumatising pain and fear is particularly unbearable, our personality may fragment into distinct parts, each of which has an identity of its own [Nijenhuis]. Some of these parts are organised around implicit memories of our traumatising experiences, and their only reality is what happened at the time of trauma. Consequently, these parts live in a world where danger is omnipresent [Nijenhuis]. Moreover, because they are largely driven by the need to find safety and avoid retraumatisation, when these parts take control of our behaviour we have no choice but to over-react [Nijenhuis].

The immense power built into our psychological defence system becomes clear when we incorporate an evolutionary perspective. We are more likely to survive if we remember our encounters with danger and avidly avoid putting ourselves in a similar situation. As a result, our psychological defence system has evolved to work on the same principle as a smoke detector: we tolerate an overly sensitive and highly reactive smoke alarm which goes off when we burn toast because the cost of a false alarm is insignificant compared to the cost of there being a real fire and the alarm not sounding [Nesse]. The metaphor of the smoke detector was developed by Nesse to explain what psychiatrists call 'panic attacks'; however, the evolutionary logic is equally relevant to reactions developed in the wake of traumatising experiences.

The smoke detector principle also suggests a possible explanation for why the brains of infants are sensitive to their parents' unconscious trauma and prone to adopting that trauma for their own [Lloyd, Schore]. Broadly speaking, children have two ways to learn about danger: first, they can learn directly from their own experiences; second, they can learn indirectly by internalising the behaviours and attitudes of parents and other adults. Both types of learning have costs. Learning directly from experience puts the child at risk of being harmed or even killed during the encounter with danger. Learning indirectly by internalising the behaviours and attitudes of adults puts the child at risk of adopting irrelevant fears, which cause them unnecessary suffering [Chisholm, Lloyd, Schore, Stromsted, Woodman]. From an evolutionary perspective the cost of indirect learning is insignificant compared to the cost of risking death; thus it makes sense for children to internalise their parents' trauma and adopt their fears.

Turning to the parents' perspective, the smoke detector principle suggests a possible reason why parents do everything in their conscious and unconscious power to prevent their children risking the dangers which they personally have faced [Chisholm, Lloyd, Stromsted, Woodman]. Regardless of the costs, it would make evolutionary sense for parents to inculcate their children with whatever beliefs and behaviours they implicitly felt were important for their own survival, including whatever made them acceptable to the group in which they lived.

So how can our healing journey be helped by these insights about why emotional trauma leaves us prone to react in ways that create new suffering? When our trauma-reactions are activated, we recreate the original traumatising situation in our internal world. We are also likely to behave in ways that recreate that situation in our external world. As a result, we become isolated from ourselves and from the situation, and end up utterly and painfully alone in a world of our own making. At this point, it is our unconsciously embodied determination to avoid retraumatisation, not our original wounds, which is destroying our lives.

After our trauma-reactions have run their course and we emerge to face the aftermath, we are often dismayed because we do not understand why we behaved as we did. At the same time, we berate and shame ourselves for being so 'stupid' and sabotaging the very things we care about most. Believing ourselves to be victims of our behaviour we feel hopeless despair, which in time can turn into self-hatred.

Further, when we castigate ourselves, we push ourselves deeper into our trauma-worlds. In response to an attack, irrespective of whether the attack comes from outside or inside us, we mobilise our defence system [Nesse, Siegel]. This leaves us disconnected from the reflective parts of our brain and increasingly at the mercy of the more crudely reactive parts, including the amygdala [Nijenhuis, Schore, Siegel].

Understanding our trauma-reactions in a layered way can help allay our fear and sense of disempowerment, prevent us from attacking ourselves and interrupt the trauma spiral. If we experience our trauma-reactions as indicative of our fundamental inadequacy, we feel that we have no choice but to fight them and try to gain power over them. In contrast, if we experience our trauma-reactions as misguided attempts to protect us from retraumatisation, we can own them cleanly for what they are, approach them with empathy and compassion, and explore them openly and without judgement [Kalsched, Lloyd, Nijenhuis, Siegel]. It is interesting that the word 'curiosity' and the word 'cure' have the same root. Fostering an internal environment in which we relate to our trauma-worlds with curiosity heralds opportunities for healing [Nijenhuis, Siegel, Stromsted, Woodman].

That said, the non-judgemental exploration and ownership of our trauma-reactions is not enough to take us out of our trauma-worlds; it is equally critical that we learn how to remain aware of present reality when these reactions are activated [Lloyd, Nijenhuis, Siegel]. We may never be able to prevent these reactions from being triggered, but if some small part of us can remain mindful and conscious of what is happening, we will not end up completely dissociated from ourselves and from our reality [Lloyd]. That can make a very real difference.

Why is it hard to make the changes that take us out of our trauma-worlds?

Change is possible. Learning occurs throughout our lives, and our brains and nervous systems can be modified and restructured by new experiences [Schore, Siegel]. However, in the wake of emotional trauma, creating lasting and meaningful change is undoubtedly difficult. Why is that? Why do we hang on to the 'terrible familiars' of our trauma-worlds, irrespective of the suffering they cause both to ourselves and others [Stromsted]? Why are we so attached to the trauma-stories which keep us chained to our retraumatising self-care system [Kalsched]? Why do we wait until our body falters before questioning what we carry [Stromsted, Woodman]? Why does our fear of not changing have to be greater than our fear of change, before we challenge our old ways [Lloyd, Woodman]?

Dissociation, a central feature of trauma, is primarily a response to experiencing pain that is so unbearable that we have to bury it in our unconscious minds and bodies [Kalsched, Lloyd, Nijenhuis, Schore, Siegel, Stromsted]. To reverse dissociation we must consciously suffer that 'unbearable' traumatising pain [Kalsched, Lloyd, Nijenhuis, Schore]. We must also suffer the secondary pain created by the dynamics put in place as a result of our traumatising experiences [Kalsched, Lloyd, Woodman]. 'Consciously suffering our pain' means that we allow ourselves to feel our pain and do not try to escape from it, while at the same time we retain an awareness that there is more to us than our pain, and that in time, our pain will pass [Kalsched, Lloyd, Siegel, Woodman]. However, pain evolved to tell us that damage is occurring; it also evolved to be all-encompassing so as to motivate us to do everything in our power to get away from the source of that damage [Nesse]. Thus, if we are to stay with our pain and consciously suffer it, we need to challenge millions of generations of natural selection.

Breaking out of our trauma-worlds similarly requires that we learn to consciously suffer our fear [Lloyd, Woodman]. By the time we are adults, we are experts at living in our trauma-worlds; to dismantle old ways of being and begin afresh feels terrifyingly risky [Lloyd, Nesse, Nijenhuis, Stromsted, Woodman]. Moreover, fear also evolved to warn us of danger and to be all-encompassing so as to motivate us to get away from the dangerous situation as fast as possible [Nesse]. Thus, the need to suffer fear also demands that we challenge anciently evolved, embodied wisdom.

Because fear and pain are indicators that our survival is at risk, natural selection has shaped us to fervently avoid anything that has caused us fear and pain in the past [Nesse]. If we were criticised and shamed for expressing particular emotions, for voicing needs, or for living certain aspects of our personality, those attacks will be seared into our implicit memory. As a result, it will take profound effort and courage to reconnect to those aspects of ourselves [Kalsched, Lloyd, Woodman]. If our pain and fear resulted from a change in circumstances, change per se may be something that our unconscious mind and body is determined to avoid [Nijenhuis, Woodman]. For example, if the loss of a parent triggered our trauma, we may hold a deep-seated, implicit belief that the dominant consequence of change is loss; or if, at birth, we found we were not wanted, we may hold a stubborn conviction that if we move into a new world, we will be rejected. Deeply held trauma-derived beliefs regarding change itself make the healing process particularly difficult.

There are other ways that implicit learning can work against change. When toddlers begin to explore, they periodically look at their caregivers to gauge whether they are safe. Relaxed and encouraging expressions from their caregivers tell them that it is fine to continue exploring, whereas frightened, discouraging expressions warn of danger [Schore]. Caregivers who experience their environment as dangerous, either because it is genuinely dangerous or because they are themselves carrying trauma and have a hypersensitive fear system, tend to discourage toddlers from exploring widely. Over time, these children implicitly learn to be wary of 'unfamiliarity' per se [Schore], and because change inevitably involves unfamiliarity [Lloyd], this makes change even harder than it would otherwise have been.

The quality and quantity of childhood play may also affect how receptive we are to new experiences. Play helps to create the neural networks which support flexible behaviour and openness to new learning [Chisholm]. Children who grow up in hostile environments generally play less [Chisholm], so their brains have fewer opportunities to develop in ways that will facilitate change.

In response to hostile environments, we tend to be oriented to the short-term and to look for immediate gratification rather than waiting for future rewards [Chisholm]. This makes evolutionary sense. In hostile environments we have a relatively high risk of dying before collecting future rewards, so it is best to grab what we can, when we can [Chisholm]. However, being oriented to the short-term makes it comparatively difficult to muster the patience and perseverance that is necessary to bring about the deep-seated changes required to heal emotional trauma.

Change requires that we leave our old world, which sometimes involves leaving our social group, family or spouse. However, deep in our anciently evolved inheritance is a profound fear of losing social relationships. Our ancestors needed to have a strong social network to survive [Hrdy, Nesse], and had no choice as to which group they belonged to. Their only option was the group into which they had been born [Nesse], and had they left that group for any reason, death would not have been far away.

The fact that change might involve leaving existing relationships does not mean we have to travel alone. In fact, when we are trying to heal emotional trauma, being accompanied is crucial [Kalsched, Lloyd, Nijenhuis, Schore, Siegel, Stromsted, Woodman]. That accompaniment can come from a therapist, counsellor, teacher, mentor, spiritual guide, healing group or friend, but ultimately it is what we *experience* within the context of healing relationships that enables us to ameliorate shame [Lloyd]; reconnect to ourselves and our emotions [Lloyd, Nijenhuis, Schore, Stromsted]; and relax our hyper-vigilance. It is through embodied, lived, relational experiences that we build the new neural networks that underlie healthier ways of experiencing ourselves and others [Schore, Siegel, Stromsted].

This has significant implications for the person we choose to accompany us on our healing journey [Lloyd, Nijenhuis, Schore, Siegel, Woodman], and one of the challenges is finding the right person. For a healing relationship to offer us the emotional environment in which lasting change can occur, those who accompany us must have worked deeply with their own trauma, fear, dissociation and shame [Lloyd, Nijenhuis, Schore, Siegel].

Healing trauma depends, in part, on gaining new experiences, and if we were unseen as children, one of the most important experiences we require is to be seen and received in an open and non-judgemental way [Lloyd, Nijenhuis, Siegel, Stromsted]. People can only offer us this if they have an embodied, non-judgemental and open understanding of their own wounds [Lloyd, Nijenhuis, Schore, Siegel].

Additionally, our body and emotional brain unconsciously mirrors and learns from the implicit emotions that are present in the body and mind of the person who is accompanying us on our healing journey [Schore, Siegel]. It follows, therefore, that if the person with whom we are working carries unconscious fear, dissociation and shame, we are likely to mirror that [Lloyd, Nijenhuis, Schore]. By contrast, if the person accompanying us relates to him or herself within a context of trust, openness, self-compassion and responsibility, our body and brain will unconsciously mirror and learn from that [Lloyd, Schore].

Because trauma creates a closed and impregnable system, we may also need another person to tell us what they are seeing in us before we can recognise it for ourselves. At times, we may even need another person to actively help us open up our trauma-world. That can be particularly true when our old trauma-derived defences are doing everything in their power to 'protect' us from the supposed dangers that they fear will befall us if we change [Kalsched, Nijenhuis]. While ultimately change has to come from the inside, Kalsched, Nijenhuis and Woodman all give poignant examples of how a therapist's compassionate and authentic anger can be invaluable in fuelling change by challenging trauma-created defences. Not all healers are experienced, connected or attuned enough to express emotions such as anger in a safe way, but when they can do so, change is greatly facilitated.

So how might this understanding of why it is so hard to make the changes that take us out of our trauma-worlds support our road to recovery? As we have seen, real change is possible, but it is not easy, and several features of trauma make it particularly difficult. Thus, one of the challenges in a healing process is managing our expectations. If we cannot do that, we face various pitfalls which risk derailing the healing process. First, when our old ways stubbornly persist, we are at risk of feeling inadequate and that can reinforce our shame-based identity. Second, in our frustration at our slow progress, we may turn to methods which purport to offer us a quick fix, and so lose the opportunity to create lasting and meaningful change. Third, we may find ourselves believing that change is impossible for us, and stop trying. Understanding why lasting change is difficult and why it takes considerable time helps us to combat these pitfalls and encourages us to foster the courage, commitment and patience that are required to persevere.

Understanding the deep-seated challenges involved in change can also encourage us both to appreciate every step we take, however small, and to respect ourselves for taking that step [Nijenhuis]. Often this is one of our first experiences of healthy self-respect, and that can initiate a positive cycle of change. Our implicit sense of ourselves is continually being recreated according to how we experience ourselves in each moment, so when we start to experience ourselves with respect, we begin to build a more empowered and healthy sense of who we are.

Concluding thoughts: transforming our trauma-worlds

When we embark on a healing journey, we typically imagine that we will reach a place where our lives are free from the pain and fear arising from our wounds. This is not what happens if we have been emotionally traumatised. The traumatising wounds endure regardless of how much inner work we do, and when something presses against these wounds our pain and fear are likely to remain intense [Lloyd, Woodman]. However, what we can change, if we engage with a healing journey, is the way that we relate to our wounds and to the associated emotions. Instead of being locked in a trauma-world in which our lives are organised around fear, dissociation and shame, we can work our way into a new world in which we live with our wounds in healthier ways [Kalsched, Lloyd, Siegel, Woodman]. Understanding trauma from a wide variety of perspectives can support us through this transformation.

At the start of a healing journey, most of us are unaware that we are living in a world defined by emotional trauma. Trauma is so deeply incorporated into our physical bodies and subjective minds that we cannot step outside it to see it for what it is. Even if we could step out, having never experienced anything else, we would not necessarily know what to look for, nor would we know what we were seeing. That lack of understanding leaves us imprisoned in our trauma-worlds and frightened. It also leaves us with no choice but to experience ourselves through disempowering, shameful and self-traumatising beliefs [Kalsched, Lloyd, Schore, Siegel, Stromsted, Woodman].

As we develop a conceptual awareness of the psychological and neurobiological dynamics that constitute emotional trauma and, more importantly, an experiential and embodied awareness of how these dynamics play out in our own minds and bodies, we are called to question our distorted ways of understanding of ourselves. If we answer that call, we begin to experience ourselves with greater clarity. Instead of feeling we are 'defective' by nature, we begin to realise that who we have become is, in part, a response to having suffered trauma [Nijenhuis, Schore, Siegel]. When we then learn that these ways of responding to trauma evolved because they enabled earlier members of our species to survive in harsh environments [Chisholm, Hrdy, Nesse], we begin to experience our humanity.

Such a shift in our deep experience of ourselves is profoundly transformative because it means we can stop attacking ourselves and start to relate to ourselves with compassion and curiosity. It is also empowering in that it invites us to dismantle the belief that we are a helpless victim to our perceived inadequacy, and encourages us to take responsibility for doing the inner work which will enable us to change.

Relating to ourselves with compassion, curiosity and responsibility sets the stage for further transformations, because it creates a safe internal environment in which we can reconnect to the parts of ourselves and experiences which were dissociated following our original wounds [Nijenhuis]. In time we can build a life that is securely rooted in the 'entirety' of who we are and what we have experienced, rather than in the compromised person we became.

Similarly, when we can relate to ourselves with compassion, curiosity and responsibility we are safe to reconnect to our previously dissociated emotions [Lloyd, Nijenhuis, Schore, Siegel]. It is a slow process, but as we get in touch with our feelings, we benefit from the guidance they provide, and so feel increasingly secure [Schore, Stromsted].

As importantly, learning how to be with our emotions frees us from having to continually scan our internal, relational and external environments for anything that might hit the fear and pain which is bound up in our wounds. We will still try to avoid fear and pain – that is natural – but once we trust ourselves to cope with these emotions in a healthy way, we can risk expanding our lives beyond the fear-driven systems put in place to prevent retraumatisation, and so move out of our trauma-worlds and begin to fulfil our potential [Kalsched, Lloyd].

It is vital to recognise that a conceptual understanding of the dynamics of trauma, even if married to a cognitive awareness of how we have been personally affected, is not enough to transform our trauma-worlds and bring us healing [Lloyd, Schore, Stromsted, Woodman]. Healing emerges out of the embodied insights that originate deep inside our own emotional brains and bodies [Lloyd, Kalsched, Siegel, Stromsted, Woodman]. It occurs at the cutting edge of where our traumatising wounds meet our present reality, and where our old fears clash with our need to live a more vibrant life [Lloyd, Woodman]. Healing happens in the present moment through lived experience [Lloyd, Nijenhuis, Schore, Stromsted, Woodman]. Just as we have to get on a bicycle to learn how to ride, we have to go to the interface with our personal trauma and find different ways of experiencing it and relating to it [Kalsched, Lloyd, Nijenhuis, Schore]. This is a frightening and painful process. While a conceptual understanding of emotional trauma is no substitute for this process, it does, however, make a powerful contribution to it, because it helps to hold and inspire us when we go to that interface. Additionally, after we have gone to the interface, being able to understand and conceptualise what we have just lived helps us consolidate and build on our new experience and insights.

One of the most harmful consequences of living in a world defined by emotional trauma is that it distorts our relationships with ourselves, other people and the world around us. The insights shared in this book, when embodied through lived experience, can help us build relationships that are more compassionate, authentic and meaningful. These relationships constitute a new world, and although this new world will not be free from pain, fear or trauma, it will be infinitely richer than anything we could ever have imagined when we started the healing journey.

Index